# Developmental Profile of Indian Education

P. Satyanarayana
Lakshmi Mantha
C. Sesharatnam

SHIPRA

₹ 1500
US$ 60
ISBN: 978-93-88691-91-8

2022, First Published in India

*Developmental Profile of Indian Education*



Published by:
**SHIPRA PUBLICATIONS**
LG 18-19, Pankaj Central Market
I.P. Ext., Patparganj, Delhi 110092, India
Tel.: +91 11 2223 5152/6152; 96500 28065
E-mail: info@shiprapublication.com
www.shiprapublication.com

# Contents

# 1

# Education Policies in the Past

"Education influences and is influenced by the context in which it is developed. This synergistic relationship implies that education must be in a constant state of change, as it responds to changing social and economic needs, and that education itself is a force for social and economic change as people become more empowered and more productive. Indeed, while education research might encompass broad themes in areas such as leadership and school improvement, teacher development and teacher quality, skills and employability, equity in education, governance and quality assurance, and citizenship education, it is ultimately policy-making that translates these domains into practice". Education policy formulation is a difficult process that can rarely claim perfection. An effective policy continuously offers scope for evaluation and modification as and when necessary. "Education policies can be useful instruments to guide decisions concerning the improvement and transformation of educational systems. Such instruments require great sensitivity to national contexts and objectives determined by their own citizens". Three reasons mentioned by the World Bank for mapping and analysing the design of education policies are:

1. Policy frameworks provide a sense of what is possible in an education system.
2. The analysis of policy frameworks allows for a better understanding of where to focus improvement efforts; and
3. The analysis of policy frameworks may support a more thorough understanding of implementation gaps.

Education policy is generally formulated having an eye on future. "The future is inherently unpredictable because it is always in the making. Long term strategic thinking in education thus needs to consider both the set of trends and the possible ways they might evolve in the future". "In today's increasingly complex systems, education systems are making considerable efforts to ensure that governance structures facilitate effective planning, implementation and delivery of education policies." Highlighting issues related to *evidence-based policy-making in education,* European Commission stated "While there is a wide range of evidence available, the challenge is to ensure that the evidence used in policy-making is pertinent to current policy issues. There are two important challenges here: timeliness and relevancy. Firstly, constant societal change implies that policies must be adapted to address new and emerging issues. As a consequence, the evidence to support policymaking often does not exist when it is needed. Secondly, the complexity and multidimensional nature of education system poses challenges to produce relevant and reliable evidence using an appropriate methodology."

Viennet and Pont stated, "Education policy implementation is a complex, evolving process that involves many stakeholders and can result in failure if not well targeted. In fact, a range of reasons can prevent implementation from being effective, such as a lack of focus on the implementation processes when defining policies at the system level; a lack of recognition that the core of change processes requires engaging people; and the fact that implementation processes need to be revised to adapt to new complex governance systems. It is therefore crucial to understand it, clarify its determinants and explore ways in which it can be more transparent and effective."

OCED stated, "Policy success depends on the design and specific features of the policies themselves, but also on the overall complexity of the policy ecosystem at the stage when implementation strategies are being developed. Here, it is important to engage actors, including students, based on a shared understanding, and supported by stronger capacities and resources. In the same way, better policy evaluation and contextual understanding should permeate the system. Evaluations can offer both summative and formative perspectives of specific reform implementation and can help identify factors that can promote success in policy implementation."

National policies generally evaluate earlier strategies and formulate future strategies in respect of various areas. Priority of an area varies from one nation to another.

## History of Policies

Nearly a century ago, in 1913, the British Rulers had brought out "Indian Educational Policy 1913. The Policy did not visualise a national pattern for the whole nation. "In view of the diverse social conditions in India, there cannot be in practice set of regulations and one set of progress for the whole of India." This policy document was based on the deliberations made at three conferences of experts and representative non-officials held during previous two years. After 18 years of having a Constitution, the nation had its first education policy in 1968 (Ministry of Education, 1968). Although this document stated that the policy would be reviewed after five years, it took 11 years to bring out a Draft Policy document after 17 years of 1968 Policy. In order to raise a debate on various issues, the Central government brought out a discussion document "Challenge of Education" that listed following constraints: (a) internal, (b) technological, (c) economic, (d) legal, (f) financial, and (g) constraints of the total system. This document made various issues to the public and pointed out the pros and cons of various strategies that could be debated.

Finally, in 1986 the National Policy on Education 1986 was brought out with approval of the Parliament. Taking note of several objections raised in various forums regarding certain aspects of the policy, the Central Government appointed a committee under the chairmanship of Acharya Ramamurti. The Central Advisory Board of Education (CABE) could not accept all recommendations of the Acharya Ramamurti (1990) and appointed a committee under the chairmanship of N. Janardan Reddy (1992). Basing on this report, 1986 policy was modified in 1992. Although the policy of 1986 modified in 1992 stated about a revision of the policy in five years, yet after 23 years, in 2016 Central Government initiated policy formulation, by bringing out a document "Some Inputs for Draft National Education Policy 2016", that invited inputs for the proposed Policy by 30 September 2016. In the same year, the Ministry brought out another document – National Policy on Education 2016 – "Report of the Committee for Evolution of the New Education Policy" (Subramanian, 2016). Based On inputs received the Ministry brought out "Draft National Education Policy 2019 (Kasturitangan, 2019). Finally, in 2020, the ministry brought out a new policy document –National Education Policy 2020.

## National Policies

India has always accorded high importance to education. The concern for the improvement of education had been at the top of India's development agenda since independence. Several commissions were appointed by the Government of India from time to time to formulate policies and programmes required to enhance access to and participation in education and improve quality of education. Important among them was the Education Commission (1964-66).

The Indian Education Commission, popularly known as Kothari Commission, was an ad hoc commission set up by the Government of India to examine all aspects of the educational sector of India, to evolve a general pattern of education and to advise guidelines and policies for the development of education in India. It was formed on 14 July 1964 under the chairmanship of D.S. Kothari, the then Chairman of the University Grants Commission. The terms of the reference of the Commission were to formulate the general principles and guidelines for the development of education from primary to the higher level and to advise the government on a standard pattern of education in India. However, medical and legal studies were excluded from the purview of the Commission. The tenure of the Commission was from 1964 to 1966 and the report was submitted by the Commission on 29 June 1966.

The Commission, under the Chairmanship of D.S. Kothari, was the sixth commission in India after independence and the first commission with comprehensive terms of reference on education. Apart from the core group, the Commission had a panel of overseas consultants numbering twenty and nineteen task forces, their sub-groups, and special panels of invitees. Nine thousand individuals covering educators, scholars, and scientists were interviewed and 2400 memoranda were examined by the Commission over a period spanning 21 months. The Commission submitted its 287-page report to M.C. Chagla, the then Minister of Education. The report had four sub-sections:

- Section I: General issues
- Section II: Stages of education
- Section III: Recommendations and programmes
- Section IV: Additional papers

The four main themes of the Commission were:

1. Increase in productivity
2. Promoting social and national integration
3. Education and modernisation
4. Developing social, moral, and spiritual values

One of the main recommendations of the Commission was the standardisation of educational system on 10+2+3 pattern, across the country. It advised that the pre-primary education which had different names such as Kindergarten, Montessori and pre-basic should be renamed as pre-primary and the primary education (renamed as lower primary) to be up to the IV standard. It further classified the schooling as upper primary or higher primary and high school (up to standard X). The undergraduate education was identified as XI and XII standards under the name higher secondary or pre-university. The graduate studies were recommended to be standardised as a three-year course.

The education system was categorised as first (primary education), second (secondary education), and third levels of education (higher studies).

The Commission recommended that a common public education system should be introduced, and that it should be vocationalised in general and special streams by introducing work experience as a part of education. It further stressed on the need to make work experience and social/national service an integral part of education. The Commission recommended that specialisation of subjects be started from higher secondary levels.

It also recommended that the days of instruction be increased to 234 for schools and 216 for colleges, and the working hours be fixed at not less than 1000 hours per academic year, preferably higher at 1100 or 1200 hours. It also advised reduction of national holidays. Linking of colleges to a number of schools in the neighbourhood, utilisation of school facilities eight hours a day all through the year, establishment of book banks, identification of talents and provision of scholarship, setting up of day study and residential facilities, and opportunities for students to earn while studying were some of the other recommendations of the commission. It also emphasised the need for free education up to and including lower secondary level of education.

The Commission stressed the desirability of ensuring women's education and advised setting up of state and central level committees for oversight of women's education. It suggested establishment of schools and hostels for women and urged identification of ways to find job opportunities for women in the educational sector. Focusing on equalisation of opportunities to all, irrespective of caste, religion, and gender to achieve social and national integration, the schools were advised to provide education to backward classes on a priority basis and the minimum level of enrolment at a secondary school was advised to be not less than 360 every year. Two sets of curricula were prescribed – one at the state level and second at the national level. The schools were recommended to experiment with the curricula. It also proposed that three or four textbooks be prescribed for each subject, and moral and religious education be made a part of the curriculum.

It also recommended the establishment of guidance and counselling centres and a new approach in the evaluation of student performances. The Commission suggested incorporating the neighbourhood school system without social or religious segregation and a school complex system integrating primary and secondary levels of education. It put forward the suggestion that state and national boards of examination be set up and state level evaluation machinery be put in place.

The Commission recommended the establishment of Indian Education Service, along the lines of Indian Administrative Service, to bring in professional management to education sector. It proposed standardisation and revision of the pay scales of the teaching, non-teaching and administrative staff and prescribed minimum pay levels based on their location. It also advised standardisation of pay scale working under different managements such as government, private and local bodies. The minimum scale was suggested to be in the ratio of 1:2:3 for teachers in the primary, secondary and higher levels of education sector. Another proposal was for the establishment of machinery for continuous on job training of the teaching staff and for efforts to raise the status of the teachers to attract talents into profession. It urged laws to be passed to legalise the educational standards and the educational expenditure to be raised from the then level of 2.9 per cent of the gross domestic product (GDP) to six per cent, to be achieved by the fiscal year, 1985-86. A significant suggestion was the issuance of a National Policy on Education by the Government of India, which should serve as a guideline for the state and local bodies in the design and implementation of their educational plans.

Formulation of a National Policy on Education was one of the important recommendations of the Commission. In 1968, the fourth Lok Sabha elected to office in 1967 under the leadership of Indira Gandhi, passed the bill. The policy covered many recommendations of the Kothari Commission such as free and compulsory education, status and pay scale revision of teachers, equalisation of educational opportunity, and science education.

Another recommendation of the Commission for the alignment of the educational system on the 10+2+3 pattern has been achieved by the government at the national level. The educational system has been modelled in accordance with the Commission's recommendation to stratify the sector with state and national bodies and a Central board, Board of Higher Secondary Education was set up in 1986.

Kothari Commission and its recommendation are also reported to have influenced the 1986 revision of the National Policy on Education by the Rajiv Gandhi government. The guidelines laid out by the Commission were revisited by the National Knowledge Commission headed by Sam Pitroda in 2005.

### 1968 Education Policy

The report of the Education Commission was widely discussed and commented upon. The result was the emergence of the National Policy of Education in 1968.

The Government of India tried to implement the policy in the following ways:

1. Fulfilment of free and compulsory education.
2. Adequate and satisfactory status, enrolment and education of teachers.
3. Protection of academic freedom of teachers.
4. Due emphasis on teacher education.
5. Development of languages – Indian and international.
6. Equalisation of educational opportunities.
7. Correction of regional imbalances.
8. Promotion of social cohesion and national integration.
9. Emphasis on education of girls.
10. Expansion of educational facilities for the physically and mentally handicapped children.
11. Identification of talent and cultivation of excellence.
12. Emphasis on work experience and national service.
13. Growth of science education and research.
14. Emphasis on education for agriculture and industry.
15. Establishing agriculture universities in all states.
16. Relating practical training to technical education.
17. Continuous review of the agricultural, industrial, and other technical manpower needs.
18. Improving quality of textbooks.
19. Reforming examination framework.
20. Extension of secondary education.
21. Increasing facilities for technical and vocational education.
22. Expansion of university education.
23. Establishing new universities.
24. Special attention to the organisation of postgraduate courses.
25. Establishing centres of advanced study.
26. Increasing support to research in universities.
27. Developing part-time education and correspondence courses.

28. Spreading literacy and adult education.
29. Emphasis on the education of practising farmers.
30. Developing games and sports.
31. Protecting the rights of minorities.
32. Following uniform educational structures (10+2+3) in all parts of the country.

## Education Policy 1986

Having announced that a new policy was in development in January 1985, the government of Prime Minister Rajiv Gandhi introduced a new National Policy on Education (NPE) in May 1986. The new policy called for "special emphasis on the removal of disparities and to equalize educational opportunity," especially for Indian women, Scheduled Tribes (ST) and the Scheduled Caste (SC) communities. To achieve such a social integration, the policy called for expanding scholarships, adult education, recruiting, more teachers from the SCs, incentives for poor families to send their children to school regularly, development of new institutions and providing housing and services. The NPE called for a "child-centred approach" in primary education and launched "operation blackboard" to improve primary schools nationwide. The policy expanded the Open University system with the Indira Gandhi National Open University IGNOU, which was created in 1985. The policy also called for the creation of the "rural university" model, based on the philosophy of Mahatma Gandhi, to promote economic and social development at the grassroots level in rural India.

### *Some Salient Features of 1986 NPE*

1. National system of education.
2. Education for equality.
3. Promotion of adult education.
4. Elementary education and operation blackboard.
5. Setting up Navodaya Vidyalayas.
6. Emphasising vocational training.
7. Recognising the status of the teacher.
8. Introduction of accountability in education.

NPE was adopted by the Indian Parliament in May 1986. In May 1990, a committee was set up under the chairmanship of Acharya Ramamurthy to review NPE and to make recommendations for its modifications. That Committee submitted its Report in December 1990. At the request of the Central Advisory Board of Education (CABE), a committee was set up in July 1991 under the chairmanship of N.J. Reddy, Chief Minister of Andhra Pradesh, to consider modification in NPE taking into consideration the Report of the Ramamurthy Committee and other relevant developments on the Policy, and to recommend regarding modifications to be made in the NPE.

The NPE 1986 was modified in 1992 by the P.V. Narasimha Rao government. In 2005, the then Prime Minister Manmohan Singh adopted a new policy based on the "Common Minimum Programme" of the United Progressive Alliance (UPA) Government. Since the formulation of earlier policies on education, significant changes have taken place in India and the world at large. India's political, social, and economic development passed through a phase which necessitated a robust and forward-looking educational system. The educational activities and learning process are no longer confined to the classroom. The educational process is not only mediated by classroom-based curriculum transaction but also by media, both electronic and print. Learners today have access to more current knowledge through non-institutionalised means.

The changing social context of education as well as the national concerns for achieving the goal of equity and inclusion demanded a changed approach to education.

### Committee for Evolution of a National Education Policy 2016

The Government of India constituted a Committee for Evolution of the New Education Policy, which comprised of T.S.R. Subramanian, former Cabinet Secretary as the Chairman and Smt. Shailaja Chandra, former Chief Secretary, NCT of Delhi, Sevaram Sharma, former Home Secretary, UT of Delhi, Sudhir Mankad, former Chief Secretary, Gujarat and Prof. J.S. Rajput, former Director, National Council for Educational Research and Training (NCERT) as members of the Committee.

The Committee for the Evolution of a National Education Policy submitted the report containing its recommendations to the Union Ministry of Human Resource Development (UMHRD) in June 2016 under the name "Some Inputs for Draft National Education Policy 2016".

The Committee examined the large body of outcome documents, recommendations and suggestions received from various consultations. The Committee also had several meetings with various stakeholders, held regional consultations and undertook field visits to educational institutions.

The online consultations on www.mygov.in portal were held from 26 January 2015 to 31 October 2015 and over 29,000 suggestions were received. The bottom-up consultative process across nearly all Gram Panchayats, Blocks, urban local bodies and districts of all 36 States/Union Territories were undertaken between May to October 2015. Thematic consultations were conducted both by the ministry and also by the institutions like University Grants Commission, All India Council for Technical Education, National Council for Teacher Education, National Council for Teacher Educational Research and Training, and several centrally funded universities and institutions, autonomous bodies, attached offices. Also, all relevant stakeholders including experts, academics, industry representatives, civil society etc. were invited for deliberations on individual themes during July-October 2015. Six zonal meeting were held by the Ministry of Human Resource Development in eastern, central, north-eastern, western, southern and northern zones covering all States and UTs in September and October 2015.

### *Major Suggestions*

1. The main objective of the new National Policy on Education is to harness the full potential of a young vibrant population and equip it to contribute meaningfully to India's development.
2. The core objectives of this Policy are to provide information, knowledge, skills, and values; also to instill social attitudes which enable a student to become a good human being, a proud citizen, and contribute to the development of the country. Besides imparting quality education, the policy seeks to emphasise the need to foster an interest in India's history, culture and traditions, a respect for all religions and acceptance for the diversity that exists in India. Through education, the policy tries to create an understanding of the need to promote social cohesion and national integration which are essential for the country's progress. In the new technology-driven environment ever more students will become conversant with the tools of modern communication and technology. The Policy recognises the immense opportunities for using these to promote education at every level.

   Despite many gains, the Indian education system faces several problems, denting its credibility. The new Education Policy has addressed all these challenges. The main factors include:
   - Absence of minimum standards in the provision of schooling facilities, processes, and student outcomes, and equity in educational opportunities.
   - Lack of professionalisation in educational planning and management.
   - Absence of requisite disaggregated data, particularly at sub-national and institutional levels for evidence-based management of education.
   - Lack of competent and committed teachers, resulting in poor quality of education.
   - Substandard quality of teacher education and training.
   - A curriculum which encourages rote-based learning.
   - Malpractices in the examination system.
   - Neglect of skill and vocational education, overemphasis on acquiring dead-end qualifications which do not lead to employment.
   - Failure to make ICT functionally integral to the management of paedagogy of education.
   - Mushroom growth of private coaching classes and degree shops.

- Corruption and politicisation of education management at all levels.
- Mediocre status of a majority of higher education institutions.
- The pursuit of degree and qualification at any cost.

3. The span of activities covered in the education sector is vast, apart from the central and state governments, the stakeholders include numerous institutions, parents, teachers, and students in a climate of rising aspirations, the developments in the education sector require exceptional attention on a continuous basis. The problems faced by the education sector are complex and necessitate independent, considered, and mature response. The Ministry of HRD requires the assistance of a high-quality think tank in the form of a Standing Education Commission to study emerging challenges, evaluate and interpret policies and programmes, and provide information and guidance to the Ministry from time to time. The Commission should prepare a National State of Education Report once in two years. The Commission should comprise of a limited number of experts and persons of eminence with special knowledge and experience of the education sector in India, supported by a small secretariat.
4. India has one of the largest systems of higher education in the country, with more than 700 universities, 37,000 colleges, and an enrolment of more than three crore students. The quality of many universities and colleges and the standard of education they provide are far from satisfactory. While there are some institutions like the IITs, IIMs, and a few others that have established a reputation as institutions of high quality, there are a large number of institutions which are mediocre, and some are no better than 'teaching shops'. The majority of higher education institutions fall in between these two extremes.
5. The process of recognition of higher education institutions, general and technical needs require considerable revamping. Accreditation is an effective system for assessing the quality of higher education institutions. Accreditation validates and provides assurance that the quality of education provided by the institutions is of satisfactory standard. Assessment and accreditation enhance the reputation and acceptability of the institution and the value of the degrees conferred by it. At present accreditation is not compulsory for all higher education institutions. It is required only for receiving grants from government agencies. According to the information available, 140 universities got themselves accredited by the National Assessment and Accreditation Council (NAAC); but only 32 per cent were rated as 'A' grade or above. Most universities have been rated average. Quality and excellence in colleges clearly leave much to be desired. A credible system of accreditation covering all institutions of higher education needs to be instituted.

6. Many private universities and colleges, professional and otherwise, flourish under the patronage of influential people backed by money power with little interest in education, taking advantage of a lax or corrupt regulatory environment. The proliferation of privately run teaching shops and so-called non-profit institutions, ill-equipped and operating with unqualified staff, is a disturbing development and needs to be addressed urgently. It is necessary to weed them out through a process of accreditation for which transparent benchmarks have to be applied.
7. At present, accreditation is mandatory only for general stream higher education institutions receiving grants-in-aid from the UGC. Accreditation should be made mandatory for all institutions of higher education, including technical education, medicine and agriculture, both in public and private sectors.
8. Most of the older universities were created by law, either by the centre or the states. Though technically these universities are autonomous, in actual practice the intervention by governments is extensive. There is a need to remove such interventions and to give freedom to universities to focus on improving their academic performance through their own initiative.
9. Although India's overall share of research publications in the world has risen in the past decade, the quality of research has not made a significant mark. Barring a few pockets of excellence like IITs, IIMs, and a few top universities and institutions, the system is marked by mediocrity. Research-minded students and faculty prefer to go abroad as they do not find the research climate in our institutions very conducive. It is estimated that nearly three lakh students go abroad every year to study in the world's best universities, spending more than $10 billion, which is twice the allocation of the Union budget in higher education. Favourable conditions need to be created in the country to promote high quality research.
10. Over the next decade at least 100 new centres for excellence, in the field of higher education both in public and private sector need to be established. If this is successfully accomplished, it will pave the way for high quality research and innovation to be undertaken. A regulatory regime which can oversee and encourage the establishment of such institutions of excellence needs to be put in place.

It is hoped that the National Educational Policy 2020, formulated after taking into consideration the suggestions made by several committees and commissions and representatives of private sector, paves the way for required transformation.

# 2

# National Education Policy 2020

The last National Policy on Education was created in 1986. During these 34 years, the world has changed in unprecedented ways. Revolutionary alterations in the world's political economy, fuelled by technological developments, have significantly contributed to the dismantling of the barriers of gender, class, caste, culture, geographical distance, and so forth. All this has created a strong sense of aspiration and hope among the people. Rapid economic developments after 1991, the year when India opened economically, have triggered a high demand for knowledge and specialised skills. The National Education Policy (NEP) 2020, released on 29 July 2020, is an ambitious document. With an eye on the future, it speaks to all aspects of education during our times. The policy envisions a 'complete overhaul' of the education system.

## Important Suggestions Made in NEP 2020

- *New Pedagogical and Curricular Structure of School Education*: The old education system follows the 10+2 structure. The new system will have 5+3+3+4 curricular structure. This system will have 12 years of schooling with three years of Anganwadi /pre-schooling.

  This change in structure does not change the years that a child spends in formal education. They remain the same as before.
- *New Examination Structure*: The new structure brings changes to the examination structure too. As per existing norms, a child gives an examination after every academic year. But once the NEP is implemented, children will give examinations only in class III, V and VIII. Appropriate authorities will conduct the school examinations for grades III, V and VIII.

  The NEP does away with annual examinations and has proposed board examinations in Grades X and XII and will be focused more on core competencies rather than memorised facts and rote learning.
- *Free Education up to XII Standard*: Earlier, schooling was mandatory for children aged between 6 and 14 years. Now education will be compulsory for children between 3 to 18 Years. Children can get educated up to XII grade free of charge at any government educational establishment.
- *Mother Tongue as the Medium of Instruction*: It is obvious that the mother tongue is the first language that a child understands. Hence, understanding newer concepts will be much easier if done in the mother tongue itself. Due to this, children are able to grasp simple concepts easily. This will be made compulsory until V grade at least or preferably until the VIII.

The NEP also includes the three-language policy. It is mandatory that at least two of the three languages should be native to India,

- *Bagless Days and Informal Internship*: According to this, students will participate in a 10-day bagless period. During this period students from Grades VI-VIII will intern with local vocational experts such as carpenters, gardeners, potters, artists, etc. A provision of vocational education with internship from Class VI has been made, which will help students to be job ready and more skill oriented.
- *Coding for Children*: Children will now be able to learn to code from Class VI as coding will be included as a part of their curriculum.
  - Coding, in simpler terms, is the language used by computers to understand our commands and, therefore, process our requests.
  - Programming is a list of codes arranged in a sequence that results in the completion of work.
- *Multi-Stream Flexibility*: The compartmentalisation of students, after X standard into Arts, Science and Commerce will be blurred. Now students will be allowed to take up courses from varied streams depending on their interests. There will not be any rigid separation between academic streams, extracurricular activities and vocational streams in schools. Furthermore, Bachelor's Programmes too will be multidisciplinary in nature with no rigid separation between arts and sciences.
- *Accreditation Framework*: A new accreditation framework will be set up along with an independent authority to regulate public and private schools.
- *Teachers' Education*: A National Curriculum Framework for Teacher Education (NCFTE), will be programmed by the National Council for Teacher Education (NCTE) in consultation with NCERT. A 4-year integrated B.Ed degree course will be the minimum degree qualification for teaching by 2030.
- *Special Daytime Boarding Schools*: Special daytime boarding school 'Bal Bhavans' to be established in every state/district in India. This boarding school will be used for participation in activities related to play, career, art, etc.

## Recommendations for Higher Education Level

- *Common Entrance Tests*: Students now will be judged by common SAT like tests that will decide the eligibility of students for different colleges.
- *4-year Bachelor's degree with Entry/Exit Options*: A student will have the right and ability to go back at a later time to complete his education and graduate with a 4-year degree. He is allowed to transfer the credits be earned in the previous degree into the degree he chooses.

  'Academic Bank of Credits' will be established which will facilitate Credit transfers. A student who decides to drop out after completing two years can do so and will be provided with a diploma certificate associated with that degree. Students who drop out after three years will receive a bachelors missing out only on research opportunities present in the final year.

- *Fee Cap for Private Institutions*: The New policy suggests a cap on the fee charged by private institutions in the higher education space.
- *Opening up Higher Education to Foreign Students*: Every year 750,000 Indian students go abroad in pursuit of higher education. There might be an increasing interest from foreign universities to invest in India. This move will not only go a long way in reducing brain drain but also help in making global education more accessible.
- *Establishment of Higher Education Commission of India (HECI)*: Higher Education Commission of India (HECI) will be established for entire higher education, excluding medical and legal education. Both the public and private higher education institutions will be governed by the same set of norms.

  The affiliation system of colleges will be wiped out in 15 years and a mechanism to be implemented for granting graded autonomy to colleges. In near future, every college is expected to develop as an autonomous degree-granting college or a constituent college of a university.
- *Multidisciplinary Education and Research Universities (MERUs) and The National Research Foundation*: Multidisciplinary Education and Research Universities (MERUS) will be established at par with IITs, IIMs as per the matching global standards.

  All the courses at undergraduate, postgraduate, and Ph.D. levels will be made interdisciplinary. M.Phil. courses will be discontinued.

  An apex body for fostering strong research culture, namely The National Research Foundation, will be established, which will serve the purpose of creating a strong research culture and building research capacity in higher education.

  The NEP offers students the ability to have a broad-based education through multidisciplinary institutions. At the moment, the students tend to focus on engineering or medicine or law streams. They miss out on exposure to other aspects of lifelike humanities, music and art, etc.
- *Shift on Focus from "Local" to "Global" Cognition*: While the 1986 policy emphasised on achieving uniformity of education across social groups, it could not consider the competitive global landscape, which became important with the beginning of and the globalisation of the Indian economy post 1991 reforms. NEP 2020 is an attempt to balance local and global human resource needs of growing Indian economy.

In the 1980s, world economies were largely local, and some were in the transient phase. Comparatively, the world economies today are operating as complex global entities. Given that in 2020, most of the organisations have reached maturity and NEP 2020 focuses on augmenting individual aspirations and achieving excellence in the field of choice by providing options for education.

### Restructuring at Higher Education Level

There will also be a major overhauling of the regulatory system like UGC and other quality control agencies. Instead of the UGC there would be a few other agencies which would look after the entire system with different mandates.

The first one is the National Higher Education Regulatory Council (NHERC) which will be an overall body for regulatory provisions for all kinds of educational institutions at higher level.

For example, a university or institution may have within its direct jurisdiction different educational institutions like engineering and technology, management, medical, education, etc. Then it will have to approach and be subject to scrutiny from various regulatory bodies with differing standards of measurements based on the specific requirements of that particular profession's needs.

On the other hand, with a single body instead of several, it would be much more convenient and effective in implementing the system. At this point, another crucial aspect needs to be given due attention. Complaints of corrupt practices, in the process of renewing or freshly considering institutions for further affiliation of their credentials, are being reported from time-to-time. It must be ensured that such corrupt practices are negated by taking care of all the loopholes in the system.

### National Accreditation Council

Secondly, there shall be a National Accreditation Council (NAC) replacing the National Assessment and Accreditation Council (NAAC). Accreditation shall depend primarily on basic norms, public self-disclosures, good governance and outcomes to be carried out by an independent ecosystem of accrediting institutions supervised and overseen by this new agency (Mishra, 2020).

Taking a cue from the provisions here, it can be expected that the new system shall facilitate a faster and more efficient assessing and accreditation process in the future. This is important because today our country has about 1000 universities in different categories including state, central, deemed and private in addition to more than a hundred IITs, IIMs and institutes of national importance, etc.

This is relevant because according to the Director of NAAC (2020), since inception in 1994, this body has been able to assess and provide accreditation to just more than 13,000 institutions only out of a total of about 45,000 of them in higher education. This includes universities, colleges and stand-alone institutions across the nation. In an in-depth interview published in *The Times of India* in May 2020, the director expressed that possibility of poor grades was the reason behind non-participation of 22% of higher education institutions (HEIs) in the NAAC accreditation process. This is followed by about 26% of institutions not applying for it as they lacked permanent faculty with another 5.5% for not having a permanent head of the institution. That leaves 600 universities and 25,000 colleges across the country 'not accredited' yet.

While this is a hard fact yet it reveals the state of affairs and ground reality that needs to be effectively tackled with innovative measures. It is expected that with a new set up and resources at its disposal, the new body should be able to cope with the situation and bridge the gap in the near future. By any standard, this is an uphill task to say the least. The other associated challenge is to constantly keep monitoring those which are already accredited so that their grades do not slip from the basic minimum at any point of time in future.

## Higher Education Grants Council

The third agency under NHERC shall be the Higher Education Grants Council (HEGC) in place of the existing Higher Education Financing Agency (HEFA) which will take care of funding and financing requirements of higher education in the future. This agency shall have a highly crucial role in the future as financial needs are a major support variable in higher education. This is necessary for almost all aspects of the educational system from infrastructure to laboratories, facilities for students, faculty members and support staff or administration. While the virtual systems have reduced the dependence on finances to some extent yet money is necessary for many works to be carried out.

Educational institutions being academic organisations cannot be expected to generate the lion's share of running the entire institution for the whole year. Yes, to some extent it is possible to generate finances from consultancy projects by teachers, researchers, fees, overhead money from research projects etc. as well as some of the costs of day-to-day running of facilities like guest house, sophisticated instruments among others.

However, the situation may be somewhat different with institutions like IITs, NITs, IIMs which have scope for generating finances to a big extent without approaching the government funding bodies for the purpose. These factors need to be considered threadbare while proceeding with constitution of HEGC's funding and financing regulations so as to put the institutions at ease and convenience for going ahead with their ambitious and regular programmes in the coming days.

At this stage, the point raised above about more industry-academia interface has a connection. That is, HEIs invariably should approach industry for organisations in the field in relevant areas from whom support for research in terms of cash or kind can be solicited. For this aspect, the academia will need to play a proactive role and provide lead in this regard to come out with potential products and concepts from which industry can take a cue for further processing, and thereby provide adequate support to the academia in return.

This shall serve three major purposes: First of all, it will open up a big scope for both these areas to come together and work in tandem to collaborate further resulting in newer products and concepts as well as improvising existing ones alike.

Secondly, the bonding and trust between these two sides would grow to a meaningful and mutually beneficial level which will ultimately facilitate passing on the benefits to the society only. This aspect of increasing the reliability between these two sides will go a long way in delivering a better product to the society. Third but the most important aspect is that students would be among the first level beneficiaries in the process as they would get an opportunity to be involved or observing the system very closely. This shall enhance their professional and academic capability in the process. This shall also boost their employability quotient in future.

However, this interaction shall have to be increased in a graded manner in the future as barring some frontline technical HEIs, this is not a strong point of a good number of universities across the board.

## General Education Council

The fourth agency under the umbrella of NHERC is the General Education Council (GEC) which shall frame the expected learning outcomes of higher education programmes to be carried out through another panel called National Higher Education Qualification Framework (NHEQF). The latter shall be in tandem with the National Skills Qualification Framework (NSQF). These two panels within the GEC are expected to perform the precarious task of integrating vocational education into the general overall scheme of education. This is expected to lead to a judicious mixture of both the areas to benefit the future students in all potential areas of studies.

This is indeed a major decision with potential for far-reaching impact on the students' community. It is because such a blended education if implemented properly will facilitate the students to become skillful in any area of study and thereby become better-equipped for employment.

It may be mentioned here that this aspect is highly important as reports from the industry are not very positive in this direction. A 2018 (March) report in *The Hindu Business Line* quoting 'Aspiring Minds' informed that around 47% graduates of the country were 'unemployable'. Further, a 2019 article from *India Today* declared that over 80% Indian engineers are unemployable with lack of exposure to new-age technology skills. Quoting *Aspiring Minds* again, the report found that they are unemployable mainly as they lack the technological skills required by employers now.

If such a ground reality is of as recent origin as of 2018 and 2019, it definitely reflects some major problems in the system which needs to be dealt with on an emergent basis. This means that there has to be a major overhauling of the entire system that has been waiting to be tapped into over so many years. This mismatch between skills, exposure to new technologies, an aspiring and enterprising mindset need to be brought into the system with the minimum loss of time as crucial moments have already been lost in the run up to the preparedness of the policies of education system over the last few decades.

Further, the professional councils like All India Council for Technical Education (AICTE), Medical Council of India (MCI), Bar Council of India (BCI), National Council for Teacher Education (NCTE), Council of Architecture (CoA) etc. shall be functioning as Professional Standard Setting Bodies (PSSB). They shall be invited for working in close coordination as members of the overall body – GEC. They would continue performing their mandated business of drawing up relevant curricula with timely interventions and improvisations, laying down academic standards and coordinating between teaching, research, extension of their domain or discipline as and when required (Mishra, 2020)

### Research Receives its Coveted Status

Another major highlight of this policy is the higher emphasis put on the aspect of research at higher education level. For this purpose, specific institutions called Multidisciplinary Education and Research Universities (MERUs) shall be set up at par with IITs and IIMs. These will be specially dedicated towards research studies as the topmost focus of their objectives (Praveen, 2020). This shall be a right step in this direction as these institutions would be mandated and focused upon research activities without any distraction. While other universities or HEIs would also be encouraged to carry out as well as further boost up their research focus the MERUs would be far more focused upon this aspect. This is expected to deliver adequate positive results in the future. Committed towards achieving this goal in a properly-planned roadmap for the future, the policy has provided for the National Research Foundation (NRF) which shall facilitate high quality research findings expected to stand peer reviews of the highest standard across the world in any platform. NRF will also act as a coordinating agency through the National Mission Projects (NMPs) as a network among the Institution's Innovation and Research Council (IRC). This will be located at different identified HEIs of the nation (Mishra, 2020). A total of 80 IRCs and 25 NMPs are being planned to be established for a smooth functioning of the whole vision plan dedicated specially for research in each and every potential and viable field.

This step, if implemented effectively can be expected to yield our HEIs the much-needed boost towards recognition of global ranking status in the coming days as it has remained a disadvantage over the decades till now. In today's research-oriented academic world, findings and their publications, patents etc. constitute a significant portion of the ranking system. This is true for both at the national and international levels.

This is more important for the fact that these findings are also a measure of good performance for potential students and their guardians as there is a higher level of competition among HEIs for attracting students from across the world. Under the liberalised platform prevailing at present, the world itself is a potential market for reputed HEIs from any corner of the globe. These strengths in the field of research publications, innovations, patents have the potential also for inviting collaborative tie-ups from reputed HEIs both from within and outside the country.

Further, discontinuation of M.Phil degree has been a well-thought out provision as the contribution of this degree towards making students proficient in the field of research has been a case for debates over the decades. Thus, to inculcate the research aptitude among the students, provision has been made for a two-year Master's degree with the second year devoted specially to research. Also, those with a four-year bachelor's degree with one year of research would be eligible for Ph.D if the student had completed a one-year Master's degree.

In addition to all these features, the linkage of the educational chain right from school level to higher level is another high point of the policy. If implemented in the right spirit, it will go a long way in delivering the results in the near and distant future, and thereby develop a strong and robust base for educational development of the society.

### National Education Policy 2020 and Innovations

Innovation is successful implementation of creative ideas within an organisation or system. From this perspective, creativity of an individual is the starting point for innovation. Management Guru Peter Drucker referred to innovation as a change that creates a new dimension of performance. Steve Jobs argued that innovation differentiated a leader from the laggard. But conventional understanding about innovation is commercialisation of invention, which refers to new concepts or products that derive from individual's ideas or from scientific research. To be called an innovation, an idea must be replicable, economic and respond to a specific need. Innovation involves deliberate application of information, imagination and initiative in deriving greater or different value from resources, and encompasses all processes by which new ideas are generated and converted into useful products. In short, an action can be identified as innovation if it is new and useful to the system, increases efficiency, is cost-effective and compatible with or adaptable by other similar systems.

In education, innovation lies in continuous march toward excellence and devising improvement in paedagogy and teaching-learning processes for improving learner's progression curve. In short, innovation is successful implementation of creative ideas for affirmative change in the lives of the people. In the context of higher education, innovation implies systemic improvement in processes of teaching-learning, learner support and knowledge management to conserve national heritage and value systems. National Education Policy seeks to:

- Use innovative teaching-learning strategies to universalise access to education and achieve 50% GER in HE by 2030;

- Integrate all streams, including professional and vocational education, leading to emergence of one coherent HE eco-system and accord them parity of esteem;
- Technology to be the major intermediary for transaction of education to enhance access equity and inclusion of all sections of society living in isolation for centuries due to gender, location and religion;
- Promote online and digital education to reach the last mile in a stratified society and innovatively use OERs and MOOCs courses and materials to save resources (financial, human and physical);
- Parity of all educational systems, practise credit exemption and promote learner mobility, and
- Design credit-based flexible and innovative curricula in conventional as well as contemporary subjects of study. For instance, environment education could include study of climate change, pollution control, waste management, biological diversity, and sustainable development and living, among other topics.

## National Education Policy 2020 and Quality

Quality in common parlance refers to "degree of excellence" of a product. It is one of the most important issues in present-day higher education ecosystem in the country, in the past it was masked by our overdrive for enhancing access and providing equitable opportunities to HE to all. The perceptions of lending educators about quality vary considerably; some consider it as fitness of purpose and conformance to standards while others look at it as value for money, relevance to world of work and perfection, and consistency in performance (Ahmed and Garg, 2015). We believe that quality is continuing march toward excellence transparently for social cause. Assessment of quality deficit and devising ways to improve quality at various stages necessary for improving the outcomes defines quality control.

Quality assurance aims to identify and address gaps which affect learner performance adversely and hinder realisation of institutional vision and mission as also self-actualisation of learners. Quality assurance comprises evaluation of policies and procedures for their efficiency, applicability, suitability and efficacy so as to guide the institution and each stakeholder. Through quality assurance, we intend to ensure that prescribed quality specifications and standards are maintained in each activity chain and try to raise the bar gradually. In the context of HE, NEP views quality assurance as an instrument for:

- review of offerings to reflect on pedagogy, improve procedures for continuous (formative) and term-end (summative) evaluation for satisfactory learner progression and reposition these to include skills needed to be globally competitive;
- cultivation of culture of ownership of the institution by every stakeholder in the system;

- development of well-rounded individuals through paradigm shift towards value-based education; and
- incremental improvement in institutional performance standards through continuous professional development of all categories of employees and academics at all levels.

The policy's vision for quality assurance also includes:

- grant of graded autonomy, with accountability, to an institution, its leader as well as teachers and office staff since creativity blooms with fragrance of academic freedom;
- improvement in institutional leadership by minimising external influences and appointing enlightened deserving individuals with pragmatic vision and impeccable integrity, and
- Creation of self-reliant (Atmanirbhar) institutions by making interactive learning materials accessible and available to all learners.

As such some of the recommendations of NEP 2020 are highly cost-intensive. Moreover, all stakeholders of university fraternity would be required to be dedicated, unlearn past practices and relearn new ones through Continuous Professional Development programmes conducted by experts. Therefore, it would be advisable that the efforts on finding ways for addressing quality concerns are driven by the wisdom of practitioners and based on solid research evidence.

COVID-19 pandemic has made it amply clear that 'disruptive innovations and collaborative partnerships are inevitable for quality assurance in every field of human endeavour, including education, research and training. The private institutions, which have been largely responsible for expansion of professional higher education in India since 1991, which marked the beginning of liberalisation era, cater to about 80 per cent learners in professional programmes. Unlike leading foreign universities like Cambridge, Harvard, Oxford, and Stanford, Indian private universities, but for a few, tend to be of small size and scope, with little emphasis on R&D. These are invariably guided by "for profit" rather than for philanthropic considerations (though justifiable returns would be in order to sustain further growth). This is a catch-22 situation government regulators tend to control rather than facilitate development and private providers like ambiguity (Kulandai Swamy, 2006). The National Education Policy accords parity of esteem to all types of HE providers by recommending acceptability and credibility for the qualifications conferred or certifications made by them.

It is now well documented that Indian Higher Education is producing unemployable graduates who pass their examinations without being deep learners. They are not trained to develop intellectual creativity needed for problem solving, independent thinking, asking probing questions and digital skills suited to 21st Century (Das et al, 2019). Moreover, conventional teachers have traditionally refrained from using technology in curricular transactions either due to their ignorance about its capabilities for value addition or they view it as an agent that would marginalise their role and adversely affect their importance (Panda and Garg, 2019). However, such impressions are misplaced technology enhances the reach of the word of mouth as also the effectiveness of a teacher in spatial as well as temporal dimensions (Garg, 2015). It facilitates interaction in a number of ways. And it would be no exaggeration to remark that growth in education and technological developments have direct correlation with the growth in education. It is despite the fact that technology could not replace, simulate or even imitate the teacher in the classroom truly and completely. But the point we wish to make is that technology improves quality by creating a rich learning environment for individualised instruction and unleash the entrepreneurial energy of our youth.

In so far as availability of technology for education is concerned, India has kept pace with developments and applications of ICTs for education and training. But the major problem has been that all these ICTs and related paedagogies/andragogies of teaching-learning have remained at the periphery, sporadically used as supplementary, and operate in a context where there is lack of a holistic and innovative use for teaching-learning. The government initiated reformative schemes such as choice-based credit system (CBCS), B.Voc degrees, Deen Dayal Upadhyay Skill Centres and UGC Regulation 2016 for SWAYAM are bound to improve quality of education for learners living in isolated and far flung areas. In parallel, there have also been developments in technologies and networks to support quality teaching-learning in information highway (Ahmed and Garg, 2015)

### Assessment, Accreditation and Quality

Experience shows that quality enhancement is facilitated by unbiased assessment and accreditation of an institution without preconceived ideas. Assessment and accreditation are viewed as complementary to quality, innovation, and autonomy by some practioners, while these are considered voluntary and self-regulatory by many educationists (Garg and Kaushik, 2020). Assessment is essentially evaluation of institutional vision, mission, core values, objectives, plans, input processes, infrastructure, and outcomes by an external agency based on certain pre-decided performance indicators with the sole purpose of improving it further. It gives an idea of the quality of the outcomes. But evaluation of quality of these aspects to qualify an institution for some status or recognition is known as accreditation (Ahmed and Garg, 2015). It serves mainly three purposes: (i) formulation of educational norms and institutional recognition, (ii) quality assurance and improvement in standards; and (iii) creation of awareness among stakeholders about the quality of education imparted by an institution.

The accreditation process can lead to a win-win situation for all stakeholders: learners get confidence that the programme being pursued by them and offered by their institution enjoys acceptability in the system; the public, including the employer groups, get satisfaction that the institution is conforming to certain standard of expectation; and the institution concerned gets a boost in its reputation and legitimacy. Moreover, by reengineering its offerings strategically with appropriate inbuilt checks and balances, an institution can boast of being trending. Also, accreditation process generates healthy competition with other institutions (Das et al., 2019).

The purpose of quality in India would be served better only if knowledgeable and reputed professors are associated in assessment and accreditation exercise because only they would be equipped with appropriate skills to guide and suggest ways for improvement. (Experience shows that those with natural tendency to bend forward find access to corridors of power and do little to justify their presence.) This highlights the need to take holistic view while framing guidelines for regulation of infrastructure, human capital, fee to be charged, and admissions, etc. so that society can get access to quality higher education at affordable cost.

It is a well-accepted fact that certain institutions of higher education enjoy definite preferences of students, parents, and employers. In India, the IITs and IIMs are institutions of choice in higher education. Of late, the process of accreditation by NAAC has undergone gradual change, so as to comply with the National Institutional Ranking Framework (NIRF) institutional ranking by government (besides assessment and accreditation by UGC) – a decision which was an outcome of disenchantment with India's showing in the world ranking of higher education institutions.

## Employment vs Employability: India's Dual Challenges

Most of the young Indians worry about the employment opportunities in the country in the Covid and post-Covid era. According to the World Bank, over 30% of Indians between the ages of 15-29 are NEETs (not in education, employment or training). In 2016, National Skill Development Corporation (NSDC) trained more than 5.5 lakh workers, only 12% of these trainees found jobs. The government has two big challenges ahead: India needs to create some 10-12 million jobs a year. The models of job creation that have worked in the past, will not work in future. Until the turn of the century, jobs were created in capital intensive sectors. Investment in manufacturing, mining, power plants etc. has created jobs before. The public sector banks have been large employers. Automation is making that opportunity disappear. Many of the jobs that have disappeared have been blue collared jobs. A good case in point is the Hyundai plant in Chennai that churned out a car every 72 seconds last year. Along with 8,500 workers five hundred robots were deployed for this job. The robots do not take days off and the employers do not need to worry about robot unions. The fact to be kept in mind is that the top five companies of the world (Apple, Alphabet, Microsoft, Amazon, Facebook) are tech companies. Their combined market value stands at $3.5 trillion. The entire stock market in India stands at $2.3 trillion. Means, the majority of jobs in future will be Tech-jobs.

As per India Skills Report 2019-20, only 46.21% students were found employable or ready to take up jobs in 2019, compared with 33 per cent in 2014, and 47.38 per cent in 2018. As per Centre for Monitoring Indian Economy (CMIE) unemployment data, unemployment rate was as high as 22.89% (May, 2020) due to Covid crisis to now somewhat stabilise at 7.65% (Aug, 2020). So, on one hand, the country has 7.65% unemployed youths, on the other hand only 46.21% of the youths are employable. Also, 56% of companies have been affected by skill shortage in the country.

According to the Manpower Talent Storage Survey – 2018, rapid globalisation and technological change have shaped the world's job market and Skill shortages have become a growing problem for employers. The scale of the problem varies hugely between countries, and it is most pronounced in Asia. Japan was the country most severely affected, with 89 per cent of companies affected with the problem. China improved their supply of skilled workers significantly since 2014, with its rate dropping from 24 per cent to 13 per cent. India also improved its performance as rate has dropped from 64% (2014) to 56% (2018). In 2015 Skill Gap analysis, expected shortfall in industry in 2022. Though the conditions has improved since 2015 as per India Skills Report 2019-20, but the projection may provide an approximation regarding the probable skill gap in 2022.

### Bottlenecks in Employability

Major bottlenecks in employability are discussed here.

- *Low Coverage*: One of the major reasons for India's Employment vs Employability, a double edge sword *syndrome, has been a very small percentage of the Indian workforce in the age group of* 19–24 (less than 5%) received formal Vocational Education whereas in countries such as the USA the number is 52%, in Germany 75%, and South Korea it is as high as 96%. These numbers only underline the urgency of the need to hasten the spread of vocational education in India.
- *The Demand-Supply Mismatch*: The current vocational programmes are largely supply-driven and still lack of relevant training for available jobs. There is a need to improve links between schools and the industry to minimise this mismatch. A divergence between the skills that the population possesses and skills required by industry is a major cause of low employability among Indian youth.
- *Poor Perception and Public Mindset*: Many Indian parents want their children to pursue a clerical job or be an office assistant, not realising

that a technician can earn more than these jobs. In countries like India Vocational Education (VE) has always been considered by the public and parents as the career choice for the less academically-qualified with the impression that VE is for school drop-outs, rather than as an important strategy to train skilled workers. Too much attention and resources are given to academic rather than vocational education. Vocational education has focused largely on Grades XI-XII and on dropouts in Grade VIII and upwards. Students passing out from Grades XI-XII with vocational subjects often did not have well-defined pathways to continue with their chosen vocations in higher education. The admission criteria for general higher education were also not designed to provide openings to students who had vocational education qualifications, leaving them at a disadvantage relative to their compatriots from mainstream or academic education. This led to a complete lack of vertical mobility for students from the vocational education stream. It is perceived to be inferior to mainstream education and meant largely for students who are unable to cope with the latter.

- *Inadequate Academia-Industry Linkage*: This results in low rates of employment due to the reason that what job providers are seeking for, are not communicated with the training sector besides it also affects the placement.
- *Lack of Updated Curriculum*: An updated curriculum which is relevant to present day need of the industry is a major requirement. The curriculum should be relevant to be need of the industry.
- *Shortage of Qualified Teachers*: Availability of good quality trained and qualified teachers and trainers is an important problem. Poor recruitment process of governments is responsible for this.

## Probable Solutions for Employment Problems as Recommended by NEP 2020

NEP 2020 aims to overcome the social status hierarchy associated with vocational education and envisions integration of vocational education programmes into mainstream education in all education institutions in a phased manner. Beginning with vocational exposure at early ages in middle and secondary school, quality vocational education will be integrated smoothly into higher education. It will ensure that every child learns at least one vocation and is exposed to several more.

By 2025, at least 50% of learners through the school and higher education system shall have exposure to vocational education. The development of vocational capacities will go hand-in-hand with the development of academic or other capacities. Vocational education will be integrated in the educational offerings of all secondary schools in a phased manner over the next decade. Towards this, secondary schools will also collaborate with ITIs, polytechnics, local industry, etc. Skill labs will also be set up and created in the schools in a hub and spoke model which will allow other schools to use the facility. The B.Voc. degrees introduced in 2013 will continue to exist, but vocational courses will also be available to students enrolled in all other bachelor's degree programmes, including the 4-year multidisciplinary bachelor's programmes.

### Light but Tight Regulation

The mushrooming of regulatory agencies in India is one of the prime reasons for India's problems in maintaining the quality of its higher education institutions. In the National Policy on Education of 1986 and Programme of Action of 1992, it was recommended that a National Higher Education Council should be established. Unfortunately, the recommendation was ignored. The National Knowledge Commission (2006-09) again raised the issue of having an autonomous regulatory body for higher education and it recommended the establishment of the Independent Regulatory Authority for Higher Education. In 2009, the Professor Yash Pal Committee Report on Renovation and Rejuvenation of Higher Education also recommended the constitution of a National Commission by merging the then more than a dozen higher education regulatory agencies.

Regulation of higher education has been too heavy-handed for decades; too much has been attempted to be regulated with too little effect. Heavy concentrations of power within a few bodies, conflicts of interest among these bodies, and a resulting lack of accountability are the major issues Regulatory system is suffering from. To address these issues, NEP envisions the distinct functions of Regulation, Accreditation. Funding and Academic standard setting will be performed by distinct, independent, and empowered bodies.

To ensure that the four institutional structures carrying out these four essential functions work independently yet at the same time and work in synergy towards common goals, an overarching umbrella institution, the Higher Education Commission of India (HECI) will be established. Regulation, Accreditation, Funding and Academic standard, these four structures will be set up as four independent verticals under HECI.

HECI will be a new avatar of UGC with a different vision, focus and powers. HECI will also have penalisation powers against the institutions on violation of rules. Substandard institutions can also be closed. Governments across political hues have advocated a single higher education regulator as this can help clean up the regulatory mess in higher education, do away with overlaps and create an ecosystem conducive to nurturing institutes of excellence.

- The first vertical of HECI will be the National Higher Education Regulatory Council (NHERC). It will function as the common, single point regulator for the higher education sector including Teacher Education and excluding Medical and Legal Education, thus eliminating the duplication and disjunction of regulatory efforts by the multiple regulatory agencies that exist at the current time. NHERC will be set up to regulate in a light but tight and facilitative manner, meaning that a few important matters particularly financial probity, good governance, and the full online and offline public self-disclosure of all finances, audits, procedures, infrastructure, faculty/staff, courses, and educational outcomes will be very effectively regulated.

- The second vertical of HECI will be a meta-accrediting body, called the National Accreditation Council (NAC). Accreditation of institutions will be based primarily on basic norms, public self-disclosure, good governance, and outcomes, and it will be carried out by an independent ecosystem of Accrediting Institutions supervised and overseen by NAC.
- The third vertical of HECI will be the Higher Education Grants Council (HEGC), which will carry out funding and financing of higher education based on transparent criteria.
- The fourth vertical of HECI will be the General Education Council (GEC), which will frame expected learning outcomes for higher education programmes. A National Higher Education Qualification Framework (NHEQF) will be formulated by the GEC and it shall be in sync with the National Skills Qualifications Framework (NSQF) to ease the integration of vocational education into higher education.
- The professional councils, such as the Indian Council for Agricultural Research (ICAR), Veterinary Council of India (VCI), National Council for Teacher Education (NCTE), Council of Architecture (CoA), National Council for Vocational Education and Training (NCVET) etc., will act as Professional Standard Setting Bodies (PSSBs). They will play a key role in the higher education system and will be invited to be members of the GEC. These bodies, after restructuring as PSSBs, will continue to draw the curricula, lay down academic standards and coordinate between teaching, research and extension of their domain/discipline, as members of the GEC.

### Public Expenditure

India's public education spending has not been enough to either attract foreign talent to the country or develop indigenous top brains, a recent World Talent ranking report 2019 by IMD showed. India spends less on education per student, and the quality of education also remains dismal in the country according to the IMD report. This has resulted in a massive dip in India's world talent ranking and the country is just ahead of four other nations in attracting and retaining top talent. India was ranked 59th among 63 countries in the 2019.

IMD World Talent Ranking released by International Institute for Management Development, a Switzerland-based business school. In 2019, India slipped by six places as compared to 53rd rank in 2018 edition of this global annual list. Switzerland topped the list. India is also lagging behind fellow BRICS countries – China ranked 42nd, Russia 47th and South Africa 50th. This is where country stands globally. When as per Economic survey 2019-20, combined (Centre and States) expenditure on education has been continuously increasing.

NEP also highlights that public expenditure on education in India has not come close to the recommended level of 6% of GDP, as envisaged by the 1968 Policy, reiterated in the NEP-1986 and further reaffirmed in the Plan of action (POA)-1992. The current public (Union and States Governments) expenditure on education in India has been around 4.43% of GDP and only around 10% of the total government spending is towards education. These numbers are far smaller than most developed and developing countries. The policy recommends to increase the public investment in education sector to reach 6% of GDP at the earliest.

## Way Forward

Padma Vibhushan Prof. Krishnaswamy Kasturirangan led National Education Policy drafting panel has accomplished its job and handed over a well drafted National Education Policy document to the country. The Cabinet has accorded approval to the Policy and implementation has actually started with the rechristening of MHRD as Ministry of Education (MoE). The Policy contains rigorously thoughtful interventions like consolidation, multidisciplinary, flexibility; autonomy and enhanced focus on research and innovation, all of them have been widely recognised as the principles of highest quality across the higher education fraternity globally. The policy provides a time frame of 20 years subject to the various recommendations. The real outcome of this entire process will definitely depend upon the implementation of the policy in letter and spirit by Union and States Government in best collaborative manner. Now, governments (Centre and States) would come forward with the roadmaps of implementation, since education being a subject of concurrent list, the Centre-States team-India and cooperative federalism spirit will a play prominent role in the policy-implementation, that truly ought to be the final destination of all the recommendations, for a lot of them, the country has been waiting since long.

## Criticisms of NEP 2020 as Cited in Social Media

Some criticisms are also observed on the NEP 2020 on social media with Reject NEP 2020 trending on Twitter. According to the Indian Constitution, regulations of different sectors of society are demarcated by three different lists, namely the Union list, the State list, and Concurrent list. As these names suggest, the Union government makes laws on matters in the Union list, the state government makes laws on issues under the State list and both the union and state government govern matters under the Concurrent list. When laws are to be made on topics under the Concurrent list, it is first put up as a draft for a threshold period. This threshold period is to encourage suggestions and discourse from the states or eminent personalities from the respective fields of the draft bill. Education is listed as a concurrent subject. Major criticism is that it was bypassed in the parliament, thereby violating the set code of conduct. A new policy introducing such substantial changes must undergo discourse in the parliament. Will this lead to centralised, communalised and commercialised education system?

The English language is not only of paramount value for global outreach, but it is also essential in connecting and communicating with people from other states within India. Career building, outsourcing technical support and skills are dominated by western conglomerates where English has utmost importance. In the new scheme, English will only be offered from the secondary level. Children from families who cannot afford to polish their children's English competence will lose out on opportunities. Discontinuing English as the main medium might make fluency in English based on whether you can afford private tutors, thus disadvantaging the population who see English as a way to escape caste hierarchy. Mainstreaming Sanskrit in India would be synonymous to the west mainstreaming Latin. Biblical Latin is a dead language; similarly, Sanskrit is used by less than 1% of the Indian population. Mainstreaming this ancient language would only be seen as a regressive step. At the time of the 2001 census on bilingualism and tri-lingualism, the number of English speakers in India was at 125 million and this number ought to have increased since then. The English language is what has given India an edge over a majority of south-east Asia. Even the Chinese government, who until recently only promoted the Chinese medium, is bringing in reforms and introducing the English language in their education system.

Under the new policy, private and self-governed colleges will receive more autonomy. When these colleges handout certifications unchecked, corporatism may follow. This will create a situation where higher studies become a privilege only for those who can afford it. A centralised education system will amount to a stepping-stone to social exclusion and dilution of the Right to Education Act. The government stated that it is proposing to improve the quality and autonomy of higher education, however, in a completely backward move; it is dismantling the University Grants Commission (UGC) which was a core structural and regulatory body for higher education. This will only accelerate the commodification and centralisation of education.

Organisations and institutions when vested with educational structure and financial autonomy will be enabled to create additional courses and departments. However, without funding from government bodies, institutions will naturally turn to the students. The tuition fee will substantially increase, not just for students in that particular department, but all the students attending that institution. This coupled with another feature offered by the NEP, i.e., multiple exit options at universities will increase the drop out rates. Under the multiple exit and entry option, if a student decides to leave mid-course, he/she will receive appropriate certification for credits earned until that point which will be digitally stored in an Academic Bank of Credit (ABC). A 'Certificate', a 'Diploma', a 'Bachelor's Degree' and 'Bachelor's Degree with Research' respectively will be awarded for each year of a four-year course. With financial autonomy resulting in financial burden on students and availability of certification each year, more students will be prompted to drop out. This creates an immense disparity between financially able and disabled students. Financially better-off students will get higher chances for studies and be able to acquire better opportunities. This would again amount to dilution of the Right to Education Act.

The government has introduced vocational and polytechnic education for school students through the new policy under the title "Reimagining vocational education, which aims to remove the hard separation between academic and vocational streams. Vocational subjects will be introduced as early as grade VI, including internship opportunities from grades VI to XII. This however ignores the importance of ensuring basic mainstream education to all students till at least grade X. Students opting for such courses will certainly not be from privileged backgrounds. Children who are economically backward and belonging to lower rungs of people who struggle in English, coding, etc. would end up opting for these streams. Introducing this at such an early age will form a barrier for first-generation learners and those from disadvantaged backgrounds to access higher education.

While NEP 2020 aims for many much-needed positive changes. The possibility of amplifying existing fault lines in Indian society needs to be looked into. The policy will seemingly increase the economic divide in a country that is already divided by religion, caste, gender, and wealth. It may make it nearly impossible for disadvantaged classes to climb up the social ladder. Are all of these move steppingstones to achieve saffronisation? It will take years before the policy goes into full swing and only then will these complexities become apparent. The method of implementation will determine its successes and failures. The flaws in this policy need to be addressed with deliberation through proper code of conduct to reduce the current shortfalls.

# 3

# National Transformation Vision

Transforming India has been the dream of many political leaders of the past and present. Pandit Nehru, India's first Prime Minister, in his 'tryst with destiny' address to the members of the constituent assembly on August 14, 1947, had appealed to them to transform India, by saying, "Awake to freedom. Long years ago, we made a tryst with destiny, and now the time comes when we shall redeem our pledge, not wholly or in full measure, but very substantially..." "We have to build the noble mansion of free India where all her children may dwell." His dream was to industrialise India using the tools of Science and Technology and developing the scientific temper amongst the people. He considered the industries as 'modern temples of India'. To generate the manpower needed to industrialise the country, he initiated the setting up of the IITs. Unfortunately, the dreams of the politicians did not percolate to energise the higher education system.

Another the then Prime Minister, Indira Gandhi, came up in 1971, with the slogan "Garibi Hatao, Desh Bachao." (Abolish Poverty, Rescue the Nation) and transform India. The role of education and skill building as precursors to economic development was also mentioned. But the slogan remained a political slogan. A subsequent appraisal suggests that all in all the "garibi hatao" (Remove Poverty) did little and accomplished less.

Once again, the Higher Education System did not participate, with vigour, in this "transformation process". The education system remained on the fringe.

One then saw the arrival of the rocket technologist, APJ Abdul Kalam as the President of India. He dreamt of a 'Developed India' by the year 2020! He remained passionate and committed to what he called Vision 2020 – transforming India with a focussed manifesto for change. He dreamt of a nation where education with a good value system is not denied to any meritorious candidates because of societal or economic discrimination. He further envisaged India as a nation which is the best destination for the most talented scholars, scientists, and investors from around the world.

The *India Vision 2020* document was prepared at the time of Prime Minister P.V. Narasimha Rao. It was given to his successor, Atal Bihari Vajpayee, who announced in Parliament as well as in one of his Independence Day addresses that India will become an economically developed nation by 2020.

The higher education system continued to be in a state of despondency and the political system did not have much faith in its role in transforming India. Prime Minister Manmohan Singh, in 2007, expressed his concern by saying:

"Our University System is, in many parts, in a state of disrepair ...higher education enrolments are abysmally low, almost two-third of our universities and 90 per cent of our colleges are rated as below average on quality parameters ... I am concerned that in many states university appointments, including that of Vice Chancellors, have been politicized and have become subject to caste and communal considerations and there are complaints of favouritism and corruption."

He immediately appointed a high-level National Knowledge Commission (NKC) to suggest major reforms and changes needed in India's higher education system to transform India's socio-economic status. He Suggested several reforms for "Expansion, Excellence and Equity" in India's higher education system. While some initial steps were taken for bringing in expansion of the system, the major challenges of reforms remained to be tackled. The concern remained as regards the non-availability of skilled manpower of quality. Indian universities were not being recognised in the top 200 universities of the world. The question of transforming India, with non-availability of talented manpower in large numbers, remained a major challenge to the higher education system,

On July 15, 2015, Prime Minister Narendra Modi, launched his pet project "Skill India Campaign" in New Delhi on the occasion of the first ever World Youth Skills Day which included the launch of the National Skill Development Mission and unveiling of the new National Policy for Skill Development and Entrepreneurship 2015.

Over the next decade, India will have a surplus manpower of 4-5 crores and the Prime Minister emphasised the need to provide this youthful manpower with skills and ability to tackle global challenges. Prime Minister Modi warned that the demographic dividend would otherwise become a challenge in itself.

The Prime Minister had further said that while in the 20th century the IITs made a name for them globally, now in the 21st century ITIs (Industrial Training Institutes) should acquire global recognition for producing quality skilled manpower. He also called for constant updating of training programmes and syllabi to ensure that the youth are exposed to the latest technology and industry environment.

The Skill Development programme also stated that the country's population pyramid is expected to bulge across the 15-59 age group over the next decade.

This is a major challenge given to the higher education system in India. Transforming India through the development and use of skilled, educated manpower is now the major challenge facing the higher education system. With these concerns, for the first time perhaps, the agenda of "Transforming India" has been directly connected with the objectives of the higher education system.

The Government of India has brought out a National Education Policy (NEP) to meet the changing dynamics of the population's requirement with regard to quality education, innovation and research, aiming to make India a knowledge superpower by equipping its students with the necessary skills and knowledge and to eliminate the shortage of manpower in science, technology, academics and industry. The responsibility of "Transforming India" is going to be squarely placed on the shoulders of the higher education system.

P.J. Lavakar discussed the role of Higher Education in Transforming India under three heads:

1. Role of Students
2. Role of Teachers
3. Role of Institutions

### 1. Role of the Students

Development of skilled manpower is the key to transforming India in the coming years. Today, about 30 million students are in the tertiary education stream in 712 universities and over 36,000 colleges. In this large pool, there are certainly some outstanding students, who are motivated, talented and hardworking and doing their bit to transform India. But this group is miniscule compared to the large number of students who, by the time they come out of their institutions, with an undergraduate degree, are not ready for the employment market. If they are not ready for the local employment market, how can India expect to supply skilled manpower to the rest of the world, as has been proclaimed by the political leaders?

The sub-sections below give the elements of the "Transforming India Matrix" that focuses on the role of the students in the functions of the three pillars of higher education – Teaching, Research and Service.

#### (a) *Student and the "Teaching" Pillar of Activity*

Based on the above analysis of the student learning shortfalls, the following steps are given as suggestions that the students would have to consider:

i. Avoid Rote Learning;
ii. Widen your reading habits;
iii. Be aware of, and also study, global issues that face us today;
iv. Acquire problem solving skills;
v. Work hard to get opportunities to study abroad for a few months;
vi. Meet and know more about international students who are going to be your competitors in the global employment market.

The students have to increasingly get into the learning mode, through national and international approaches and through the use of modern technologies

#### *(b) Student and the "Research" Pillar of Activity*

Having observed that the "research culture" is lacking in our undergraduate education, the students have to be conscious that their counterparts in other parts of the world already have exposure to research by the time they graduate.

Hence are able to directly develop problem solving skills as soon as they enter the real life of employment. Following measures are suggested for the students to imbibe some aspects of research by the time they complete the graduation:

i. Develop a sense of curiosity about the topics in your syllabus;
ii. Discuss new and interesting topics with other students;
iii. Use Internet to gather new information on your course contents;
iv. Think how your classroom knowledge can be applied in real life situation;
v. Dream new ideas and innovate new approaches to learning by doing;
vi. In the final year of your undergraduate degree undertake a research project with your teacher and write a paper on your findings.

Students must accept the "research" agenda more seriously, if they wish to transform India.

### *(c) Student and the "Service" Activity*

The undergraduate Indian students do not get any opportunity of being immersed, on a sustainable basis, in any of the societal issues or problems that face India. The National Social Service (NSS) programme does not have the rigour and emotional commitment that is required today. Following are some suggestions for action by the students:

i. Study and understand your country its social, economic and political status.
ii. Study your surrounding localities and identify the developmental issues that you can try to solve with your knowledge.
iii. Analyse the various national missions like, "Swachh Bharat", "Make in India, Digital India" and identity projects that you can formulate in your own surroundings.
iv. Devote specific time for doing focussed community service project over your academic years.

Finally, become "Global Citizens" with Indian Ethos. Remember the three important 'H's in your life Honesty, Hard work and Humility. Cultivate them with passion. Remember you can change and transform India if you pursue this ambition with zeal . . . . and remember the three-word advice of a Nobel laureate... to succeed "Don't Give Up!"

## 2. Role of the Teachers (Faculty)

If one is expecting the large population of students to "Transform India", it must be recognised that the teachers will have to take greater responsibilities in energising the students to the new challenges that will be involved in transforming India. Following sub- sections will look at some of the challenges and opportunities that will have to be considered by the teacher community to fulfil their role of "Transforming India" through the three higher education pillars of activity viz. "Teaching", "Research" and "Service".

#### *(a) Teachers and the Pillar of Teaching*

With the availability of Internet and the advent of Information Technology, teaching/learning activity has become fairly advanced. With the availability of massive open online courses (MOOCs and Coursera); students have access to knowledge without the presence of the teacher in the classroom. At the same time, the students are expecting the teachers to give them their perspective based on their experience and maturity.

#### *(b) Teachers and the Pillar of Research*

In taking up these dynamic challenges, the teacher community has to immerse itself more than ever before into the realm of research and innovation. All teachers must be introduced to (if not already familiar with) the research methodologies that help in creating new approaches to finding the unknown and improving the knowledge base for teaching. If the teachers themselves get involved in research activities, the student would automatically get interested in such efforts.

#### *(c) Teachers' Responsibility to the Society: The Third Pillar of Service*

"Transforming India" is very much connected with understanding the society that has to be transformed, its needs and the tools that could be effectively used for this transformation. Following are some suggestions for the consideration of the teacher community in their efforts to ensure commitment to the 'Service' function of higher education:

1. Get socially involved with the local community that may be able to use your knowledge and expertise.
2. Encourage students to get involved in planned and sustainable community service in the neighbouring community of NGOs, development organisations, local public schools, orphanages, etc.
3. Be a mentor to a community development project selected by the students. Devote part of your holidays and spare time to well conceived community service projects in your neighbourhood.

### 3. Role of the Institutions

The students and the teachers can be important "actors" in the mission of "Transforming India". But they cannot be effective unless the educational institutions and the management of the institutions provide the policy framework and necessary support system for them to get involved in the proposed transformation process. Some of the initiatives that the institutions can take up under each of the pillars of higher education are suggested in the following sub- sections:

#### *(a) Institutions and the 'Pillar' of Teaching*

It is unfortunate that the quality of teaching in our higher education system has been criticised time and again by the society, particularly by the Industry, who is perhaps the main users of the products of higher education. Even internationally, our educational institutions are not being recognised amongst the top ranking world institutions. At the same time, one must admit, that the same education system is producing some outstanding students who excel in their careers as they cross the national boundaries and enter a new competitive environment outside. Examples of Indian origin academicians are often quoted to make India proud. But these examples are small in number compared to the large population of India. There is no question that the Indian academic institutions have to put their best foot forward, particularly if they want to take up the bigger agenda of "Transforming India", as proposed now.

### *(b) Institutions and the 'Pillar' of Research*

One of the major initiatives of our educational institutions to be able to "Transform India" would be to pay greater attention to the activity of "Research" than what has been done so far. In the knowledge society of the 21" century, creating new knowledge in the higher education system, and ensuring that it is usable and applied to produce economic benefits, could be major 'Transforming India' initiative.

One of the important reasons why Indian educational institutions are not figuring in the top ranking institutions of the world is the fact that the research output from our universities is insignificant to what one sees in the other world class universities. It is suggested therefore that the educational institutions and their managements, take into account some of the suggestions made above to transform India's position in the world.

### *(c) Educational Institutions and the Pillar of 'Service' to Society*

Many of the higher education institutions have taken an elitist approach of pursuing knowledge through Teaching and Research activities. This has eluded their contact with the daily life of the society in which they operate. The government is now looking at the educational institutions to contribute to its major programme of development of skilled manpower to transform India. Developing skilled manpower without understanding the skills required for development of the society, would not result in the "transforming India" agenda that the higher education system seems to be setting up for itself.

The vast infrastructure of our universities and colleges spread across various states of India can definitely contribute to the development of the society and "Transform India", provided a conscious strategy towards this goal is adopted.

## Transforming Higher Education Quality

By 2030, India will be amongst the youngest nations in the world. With nearly 140 million people in the college-going age group, one in every four graduates in the world will be product of the Indian higher education system. By 2030, the already existing challenges for Indian higher education – access, equity and quality – will only be greatly exacerbated unless we significantly transform our higher education model. Needless to say, 2030 calls for a new vision and a new aspiration, and this is the genesis of the "Higher Education in India: Vision 2030" report – to articulate an ambitious vision for higher education reform and lay out a roadmap to achieving it.

Indian demography is characterised by significantly high proportion of youth. Whether this demographic advantage would be translated into a powerful engine of growth or be a major drag on our development is largely dependent on empowerment of our youth through quality higher education. Such an education should be holistic incorporating teaching at the frontiers, translation of knowledge to cutting edge technology through nurturing of conductive innovation ecosystem and application of technology to understand and solve problems before the society and industry. Besides, a holistic learning environment should enable acquisition of relevant skills and develop sensitivity to surrounding environment comprising of human beings, life and nature.

M.C. Patel and R.M. Patel in an article in *University News,* 54(05) 2016 offered the suggestions for transforming Indian Higher Education quality, under the following heads:

*Towards a Learning Society*
*Industry and Academia Connection*
*Incentives to Teachers and*
*Innovative Practices*
*To Mobilise Resources*
*Coming of information age*
*Student centred education and dynamic method*
*Public private partnership*
*Provide Need Based Job-Oriented Courses*
*International Cooperation*
*Towards the New Vision*
*Cross Culture Programmes*
*Action Plan for Improving Quality*
*Individuality*
*Privatisation of Higher Education*
*Quality Development*
*World Class Education*
*Personality Development*
*Status of Academic Research Studies*

# 4

# Promotion and Expansion of Higher Education

India has a long and venerable history of higher education. In ancient times, the country was home to the oldest formal universities in the world. Higher education in Ancient India was considered religious. The basic religions were Hinduism, Buddhism and Jainism. Religion-based education in Ancient India had an outstanding role in creating, transforming and transmitting knowledge to the people in society. These were in the early times of Indian civilisation and attracted students from all parts of India, Central Asia, China and South-East Asia. The history of higher education in India had thus begun its journey quite with a bang.

The socio-historical journey of higher education started with an ancient system of education in the Vedic period. In pre-British days, Hindus and Muslims were educated through Pathshala and Madrassa respectively. The ideas and pedagogical methods of education during the colonial period, from 1757 to 1947, were contested terrain. A commercial company, the British East India Company ruled parts of India from 1764 to 1858. A few eighteenth-century company officials became scholars of Sanskrit, Persian and Tamil, and promoted Oriental learning and advocated the introduction of institutions for Western learning based upon the British curriculum with English as the medium of instruction. By the early nineteenth century, when English was made the official language of government business, British policy promoted a cheap, trickle-down model for colonial education. When the British crown abolished company rule in 1858, government universities existed at Mumbai, Kolkata, and Chennai.

## Post-independence Scenario

After independence, India made concerted efforts to improve access to higher education and the system grew rapidly after independence. By 1980, there were 132 universities and 4738 colleges in the country enrolling around five per cent of the eligible age group in higher education till 1980. The growth of higher education was largely confined to liberal arts, science and commerce. Not only the government supported higher education by setting up universities and colleges, but also took over the responsibility of running the institutions set up through private sector, which were known as Grant-in-aid institutions or private aided institutions.

Privatisation of higher education has been natural outcome of several policy changes such as liberalisation, privatisation, etc. during 1991. All these set a pace for accelerated growth of higher education by the private sector in the country. Yet, there was realisation amongst the promoters of private institutions about the powers of the regulatory mechanism of the universities and the state governments with regard to checks and balances on key items such as admissions and fee regulations. Thus, the autonomy of private institutions was not questioned and the efforts towards moving out of the affiliating universities led to the establishment of deemed-to-be universities and a way to get the degree granting powers. By early 2005, seven private universities were set up in different states and were also recognised by the UGC.

## Notable Commissions in Promoting and Expanding Higher Education

Various commissions and study reports were generated after studying the status of higher education in India, its need for expansion, the problems and lacunae faced in the existing system of both the education and the society in general and keeping the needs of the developing India.

### *Radhakrishnan Commission*

As Chair of the Commission, Dr. S. Radhakrishnan recommended the reconstruction of university education as essential to meet the demand for scientific, technical and other human power needed for the socio-economic development of the country. For this, the Commission had given the following recommendations: Covering all aspects of university education in India, they emphasized the 10+2 structure at the pre-university stage, correction of the "extreme specialization" in the courses, development of research to advance the frontiers of knowledge and of professional education in agriculture, commerce, law, medicine, education, science and technology including certain new areas such as business and public administration and industrial relations and suggested reform of the examination system by assessment of the students' work throughout the year and introduction of courses on the central problems of the philosophy of religion. They also emphasised the importance of students welfare by means of scholarships and stipends, hostel, library and medical facilities and suggested that they should be familiar with three languages-regional, federal and English at the university stage and that English be replaced as early as possible by an Indian language. The Commission was also in favour of the idea of setting up rural universities to meet the need of rural reconstruction in industry, agriculture and various walks of life. The universities should be constituted as autonomous bodies to meet the new responsibilities, (Central) University Grants Commission be established for allocating grants, and finally, university education be placed in the concurrent list. The report was considered by the Central Advisory Board of Education (CABE) in 1950 and most of the recommendations were accepted.

Right from the time of the first five-year plan, major changes prompted reform of the university system. The third five-year plan observed that: "Education is the most important single factor in achieving rapid development and technological progress and in creating a new social order based on values of freedom, social justice and equal opportunities". There have been various commissions and committees appointed by the Government of India and the University Grants Commission from time to time.

### *Kothari Commission (1964-66)*

The most important document on Education in India is the report of the Education Commission under the chairmanship of Dr. D. S. Kothari, then Chairman, University Grants Commission, to advise the Government of India "On the national pattern of education and on the general principles and policies for the development of education at all stages and in all aspects".

The Report made very important recommendations covering all aspects for the future development of national education. The Report emphasised the need for a built-in flexibility in the system of education, and for the necessity of education to be science-based and coherent with Indian culture and values. It also visualised education as an instrument for the nation's progress, security and welfare. The Report stressed:

- there had to be a radical improvement in the quality and standard of higher education and research,
- expansion of higher education to meet manpower requirements of the Nation and the rising social ambitions and expectations of the people, and
- improvement of university organisation and administration.

The Commission recommended special measures for major universities to ensure quality of research development of other universities and affiliated colleges improvement in teaching and evaluation by re-organisation of courses and examinations, opportunities for part-time education, and special attention to women's education. As far as the implementation of the Kothari Commission is concerned, the recommendations were discussed in both the Houses of Parliament and there emerged the first national policy in independent India in the form of a resolution in July 1968. The policy that was born out of them remained the basic framework for all governmental action despite an attempt by the Janata Government to revise it in 1979. The new education policy appeared in May 1986.

### *National Policy on Education 1986*

The policy aims at not only developing human power for serving the economy but also at developing crucial values. The policy envisages education for equality and an understanding of the diverse socio-cultural systems of the people while motivating the younger generations towards international co-operation and peaceful co-existence. As regards higher education, the document expressed great concern regarding the conditions of the colleges and universities, and hence the policy emphasised consolidation and expansion of facilities. In fact, the policy indicates a major thrust in higher education incorporating:

- Expansion of higher education,
- Improvement of the quality of higher education, and
- Increased relevance and job orientation in higher education.

It is evident that much thought has been given to identifying the problems faced by higher education in India and to formulating policies and programmes for their mitigation. However, India has not been very successful in implementing the reforms.

### *Ministry of Human Resource Development**

Higher Education in India is monitored by an apex body which has classified higher education in mainly two streams: (1) Universities, which include "Central-State-Deemed universities and other national, research and institutions of national importance" Institutes; and (ii) Colleges, include all general, Engineering, Medical, Teacher-Training and other Law/Management/MCA types.

Accreditation for higher learning is overseen by following fifteen autonomous institutions established by the University Grants Commission:

- All India Council for Technical Education (AICTE)
- Distance Education Council (DEC)
- Indian Council of Agricultural Research (ICAR)
- Bar Council of India (BCI)
- National Council for Teacher Education (NCTE)
- Rehabilitation Council of India (RCI)
- Medical Council of India (MCI)
- Pharmacy Council of India (PCI)
- Indian Nursing Council (INC)
- Dental Council of India (DCI)
- Central Council of Homoeopathy (CCH)
- Central Council of Indian Medicine (CCIM)
- National Council for Rural Institutes
- State Councils of Higher Education

## Other Professional Councils that Facilitate Higher Education

### *Indian Council of Social Science Research (ICSSR)*

The Indian Council of Social Science Research (ICSSR) was established in 1969 for promoting social science research, strengthening different disciplines, improving quality and quantum of research and its utilisation in national policy

* Now Ministry of Education

formulation. To realise these objectives, the ICSSR envisaged development of institutional infrastructure, identifying research talents, formulating research programmes, supporting professional organisations and establishing linkages with social scientists in other countries. The ICSSR provides maintenance and development grants to various Research Institutes and Regional Centre across the country. Regional Centres have been set up as extended arms of the ICSSR to support research and development of local talents and its programmes and activities in a decentralised manner.

### *Indian Council of Historical Research (ICHR)*

Indian Council of Historical Research is an autonomous organisation which was established under Societies Registration Act, 1972. The prime objectives of the Council are to give a proper direction to historical research and to encourage and foster objective and scientific writing of history. The broad aims of the Council are to bring historians together, provide a forum for exchange of views between them, give a national direction to an objective and rational presentation, interpretation of history, to sponsor historical research programmes and projects and to assist institutions and organisations engaged in historical research. It has a broad view of history so as to include in its fold the history of Science and Technology, Economy, Art, Literature, Philosophy, Epigraphy, Numismatics, Archaeology, Socio- Economic formation processes and allied subjects containing strong historical bias and contents.

### *National Council of Rural Institutes (NCRI)*

The National Council of Rural Institute is a registered autonomous society fully funded by the Central Government. It was established on October 19, 1995 with its Headquarters at Hyderabad. Its main objectives are to promote rural higher education on the lines of Mahatma Gandhi's vision for education so as to take up challenges of micro planning for transformation of rural areas as envisaged in National Policy on Education (NPE) 1986. In order to achieve its objectives, the NCRI has been identifying various programmes for providing support and financial assistance, to be taken up by suitable institutions including voluntary organisations.

### *Indian Institutes of Technologies*

In this vast array of universities, one group of very special institutions stands out: the Indian Institutes of Technology. Conceived in 1946, a year prior to India independence from British rule, the blueprint for the institutes was prepared by the Sarkar Committee, composed of leading academics, scientists, industrialists and government officials. In 1961, the Institutes of Technology Act was passed by the Indian Parliament, with many of the committee's recommendations enshrined in law.

Between 1951 and 1960, five IITs were set up across the country, and within two to three decades the model gained national and international acclaim, primarily as a result of the achievements of IIT alumni. Strong public demand for an IIT education has resulted in the setting up of more institutes.

### *Indian Institutes of Management*

Indian Institutes of Management (IIMs), established over different periods, have emerged as great teaching institutions and their products are in high demand in India and abroad. IIMs enjoy complete academic freedom and admission to them is strictly on merit.

## Other Efforts by the Government to Enhance Higher Education

With the initiation of various commissions and their functioning, higher education in India radically expanded the reach and quality of education. This in turn has improved the quality of parameters in various fields, which has taken India to a different strata and helped move towards a developed nation. Let us take a look at developments in various fields.

### *Technical Education*

Higher education is of vital importance for the country, as it is a powerful tool to build knowledge based society of the 21st Century. In fact, the institutions of higher education included not only colleges and universities but also professional schools in the field of law, theology, medicine, business, music, and art. Higher education also includes institutions like teacher training schools, community college and institutions of technology. The term higher education also has in its fold training of highly skilled specialists in the fields of economics, science, technology and culture at various types of higher schools who accept the candidates who have completed secondary general education.

Several new measures have been taken to implement the Government vision of providing increased access with equity and excellence. Eight (8) new IITs, five (5) new IIMs and ten (10) new NITS have been set up and are functional. Twenty new IIITs will be set up in Private-Public Partnership (PPP) mode Technical Education Quality Improvement Programme envisages on focus in strengthening the Institutions to produce high quality engineers for better employability, establish centres of excellence for focused applicable research, training of faculty for effective teaching, enhancing institutional, and system management effectiveness.

### *National Scheme of Apprenticeship Training*

The basic objective of the Scheme is to fulfill/match, any gap, in so far practical hands on experience of fresh Graduate Engineers, Diploma holders and 10+2 vocational pass-outs and also to enhance their technical skills for making their suitability in job absorption as per the needs of the Industry.

### *Indian National Digital Library in Engineering, Science and Technology (INDEST- AICTE) Consortium*

The Ministry of Human Resource Development set up the "Indian National Digital Library in Engineering Sciences and Technology (INDEST-AICTE) Consortium". The Ministry provides funds for access to electronic resources and databases to centrally funded institutions. The benefit of consortia-based subscription to electronic resources is also extended to all educational institutions under its open-ended proposition. AICTE approved Government/ Government-aided engineering colleges are getting access to selected electronic resources with support from the AICTE and a number of other engineering colleges and institutions have already joined the consortium on their own. A mechanism is in place wherein this consortium takes advantage of collective bargaining and passes on the benefit of e-journals to subscribing members (indest.iitd.ac.in).

### *Technology Development Mission*

In 1993, the Technology Development Mission (TDM) started at all the IITs and IISc with the objective of a concerted national effort towards technology development with direct involvement and participation of industries. Several mission projects, with well-defined goals, milestones and deliverables were identified in areas of national importance. Two or more academic institutions and industries collaborated in most of the mission projects. The funding to these mission areas was as follows:

Ministry of Human Resource Development (MHRD) funded these projects. The most important aspect of this mission was a significant effort on the part of the Government in encouraging industry-institute interaction as well as assisting industry in developing the latest technology. This was first time that mission oriented programmes were successfully taken jointly with industry.

The TDM-I was successful and highly appreciated in the National Steering Committee meeting of the Planning Commission held on August 06, 1999 at New Delhi. TDM-I resulted in development and transfer of several technologies to Industry viz:

- Automation of power distribution,
- An immuno diagnostic test for AIDS,
- Vaccine for Hepatitis-B,
- Supercritical fluid extraction technology,
- Controlled atmosphere storage technology for food grains,
- The first 50 kg payload robot,
- Automated monitoring systems,
- Squeeze casting technology for metal matrix composite piston,
- Environment friendly vapour compression heat pump assisted dryer for agricultural products, etc.

Most of the deliverables were achieved. Subsequent increase in industry-sponsored research at IITs and IISc confirmed that the TDM-I programme fostered an environment of faith in capabilities of Indian academic institutions to solve current technology problems of the industry and help them in developing newer technologies and products. Some of the significant benefits from TDM-I were:

- Industry and IITs collaborated on such mission-oriented programmes for the first time,
- Industry was convinced about the capabilities of IITs and IISc in solving technological problems and to undertake development of new products successfully,
- Increase in the number of Industry-sponsored research at IITs and IISc,
- Enhanced academic collaboration among these top Institutes.

### *Setting up 20 New IIITs*

To address the challenges faced by the Indian IT industry and growth of the domestic IT market, the Ministry of Human Resource Development (MHRD), Government of India intends to establish twenty Indian Institutes of Information Technology (IIITs), on a Not-for-profit Public Private Partnership (N-PPP) basis. The partners in setting up the IIITs would be the Ministry of Human Resource Development (MHRD), Government of the respective States where each IIIT will be established, and the industry. A major objective in establishing IIITs is to set up a model of education which can produce best-in-class human resources in IT and harnessing the multidimensional facets of IT in various domains. While the number of students produced by these IIITs would be small, the impact they create would be great.

## Achievements of Higher Education Plans and Schemes Enacted by the Government

The Indian higher education system has undergone rapid expansion. In less than 20 years, the country has created additional capacity for a mammoth 40 million students. India's higher education system has finally broken free of decades of colonial overhang. In recent years, the country has undertaken massive structural and systemic changes that have started to yield encouraging results. About 15 years ago, India consciously moved to a differentiated academic system with a three-tiered structure comprising highly selective elite research universities at the top, comprehensive universities and specialised institutions in the middle, and an array of highly-accessible and high-quality colleges at the bottom. While the first tier caters exclusively to furthering India's intellectual capital, the other two focus on delivering economic and social values respectively.

India possesses a highly developed higher education system which offers facility of education and training in almost all aspects of human creative and intellectual endeavours: arts and humanities; natural, mathematical and social sciences, engineering; medicine, dentistry, agriculture, education, law; commerce and management; music and performing arts; national and foreign languages; culture, communications etc. From the times of ancient India, which was the home of prestigious universities to the present higher education system, our higher education has witnessed a tremendous improvement in increase in the number of Universities/University level Institutions and Colleges since Independence. There has been an explosive number of universities, colleges and student enrolment. This has been made possible by the various academic and professional councils that have been set up and the regulations that have been put in place and enacted. Higher education is the driving force behind economic development and the focal point of learning in a society. It is both a repository and a generator of knowledge and is the chief agent of passing on the accumulated experience, both cultural and scientific to society. The emerging world view suggests that in the days to come, the role of knowledge capital in the process of development will predominate the physical capital and this clearly indicates that the importance and relevance of higher education are going to grow further. All these achievements in Higher Education have resulted in commendable accomplishments in various walks of life which have made India proud and put it on a path to becoming a superpower economically and otherwise.

## Conclusion

Higher education system in India has shown a massive increase in the number of institutions both colleges and universities after independence leading to a significant increase in the number of students enrolled in the higher education institutions. This is evident from the Gross Enrolment Ratio which was less than one per cent in 1950-51 and at present it is above twenty per cent. If we look at the higher education participation, we find that the women enrolment in higher education in India has witnessed an increase from 14 women enrolment per hundred men in 1950-1951 to 88 women enrolment per hundred men now. Similarly, due to various policy initiatives the GER of SCs and STs students has improved a lot but still these sections of the society are far behind the general category students.

One distinguishing feature of this expansion in higher education is the rise of private sector. Undoubtedly, private sector is contributing towards improving accessibility to higher education by increasing the number of seats in various courses, and introducing new courses. But, the fact of the matter is that it has improved access to higher education only for well-off sections of the society and for the diverse socio-economic strata the private sector is not equitable. Besides, improved accessibility is only of lower quality. Private institutions admit students by charging exorbitant amount of fee and ignore standard admission procedures like entrance tests, merit list and interviews etc. thus depriving poor but brilliant students of higher education. Thus, expansion of higher education through private participation is not an organised programme with social objectives and it has led to crass commercialisation of higher education.

Further, utility of higher education in assuring employment is questionable. Many graduate and post-graduate students do not get jobs in their respective fields even after spending several years in acquiring higher education. The quality of Indian universities is also below excellence as no Indian university found a place in the top 200 positions in the global ranking of the universities (MHRD, 2016). Thus, the major issue before Indian higher education is no longer of 'mere expansion and access' but access to a quality and equitable higher education which in future could translate into good employment.

# 5

# Profile of Higher Education

## Gross Enrolment Ratio in Higher Education

The Gross Enrolment Ratio (GER) in higher education of India is about 27.4% according to latest All India Survey of Higher Education (AISHE). GER is statistical measure for determining the number of students enrolled in undergraduate, postgraduate and research-level studies within country and expressed as a percentage of population. India is aiming to attain GER of 50% by 2030, but it is still far behind countries like China with GER of 43.39% and the US with 85.8%.

Six states have registered GER higher than national average (25.2%), with their share of students entering higher education is growing twice as fast as overall rate. These states are Tamil Nadu (46.9%), Himachal Pradesh (36.7%), Kerala (34.2%), Andhra Pradesh (32.4%), Haryana (29%) and Punjab (28.6%).

However, eight states UP (24.9%), Madhya Pradesh (20%), Odisha (21%), Bihar (14.4%), Gujarat (20.2%), Rajasthan (20.5%), Mizoram (24.5%) and West Bengal (18.5%) had GER ratio far less than the national average. Bihar has lowest GER with just 14.4% of its eligible population (in age group of 18 to 23 years) pursuing higher education.

## Gender Parity Index (GPI)

India registered its best performance on the GPI in last seven years 0.94 in 2016-17 from 0.86 in 2010-11. GPI is calculated as quotient of number of females by number of males enrolled. GPI equal to 1 indicates 1, value less than 1 indicated disparity in favour of males. In Seven states – Goa, Himachal Pradesh, Meghalaya, J&K, Nagaland, Sikkim and Kerala – women in higher education have outnumbered men.

## College Density

States in south India have higher college density. It is defined as number of colleges per lakh eligible population. The college density in top three states/ UTs is Puducherry (49), Telangana (59) and Karnataka (53). Bihar (7 colleges/1 lakh population), Jharkhand (8) and West Bengal (11) on the other hand, are at the bottom in terms college density.

## Foreign Students

There has not been much improvement in the internationalisation of education in the country. There is marginal improvement in number of foreign students

47,575 in 2016-17 from 45,424 in 2015-16 with 31,779 men and 15.796 women. The highest share comes from the neighbours Nepal (23.6%), Afghanistan (9.3%), and Bhutan (4.8%).

### Indian Students Studying Abroad

*(Source UNESCO Institute for Statistics, 2016)*

A total number of 181,872 Indian students are currently studying abroad for a higher education degree. The most popular study abroad destinations among students from India are:

| | |
|---|---|
| USA | 92,597 students |
| UK | 22,155 students |
| Australia | 16,150 students |
| Canada | 9,582 students |
| UAE | 9,273 students |
| New Zealand | 6,845 students |
| Germany | 5,645 students |
| Ukraine | 3,587 students |
| France | 1,828 students |
| Saudi Arabia | 1,817 students |

### World Class Higher Education Institutions in India

#### *Times Higher Education World University Ranking 2020*

The Times Higher Education World University Ranking 2020 features six Indian institutes among the top 500 in the world, an increase from last year's five institutes. IIT Ropar made a surprise entry and takes the number one spot among Indian varsities alongside IISc Bangalore.

However, we need to note that this is for the first time since 2012 that not a single Indian institute featured among the top 300 educational institutes in the world.

After the first 200 ranks, the World University Ranking puts institutes into rank groups rather than individual ranks. Here are the top 10 Indian universities ranked in World University Rankings 2020

IISc Bengaluru

- Grouped among the top 301-350 universities of the world. Overall score: 44.5-46.8
- IISc Bengaluru shares the top spot among Indian universities along with IIT Ropar.

IIT Ropar

- Grouped among the top 301-350 universities of the world. Overall score: 44.5-46.8

- IIT Ropar shares the top spot among Indian universities with IISc Bangalore.

IIT Indore

- Grouped among the top 351-400 universities of the world. Overall score: 42.4-44.4
- IIT Indore is the second-best university in India after IIT Ropar and IISc Bangalore.

IIT Bombay

- Grouped among the top 401-500 universities of the world. Overall score: 38.8-42.3
- IIT Bombay is the third-best university in India alongside IIT Delhi and IIT Kharagpur.

IIT Delhi

- Grouped among the top 401-500 universities of the world. Overall score: 38.8-42.3
- IIT Delhi is the third-best university in India alongside IIT Kharagpur and IIT Bombay

IIT Kharagpur

- Grouped among the top 401-500 universities of the world. Overall score: 38.8-42.3
- IIT Kharagpur is the third-best university in India alongside IIT Delhi and IIT Bombay.

Institute of Chemical Technology

- Grouped among the top 301-350 universities of the world. Overall score: 35.3-38.7.
- Institute of Chemical Technology is the fourth-best university in India alongside IIT Gandhinagar and IIT Roorkee.

IIT Gandhinagar

- Grouped among the top 301-350 universities of the world. Overall score: 35.3-38.7
- IIT Gandhinagar is the fourth-best university in India alongside Institute of Chemical Technology and IIT Roorkee.

IIT Roorkee

- Grouped among the top 301-350 universities of the world. Overall score: 35.3-38.7
- IIT Roorkee is the fourth-best university in India alongside Institute of Chemical Technology and IIT Gandhinagar.

Amrita Vishwa Vidyapeetham

- Grouped among the top 601-800 universities of the world. Overall score: 28.3-35.2
- Amrita Vishwa Vidyapeetham is the fifth-best university in India.

India has jumped significantly in the Times Higher Education World University Rankings 2020, with 56 Higher Education Institutions making it to the list, up from 49 previously. However, for the first time since 2012, not a single Indian University made it to the top 300 list.

The Indian Institute of Science, Bangalore still ranks the highest but now shares this position, after dropping into the 301-350 bracket (from 251-300), due to a significant fall in its citation impact score, negating improvements in research and teaching environment and industry income. Newcomer IIT Ropar shares the joint top spot with IISc, Bangalore, pushing IIT Indore, which remains in the 351-400 band, into the third spot.

The older IITs, Bombay, Delhi and Kharagpur – are in the 401-500 bracket, IIT Roorkee is in the 501-600 and IIT Guwahati, IIT Kanpur and IIT Madras in the 601-800 category. So why do the much younger IITs one set up in 2008 and the other set up in 2009 outperform their older, much more established counterparts on the ranking front?

"IIT Ropar and IIT Indore performed very well in the citation score, the best in India. In fact, as this measure is heavily weighted, performing well here helps ranking performance greatly," a Times Higher Education spokesperson told *Economic Times* to an emailed query. IIT Ropar and IIT Indore are also smaller institutions, which mean that they have a better student/staff ratio which also helps improve their ranking tally.

Overall, seven Indian universities fall in the lower band this year, while the bulk of the country's institutions remains stable. But there are a few institutions that have moved up in the ranking table, including IIT Delhi, IIT Kharagpur and Jamia Millia Islamia.

The best Indian institutions are generally characterised by relatively strong scores for teaching environment and industry income, but perform poorly when it comes to international outlook compared with both regional and international counterparts.

"India has a huge amount of potential in global higher education, given its rapidly growing youth population and economy and use of English language instruction. The Indian Government has strong ambitions to boost the global standing of its top universities and attract foreign students, academics and research collaboration. It now needs to back up these aspirations with high level of investment – or risk declining further amid increasing global TV competition, especially from other parts of Asia," said Ellie Both Well, the ranking Editor.

Now in 16 years, the ranking includes over 1300 universities from 92 countries. Rankings are done across 13 performance indicators grouped into five areas: teaching (the learning environment), research (volume, income, reputation), citation (research influence), international outlook (staff, students and research) and industry outcome (knowledge transfer).

University of Oxford took the first place in the overall rankings, followed by California Institute of Technology, University of Cambridge, Stanford University and Massachusetts Institute of Technology.

### Institutions of Eminence

The UGC, in its 542nd meeting held on 02 August 2019 has considered the reports of the Empowered Expert Committee (EEC) appointed by Government under the Chairmanship of Shri N. Gopalaswami recommending (15) Public Institutions and (15) Private Institutions for considering to give status of Institutions of Eminence.

Since the scheme has only provided for (10) Public and (10) Private Institutions, the UGC has examined the list of (15) Public and (15) Private Institutions using transparent and verifiable criteria.

The following were the principles used for identifying the (10) Public and (10) Private Institutions from the list of (15) Public and (15) Private Institutions recommended by the EEC:

a. Since the thrust of the scheme is to prepare institutions for the global rankings, no existing institution which has NOT figured in any of the global/national ranks shall be recommended for the IoE status.
b. Only after exhausting the above criterion, if any slot remains vacant, consideration shall be given to 'yet to be established (Greenfield)' proposals.

### Public Institutions

In accordance with the above principles, the UGC has ranked the list of (15) recommendations as per the QS-2020 World Rankings. Wherever there is a tie, used the QS-2019 India Rankings as a tie-breaker. Accordingly, the Public Institutions recommended for grant of IoE status have been shown in Table 1.

### State Universities

Jadavpur University and Anna University can be considered for issue of the IoE status only after the respective State Governments have issued an official communication allocating their share of the funds (up to 50%).

### Private Institutions

UGC has ranked the list of the (15) private institutions recommended by the EEC by taking their ranking in the QS India or NIRF rankings, and NIRF

Table 1: Public Institutions Identified as Institutions of Eminence

| *S. No.* | *Institution* | *World Ranking (QS 2020)* | *India Ranking (QS 2019)* | *Recommended of UGC* |
|---|---|---|---|---|
| 1. | IIT Bombay (INT) | 152 | 1 | Already declared IoE |
| 2. | IIT Delhi (INT) | 182 | 4 | Already declared IoE |
| 3. | IISc Bangalore (Deemed Univ.) | 184 | 2 | Already declared IoE |
| 4. | IIT Madras (INT) | 271 | 3 | Recommended for declaring as loE |
| 5. | IIT Kharagpur (INT) | 281 | 5 | Recommended for declaring as loE |
| 6. | University of Delhi (Central Univ) | 474 | 8 | Recommended for declaring as loE |
| 7. | University of Hyderabad, Hyderabad (Central Univ.) | 601-650 | 7 | Recommended for declaring as loE |
| 8. | Jadavpur University, Kolkata (State Univ.) | 651-700 | 12 | Needs consultation with State Govt. prior to consideration |
| 9. | Anna University, Chennai (State Univ.) | 751-800 | 13 | Needs consultation with State Govt. prior to consideration |
| 10. | BHU, Varanasi (Central Univ.) | 801-1000 | 15 | Recommended for declaring as loE |
| 11. | Savitribai Phule Pune University, Pune (State Univ.) | 801-1000 | 19 | |
| 12. | AMU, Aligarh (Central Univ.) | 801-1000 | 33 | |
| 13. | Tezpur University (Central Univ.) | Not ranked | 36 | |
| 14. | Panjab University, Chandigarh (State/Central Univ.) | Not ranked | 49 | |
| 15. | Andhra University, Visakhapatnam (State Univ.) | Not ranked | 46 | |

ranking has been used as tie-breaker. In case there is any vacant slot after considering all the ranked institutions, the same was used for 'yet to be set up (Greenfield)' institution (Table 2).

In case of the private institutions proposed as Institutions of Eminence, there will be no financial support, but they will be entitled for more autonomy as a special category Deemed University.

The Greenfield Institutions would get three year period to establish and operationalise the institution, and thereafter, EEC will consider giving IoE status to such institutions.

Reality is out there and it is independent of the investigators who investigate it. Then why should there be significant differences amongst the ratings of higher education institutions by various agencies. There ought to be congruence in the criteria of ratings and competencies of the rating agencies.

### *Banaras Hindu University (BHU)*

*Ethos of Select Indian Universities*: Mahamana Madan Mohan Malaviya realised his vision as a philosopher and practitioner that the emphasis on the process of education was the sole solution to prevailing personal, social and national problems of Indian people. Therefore, in the year 1904 he visualised to establish a national university in Kashi.

1. The philosophy and the ideas of Malaviya Ji which were the foundation of this new university and its scheme of education were based on the Gurukul System of Education in India.
2. The philosophy states that the Parmatma is the sole creator of the Universe and its beings, and Sanatana Dharma practices are most ancient and best ever practices of Dharma.
3. On the other hand, for worldly growth the skills related to modern science, technological and industrial growth are the need of the hour which can be best learnt by integration of the Western education with the ideals and values of the Sanatana Dharma. Therefore, the new university should revive the best traditions of the ancient gurukuls of India – like those of Takshasila and Nalanda where Hindu sages taught and fed ten thousand students at a time – and which should at the same time combine with them the best traditions of the modern Universities of the West where the highest instruction is imparted in Arts, Science and Technology. Further such a scheme will integrate religion and ethics as an integral part of education of the youth so that they come out as the persons of invincible moral character. Hence, such an attempt of amalgamation of best thoughts and practices of Oriental-Western and Traditional-Modern was unique owing to its newness in the contemporary world history of higher education institutions. Malaviya Ji sacrificed his life ambitions and made it as the only ambition to establish such a unique university as a mark of his patriotism and the love for the motherland.

Table 2: Private Institutions Identified as Institutions of Eminence

| *S. No.* | *Institute* | *India Rankings (QS 2019)* | *India Ranking NIRF 2019* | *India Ranking NIRF 2018* | *UGC Recommendation* |
|---|---|---|---|---|---|
| 1 | BITS Pilani, Rajasthan | 17 | 23 | 17 | Already selected and given Letter of Intent |
| 2 | Manipal Academy of Higher Education | 26 | 9 | 11 | Already selected and given Letter of Intent |
| 3 | Jio Institute (Reliance Foundation, Maharashtra) | Green Field (yet to be established) | | | Already selected and given Letter of Intent |
| 4 | Amrita Vishwa Vidyapeetham, Bangalore | 40 | 8 | 8 | Recommended for issue of LoI |
| 5 | VIT Vellore, Tamil Nadu | 44 | 19 | 16 | Recommended for issue of LoI |
| 6 | Jamia Hamdard, New Delhi | 51-55 | 18 | 23 | Recommended for issue of LoI |
| 7 | Kalinga Instt. of Industrial Technology, Bhubaneswar | 61-65 | 31 | 42 | Recommended for issue of LoI |
| 8 | O.P. Jindal University, Haryana | 66-70 | – | – | Recommended for issue of LoI |
| 9 | Shiv Nadar University, Uttar Pradesh | – | 52 | 48 | Recommended for issue of LoI |
| 10 | Bharti (Satya Bharti Foundation), Delhi | | | | Recommended for issue of LoI in the vacant slot |

4. His sole purpose was to regain lost faith in the heritage of India and to excel skillfully through technological growth in the modern world. Since 1904 till 1916 Malaviya Ji made a Herculean attempt and succeeded in mobilisation of common masses, contemporary royal personalities, foreign appreciators of Indian culture and Hindu thought, people of all religious communities in aggregating mind, spirit and money altogether to achieve the goal by construction of this truly national university being developed by Indians themselves. Lala Lajpat Rai said, "charter or no charter the university will exist". Malaviya Ji said, "charter and charter and university will exist". Malaviya Ji was so confident that the Government will have to support his move. He with all other likeminded personalities moved to all corners of India including today's Pakistan and Burma. Hence the people of Akhand Bharat truly supported the move and contributed funds. The university finally came into existence on 4 February 1916 but it did not end the task of the founder.
5. Malaviya Ji worked incessantly for construction of student hostels, institutional buildings, residential quarters, marvelous grassy playgrounds, production units of electricity, other daily products and search for scientists, engineers and knowledgeable scholars of repute from all corners of India and abroad. Today's Institutes of Technology, Medical Science, Agricultural Science, Science, Sustainable Development, Management and the Faculties of Law, Education and Performing Arts with hundreds of Departments are living testimony to its realisation and continuance of his memorable vision.
6. Since 1916 more than hundred years have led to production of thousands of patriotic Engineers, Doctors, Managers, Social Scientists, Politicians, Educational Administrators, Educationists, School and University Teachers, Agriculturalists, Lawyers, Judges and enlightened citizens who are continuously contributing to the development of the nation.
7. The different fields of study in the curriculum and their integration with a variety of co-curricular activities related to religious festivals, religious discourses, foundation day celebration, Janamashtami Celebration have excellent achievement through his unique educational endeavour. This is all due to the vision of the great founder who could visualise the need of the big human resource for the modern India for all material development. The contemporary problems of corruption, violence, inefficiency of educated degree holders, political bankruptcy, endless sensual pleasure, emotional deviation were also visualised by him. As a solution he expected the students of this great centre of 'life and light' to be persons of invincible moral character by developing their mind and spirit through devotion of their time to it. He never wanted students on campus to take part in active politics and expected that they will

strengthen themselves holistically keeping away from politics, so that in their later real life they turn out to be more effective and efficient to handle challenges.

8. Mahamana expected that all students devote atleast one and half hour per week for the study of Dharma. This was his Guru-Dakshina. He wanted all to excel in life through self study (Swadhayay). He also expected the alumni to contribute generously to the institution monetarily and to the society through their honest services. Owing to his thought and acts this new university (centre of life and light) of Mahamana has produced Bharat Ratna, Padma Awardees, National awardees and several Vice Chancellors and Teachers of repute which is evident through contribution of alumni in national reconstruction.

There is an immediate need to renew and renovate the Banaras Hindu University converging on its vision as envisaged by Mahamana Madan Mohan Malviya, so that the globe as a whole emulates it as a university with universal ethos. Along with opening new universities there is a need to strengthen the already established universities.

### *Banasthali Vidyapith*

Banasthali Vidyapith is World's largest fully residential university for women. It is now recognised by the Times Higher Education World University Rankings 2020 as the second best women's university in the world. It was on 6 October 1935 that Smt. Ratan Shashtri and Pandit Hiralal Shashtri founded Banasthali to fill up the vacuum caused by the sudden death of their highly talented and promising daughter Shantabai. They had high expectations that she would work for women's cause when she would grow up. But destiny ordained otherwise. The Banasthali owes its existence neither to the zeal of an educationist, nor to that of a social reformer. It is also not the creation of a Philanthropist's purse. It has arisen like the fabled phoenix from the ashes of a blossoming flower Shantabai. Banasthali is one of the five higher education institutes in India meant exclusively for Women. Over these about 85 years Banasthali has developed into a National centre for women's education. Banasthali educational programme aims at an all-round development of the student's personality. It has evolved five-fold educational programme (Panchmukhi Shiksha) comprising of physical, practical, aesthetic, moral and intellectual aspects. Banasthali Vidyapith has thousands of students from abroad.

### *Visva Bharati*

According to Sabujkoli Sen, Director of Studies, Educational Innovations and Rural Reconstruction and Principal, Vinay Bhavana, "There could be none in India parallel to Rabindranath Tagore who dared to discontinue his school education as a rebel child against colonial education and later founded Visva Bharati to practically experiment and demonstrate that an indigenous method of education in the spirit and culture of Tapovan of India is not only possible but quite potential and promising without being ever obsolete and outdated. He strongly believed that education, devoid of one's soil, people, climate Edu and culture suffers from infirmity and impermanence affecting the very vitality of life and spirit". He has been second to none being a staunch nationalist and vouching for a nationalistic education on the eve of Swadesi movement in India. At the same time he has never imagined a system of education confined to the narrow domestic walls. He, being a lofty visionary and lover of mankind, has always gone beyond the geographical and territorial boundaries of the nation being always enamoured by the open invitation of the people of the world. In fact, his grand vision of Universal Man is over and above all kinds of short-sighted nationalism, the narrow nationalistic fundamentalism and extreme sentimentalism. Unlike others, he wanted to make in Visva Bharati a cultural hotspot where two streams of knowledge from east and west can merge and people from all over the world can make their home in a single nest.

### *Gujarat Vidyapith*

In August 1920, Gandhiji started non-cooperation movement. Gandhiji asked everybody to boycott the Honours and Awards of the British empire, schools and colleges imparting English education, Courts and Legislative Assemblies. One of the most important issues of this non-cooperation movement was to boycott all schools and colleges under British Government's control and to liberate the Indian youths from the shackles of British colonial education system, propounded by Macaulay, that produced human resources for the oppressive British empire. There was a great response to Gandhiji's command to vacate the English teaching schools and colleges. Now, in order to see that the students who left their education half way are not deprived of the education, it was decided to establish national vidyapith. Out of those five Vidyapiths established during that period, Gujarat Vidyapith was the one, established by Gadhiji himself on 18 October 1920. Gandhi wanted his vidyapith to prepare the youths for the task of national reconstruction and usher in 'Hind Swaraj', the India of his dream. Today, it is one of the national universities with a charter from the Government of India and seeks to promote Gandhiji's ideals of service-oriented education. Higher Education along with knowledge seeking ought to emanate into entrepreneurship with service motive.

## Scenario of Indian Institutes of Higher Education

Indian Higher Education has a mixed scenario. The scenario of ancient Indian Universities and some of the apex institutions of higher education has already been presented above. But as a whole, the Indian Higher Education has a mixed scenario. Rather than having universal distinction, most of the universities have distinction discipline-wise. Some are known for Faculty of Fine Arts, whereas some for School of Economics. Some of the universities have the focus on the east, whereas some have focus on the west, whereas, there are some which focus on both the cast and the west. Some of the universities are excelling in liberal arts, whereas, others are excelling in science and technology. Some of the institutions focus on Indian Languages, whereas, others focus on English and Foreign languages. There are public universities, private universities and public-cum-private universities. There are IIMs, LITs, IIITs, AIIMS, CDRI, HBCSE, TIFR, Azim Premji University. Indian graduates find significant expression globally in various fields. Indians have been contributing significantly in many international company. We are very good at problem solving. We have significant places in almost most all the domains – germination, incubation, creation, construction and connection. The ultimate aim of Indian education is development of universal beings having interrelation, interdependence and healthy co-existence with all the entities. We are transcending from Human Development Index (HDI) to Universe Development Index (UDI). Indian Higher Education has healthy global scenario.

# 6

# University Typology

The higher education system in India includes both Private and Public universities. Public universities are supported by the Government of India and the state governments, while private universities are mostly supported by various bodies and societies, Universities in India are recognised by the University Grants Commission (UGC), which draws its power from the University Grants Commission Act, 1956. In addition, 15 professional councils were established, controlling different aspects of accreditation and coordination.

The types of universities include:

- Central universities, or Union universities, are established by an Act of Parliament and are under the purview of the Department of Higher Education in the Union Human Resource Development Ministry (now Ministry of Education). The UGC lists 47 central universities,
- State universities are run by the state government of each of the States and Union Territories of India and are usually established by a local legislative assembly Act. As of 25 May 2016, the UGC listed 347 state universities. The oldest establishment date listed by the UGC is 1897, shared by the University of Mumbai, the University of Madras, and the University of Calcutta. Most state universities are "affiliating universities" in that they administer a large number of "affiliated colleges" (many located in very small towns) that typically offer a range of undergraduate courses, but may also offer postgraduate courses. More established colleges may even offer Ph.D. programmes in some departments with the approval of the affiliating university,
- Deemed university or "Deemed to be University", is a status of autonomy granted by the Department of Higher Education on the advice of the UGC, under Section 3 of the UGC Act. As of 25 May 2016, the UGC listed 130 deemed universities. According to this list, the first institute to be granted deemed university status was Indian Institute of Science at Bengaluru which was granted this status on 12 May 1958. The same listing by the UGC covers several institutes. For examples, the listing for Homi Bhabha National Institute covers the Institute of Mathematical Sciences, the Indira Gandhi Centre for Atomic Research and other institutes.

- Private universities are approved by the UGC. They can grant degrees, but they are not allowed to have off-campus affiliated colleges. The UGC list of private universities as on 25 May 2016 listed 237 private universities.

India has 754 universities. There are universities of some kind in each of the 29 States of India as well as three of the Union Territories: Chandigarh, Delhi, and Puducherry. The state with the most universities is Rajasthan with 71 universities. Tamil Nadu is the state with the most deemed universities, numbering 30. Gujarat and West Bengal have the most state universities, 25 each and Uttar Pradesh has 24 state universities. Rajasthan has the most private universities – 41. Uttar Pradesh has six central universities and Delhi has five central universities.

Apart from the above universities, other institutions are granted the permission to autonomously award degrees. These institutes do not affiliate colleges, and are not officially called universities, but are autonomous organisations or autonomous institutes. They fall under the administrative control of the Department of Higher Education. These organisations include the Indian Institute of Technology, the National Institute of Technology, the Indian Institute of Science Education and Research, the Indian Institute of Engineering Science and Technology, the Indian Institute of Management, the National Law School, the All India Institute of Medical Sciences, and other autonomous institutes.

The regions with the most central universities in India are Delhi (namely University of Delhi, Jamia Millia Islamia, Jawaharlal Nehru University, IGNOU, and South Asian University) and Uttar Pradesh also with five central universities namely BHU, AMU, Allahabad University, BBAU, and Rajiv Gandhi National Aviation Institute. There are central universities in all of the states of India except Goa, Andhra Pradesh, and UT of Chandigarh. Of the Union Territories, there are central universities in Puducherry. Universities at Calcutta, Bombay, and Madras.

## Central Universities

The British Government in India passed Acts in 1857 to establish Central Universities.

So also, the universities of Punjab (1882), Allahabad (1920), Banaras (1916), Patna (1917), and Aligarh (1920) were established by the central legislature. They were central universities when established. In fact, the Calcutta University had the status of Central University for a long time as it was located in the capital of the country and the Governor-General was its chancellor. It continues to be a central university even after the capital was later shifted to Delhi.

| *State* | *Central Universities* | *State Universities* | *Deemed Universities* | *Private Universities* | *Total* |
|---|---|---|---|---|---|
| Andhra Pradesh | 0 | 20 | 5 | 0 | 25 |
| Arunachal Pradesh | 1 | 0 | 1 | 7 | 9 |
| Assam | 2 | 12 | 0 | 4 | 18 |
| Bihar | 3 | 15 | 2 | 0 | 19 |
| Chandigarh | 0 | 1 | 1 | 0 | 2 |
| Chhattisgarh | 1 | 13 | 2 | 8 | 22 |
| Delhi | 5 | 7 | 10 | 0 | 22 |
| Goa | 0 | 1 | 0 | 0 | 1 |
| Gujarat | 1 | 25 | 2 | 24 | 52 |
| Haryana | 1 | 14 | 6 | 19 | 40 |
| Himachal Pradesh | 1 | 4 | 0 | 17 | 22 |
| Jammu and Kashmir | 2 | 7 | 1 | 0 | 10 |
| Jharkhand | 1 | 7 | 2 | 3 | 13 |
| Karnataka | 1 | 25 | 15 | 12 | 52 |
| Kerala | 1 | 13 | 2 | 0 | 16 |
| Madhya Pradesh | 2 | 21 | 3 | 20 | 44 |
| Maharashtra | 1 | 21 | 21 | 5 | 48 |
| Manipur | 2 | 0 | 0 | 1 | 3 |
| Meghalaya | 1 | 0 | 0 | 8 | 9 |
| Mizoram | 1 | 0 | 0 | 1 | 2 |
| Nagaland | 1 | 0 | 0 | 2 | 3 |
| Odisha | 1 | 13 | 2 | 3 | 19 |
| Puducherry | 1 | 0 | 1 | 0 | 2 |
| Punjab | 1 | 9 | 2 | 13 | 25 |
| Rajasthan | 1 | 21 | 8 | 41 | 71 |
| Sikkim | 1 | 0 | 0 | 5 | 6 |
| Tamil Nadu | 2 | 22 | 30 | 0 | 52 |
| Telangana | 3 | 16 | 2 | 0 | 21 |
| Tripura | 1 | 1 | 0 | 1 | 3 |
| Uttar Pradesh | 6 | 24 | 10 | 24 | 63 |
| Uttarakhand | 1 | 10 | 4 | 11 | 25 |
| West Bengal | 1 | 25 | 1 | 8 | 35 |
| Total | 47 | 347 | 130 | 237 | 754 |

Later, all universities except Banaras Hindu University were transferred to the provincial governments. When Delhi University was set up in 1922, it was outside the jurisdiction of provincial government. Hence, it came under central legislature and in 1935, by the Government of India Act, these three universities (Aligarh, Banaras, Delhi) were included in List-1 and remained central universities.

When the Constitution was framed, there were heated discussions on listing education under Union or State jurisdiction, and finally it found a place in all the three lists – Union, State, and Concurrent. Central universities have unique objectives of serving specific needs, apart from being institutions of national importance, attracting students and faculty from all over the country.

Visva Bharati was set up in 1951 as a central university and the objectives of the University were clearly enunciated as the objectives under which Tagore had founded the Visva Bharati at Santiniketan in 1921.

The objectives of Visva Bharati are:

i. To study the mind of man in its realisation of different aspects of truth from diverse points of view.
ii. To bring into more intimate relations with one another through patient study and research the different culture of the east on the basis of the underlying unity.
iii. To approach the west from the standpoint of such unity of life and thought of Asia.
iv. To seek to realise in a common fellowship of study the meeting of the east and the west, and thus ultimately to strengthen the fundamental conditions of world peace through the establishment of free communication of ideas between the two hemispheres; and
v. With such ideals in view to provide at Santinikentan aforesaid a centre of culture where research into a study of religion, literature, history, science, and art of Hindu, Buddhist, Jain, Islamic, Sikh, Christian, and other civilisations may be pursued along with the culture of the West for true spiritual realisation, in amity, good fellowship, and cooperation between the thinkers and scholars of both Eastern and Western countries, free from all antagonism of race, nationality, creed or caste.

### *Overall Objectives of Central Universities*

The Banaras Hindu University Inquiry Committee (1969) enunciated in its Report the objectives and role of central universities as follows:

> "In this connection there is one point of some importance to which we wish to refer. The Banaras Hindu University like the Aligarh Muslim University, the Delhi University, Vishwa Bharati, and Jawaharlal Nehru University are central universities and the Union Government fully finances, through the UGC, the

> expenditure incurred by these institutions. The question which arises is what should be the specific features of a central university? Central universities should not be described as central merely because the central government finances them. They should have a distinctive character of their own. 'The central universities should seek to supplement, and not always duplicate the facilities and achievements of state universities. The state universities, though they should function in every possible way as all-India institution, have a basic responsibility to address the needs of the state and the local community. Sometimes these may not coincide exactly with the order of priorities and demands of other parts of the country or the country as a whole. However, in the case of central universities, their role and responsibility is clear – it is to function effectively and vigorously on an all-India basis to help build up a corporate intellectual life in the country and to further national integration. Broadly speaking, the central universities should provide courses which need facilities in terms of staff and equipment ordinarily beyond the reach of state universities, or for which the demand would be too small if limited only to the requirements of an individual state. There is another aspect which we would like to refer as it has reference to the special function and responsibilities of central universities. It is well known that in our country, just as some areas are economically backward, so are some areas educationally backward, and we feel that the central universities should regard it as a part of their special function to contribute towards removal of imbalances from the academic life of our country and take suitable action to help deserving students from educationally backward areas. In order to achieve this object such facilities as may be necessary should be made available to the central universities."

The Report of the Committee to enquire into the working of the central universities (1984) commented:

> "The central universities are in a state of perpetual crisis and are faced with problems some of which are beyond their competence to solve. We have to ask many questions in order to appreciate the causes of crisis. Is it due to lack of clarity in understanding the aims of university education on the part of the people, the academics, or the decision makers? Unfortunately, the intellectual, cultural and ethical values, which the universities are expect to uphold and preserve are easily subordinated to lesser concerns on the part of the university community."

## State Universities

State universities are still the backbone of higher education. Majority of students get enrolled there. State governments are to shoulder the responsibility of maintaining and developing them. Presently, many colleges are affiliated to state universities. This has burdened many universities with the management of academic content, examination, and quality maintenance issues. Good affiliating colleges should be converted into autonomous colleges. There is a view that the optimum size of a university has not only a quantitative, but also a qualitative dimension.

What is interesting is the manner in which academic practice is structured in the typical university. There is little chance that someone who has managed to get admission will not come out with a degree. What is more remarkable is that, given the already low levels of academic work that is required of students, an undergraduate student normally has to work harder than a typical Master of Arts (M.A.) student to get his degree. The M.A. student once admitted has a higher probability of finishing the course even with less of an academic input. And if s/he manages to get into a Ph.D. programme, a degree is assured with the most minimal inputs by the student. This illustrates the anomaly in our state universities. Similar conditions prevail in the recruitment and promotion of faculty. At the entry point itself there is a deficit of professional and academic skills of those who are in state universities and colleges. Once someone enters as a lecturer in any university, it is highly unlikely that the person will not rise, given time to become reader and then a professor, not withstanding academic achievements or lack of these. Instead of the pursuit of knowledge, the chase for power and petty politicking has become the principal axis of the state university system. Even at the cost of advocating nihilism, it may be stated that in the prevailing anomalous conditions there is no escape for the Indian state universities.

National Policy on Education, 1986 and RUSA, 2013 proposed the establishment of State Council of Higher Education in all states to increase the coordination among state and centre, and also among college and state universities. National Knowledge Commission, 2008 argued that the existing governance and regulation have an adverse effect on the development of the higher education system. Knowledge Commission proposed the establishment of an independent regulatory authority for higher education. The Yash Pal Committee also recommended replacing multiple bodies for accreditation with a single regulatory body.

### Deemed Universities

The main idea behind the concept of deemed university is to promote, strengthen, and bring those institutions under the purview of the UGC, which for historical or any other circumstances are not universities; yet are maintaining high standards of work in specialised academic fields comparable to a university. The UGC Act provides for the possibility of an institution being granted a deemed university status under Section 3 of the Act.

Till 1970, only seven institutions were notified as deemed to be universities. Between 1970 and 2000, 36 more were granted the status of deemed to be universities. Now, the total number is 130. This unusual growth has created a problem of equity, quality, and excellence. Various committees constituted by UGC, MHRD, and other bodies suggested measures for strengthening private deemed universities and resolving quality issues.

The Yash Pal Committee expressed great concern over the mushrooming of deemed universities. Though the deemed universities do not have affiliating powers; many of them have a number of campuses spread throughout the country. The Yash Pal Committee suggested that in view of misuse of the provision for deemed university status; the granting of such status should be put on hold till unambiguous and national guidelines are evolved. The committee further suggested that institutions wishing to get deemed university status should demonstrate special capabilities as was originally intended.

## Private Universities

Private universities are mostly supported by various bodies and societies. They are regulated under UGC Establishment and Maintenance of Standards in Private Universities Regulation, 2003. They are established by an Act of local legislative assembly and listed by the UGC in the gazette upon receiving the copy of the Act. As confirmed by the ruling of the Supreme Court, recognition by the UGC is required for the university to operate. Also, as per the 2003 Regulation, the UGC sends committees to inspect the private universities and publishes their inspection report. The earliest date of notification is that of Sikkim Manipal University, 11 October 1995. The earliest inspection report is that of Nirma University of Science and Technology, 15 May 2004. Private universities were established in 22 of the 29 states of India, and in none of the Union territories. The State with the most of private universities listed is Rajasthan.

Private universities are competent to award degrees as specified by the UGC under 22 of the UGC Act, with the approval of the statutory councils, wherever required through their main campus. Whenever the approval of the statutory council is not a prerequisite to start a programme, the universities are required to maintain the minimum standards regarding academic and physical infrastructure as laid down by the concerned statutory council. They cannot affiliate an institution or college. They cannot establish off-campus centres beyond the territorial jurisdictions of the concerned state. However, they can establish off-campus centres within the concerned state after five years of functioning as a private university recognised by the UGC, and with the prior approval of the UGC. A private university shall provide the relevant information relating to the first degree/diploma programmes, including the curriculum structure, contents, teaching and learning process, examination and evaluation system, and the eligibility criteria for admission of students, to the UGC on a Proforma prescribed by the UGC prior to beginning these programmes. The UGC gives clearance before starting the university.

Philip Altbach, who has studied higher education around the world for nearly five decades, notes that with some exceptions, there are no successful private research universities outside of the U.S. and Japan.

While private institutions do have the potential to make a contribution in the production of new knowledge, it is quite unlikely that they will actually do so in the foreseeable future.

It is also unlikely that India's private institutions will emulate the American or Japanese models. This is because the majority of private institutions are run by two sets of entrepreneurial social groups – business people and politicians – who are in the game for one simple reason: higher education is a great business opportunity.

Not surprisingly, private institutions have proliferated across the country to meet the high demand for education, especially in professional streams such as engineering and management. Labeled "teaching factories" by their detractors, they charge high fees, and often demand a lump sum amount by one name or by multiple names.

Here is the list of top 10 private and deemed multidisciplinary universities in India. The list is made by a survey conducted by *The Week* and Hansen research for the year 2015.

| *Rank* | *Name of the Institution* | *Places* |
|---|---|---|
| 1. | Manipal University | Manipal |
| 2. | Amity University | Noida |
| 3. | Symbiosis International University | Pune |
| 4. | Banasthali Vidyapeeth University | Banasthali |
| 5. | Amity Viswa University | Coimbatore |
| 6. | SRM University | Chennai |
| 7. | Christ University | Bengaluru |
| 8. | D.Y. Patil University | Mumbai |
| 9. | SASTRA University | Thanjavur |
| 10. | SVKM's NMIMS University | Mumbai |

## Establishing Research Universities

The idea of establishing research universities by RUSA (Rashtriya Uchhater Shiksha Abhiyan) is welcome. It may elevate the status of existing promising universities or set up new ones. In any case, the idea behind the concept is excellent. Setting up of research universities requires well defined vision and perspective. It should be based on developing a bond between research and education, research should extend the boundaries of education, and education in turn nurture creativity and innovative outlook among learners. They should work in close collaboration with various sectors: government, society, business, industry, etc.

Organisation for Economic Cooperation and Development (OECD) reports that out of 50 world class universities, 40 are in America with the highest research input. Though we have more than 700 universities, none of these is included in top 100 universities of the world. We have models of research universities in developed countries, various features of which can be adapted and followed.

### Establishing Navratna Universities

Some Indian universities have enormous potential to reach world standards in teaching and research. Identification of such universities, based on stringent parameters identified by a Committee of Vice-Chancellors, could be taken up during the Twelfth FYP. The salient features that may determine a university's eligibility to be rated "Navaratna" could be: (a) the number of programmes offered and departments existing in the university; (b) the rate of expansion during the last five years; (c) visibility assessed by the number of students seeking admission; (d) plurality and demographic diversity of faculty and students; (e) number of SAP departments, CAS advancements, national facilities, centres of excellence; (f) extramural funding and research projects carried out; (g) number and quality of publications in impact factor journals, Average Citation Index, Average H Index; (h) international collaborations. Such top universities to be identified in the Twelfth FYP will function under total autonomy and relaxation of rigid regulations in respect of faculty, appointment of overseas professors, and international partnership. Such universities may have to be provided an annual additional grant of ₹50.00 crore over and above the normal grant provided for five years.

Jandhyala B.G. Tilak put forward seven prepositions for the rejuvenation of Indian universities.

1. It is important to realise that public higher education forms the foundation for an equitable, just, and human society nation with weak public higher education system remains backward intellectually, socially, economically, and politically.
2. The classical model of university is still the best and most relevant of developing universities.
3. University should be designed to be universal in character scope and jurisdiction, with students and faculty drawn from various socio-economic echelons, different cultural backgrounds, diverse ideological milieu and from various regions of the country and even the globe.
4. The main function of universities include the production of knowledge through research, dissemination of knowledge through teaching social responsibility. Universities produce brilliant teachers, inspiring researches and socially responsible citizens.

5. A set of minimum requirements for university to function like a university is identified, in terms of faculty members, classrooms, hostels, faculty residences, libraries, labs, playgrounds, parks, canteens, etc.
6. Open Universities are not the effective alternative for a good formal university. Distance education may be good for skill inculcation.
7. Universities require sustained liberal state funding, ensuring adequacy, quality, diversity and equity in higher education. Within the university system, sizeable resources need to be allocated to enhance quality and excellence in teaching and reserve and scholarship programmes to ensure equality and promote inclusiveness.

### Vision World Class University

Chaya Goel and Devraj Goel, popular educationalists, highlighted the vision of a world class university in the following way:

i. Any university should be constructed, developed and established considering the global profile, that is, needs of various people, conditions of various people aiming at development of Universal Beings.
ii. The university should offer Choice Based Credit System, not for name sake, out of the given, but, out of the desired.
iii. The universities globe over should have complete Networking.
iv. The university should be a miniature of the Universe, different cultures, ideas, ideologies and philosophies. All these should find a place on a single campus and all should be fully valued, accepted and inculcated.
v. Ideas ought not to have labels. There are no limits and boundaries for knowledge generation and sharing. Universities should provide congenial environment for all these.
vi. Innovative Research and Development should be the essential features of all the universities.
vii. There should be utilisation of all innovations irrespective of their origin. Every innovation should become universal through the universities.
viii. A sense of equality among all students from various countries should be acculturated in the campus. The ultimate goal of Higher Education ought to be universal citizenship.
ix. The universities should own their own products. There should be adequate focus on Process Norms, along with Input Norms and Output Norms. If the process norms are perfected and observed honestly, then, the output quality and yield are almost ascertained.
x. The universities should have a vision of the unseen, and skills and competencies to regulate to lead the universe.

xi. Universities should produce the capital for the Nation, Globe and Universe.
xii. A university should be a blend of the Orient, Modern and Vision.
xiii. Universities should be Centres of Construction, Connection and Learning,
xiv. Universities should abstain from becoming Political Hubs. Universities ought to be autonomous.
xv. Universities in India should do away with Anti Plagiarism Software (APS), API (Academic Performance Indicators), SLETs and NETs. Universities ought to be Quality Centres. We should learn to own our own products.
xvi. Assessment and Accreditation by NAAC ought to be perfected if at all it is to be sustained. The grading rather than merely the function of the Peer Team, ought to be the function of the Educational Institution Reality.
xvii. Infrastructure should be of High Quality.
xviii. University campus should be peaceful with healthy ambience.
xix. Every Individual and Institution of India should observe the Preamble of Indian Constitution, that, India is a Sovereign, Socialist, Secular, Democratic, Republic, in thought and action.
xx. Developing Caring, Sensible, Responsible, Honest and Humble Citizens ought to be the major objective of the universities.
xxi. Universities ought to be fair in their dealings.
xxii. Universities should be centres of Higher Learning. Every Moment to sustain their identity.
xxiii. Internal Quality Assurance Cells (IQAC) of the universities should assure and ensure quality.
xxiv. The Curricula and modes of Transaction need to be perfected.
xxv. Convocations without invocation are useless. Let us really mean Graduation and Degrees.

World Class Universities ought to be universal in character. What use are colourful citations, unless there is scaled expression at the field and functional levels? What use is the International Outlook unless there is emancipation and liberation of the universal constituents and entities of the miserable painful states? World class universities are where ideas germinate and spring, feelings flow, motor creates, the soul spirit reins, and the self resonates within and with the universe, where the Human Beings Transcend from Human Development Index (HDI) to Universal Development Index (UDI) and Human Beings tend to be Universal Beings, where we have unconditional love for the nature with super inner control. Let us cleanse ourselves with all compatible rinsing agents and submit fully, with complete immersion for understanding the manifestations of the universe. With this prayer India has the potency to establish Universities, which are true Universities, universal in character and expression. The World Class Universities should aspire to be Universal Universities.

## Global University Features

In India, the public are continuously echoing their desire that at least some of the Indian universities appear in the top 100 in global ranking systems. In this context, it is necessary to examine what it takes to become a global university

A university aspiring to become a global university may have to adopt systems and practices that are globally relevant. A global university may constitute a governing body with members from different nationalities to reflect international positioning and outlook. The University will have to engage a truly international mix of faculty members reflecting diverse communities and provide education to students coming from different countries with their own cultural backgrounds. A global university require to have financial capacity and human resources frame works and systems that can attract international talent.

S.R. Shankapal, Vice Chancellor of M S Ramaiah University of Applied Sciences narrates the characteristic of a global university in the following words:

A global university requires a global brand to project itself internationally. Harvard and Cambridge are truly global universities, as they have associated by the audience across the world with attainment and educational excellence. The creation and working of a global brand requires enormous efforts to address concerns and perceptions of a given cultural and geographic setting and a vision for placing the institution in a global context.

Global universities address global issues. Education should make humanity more intelligent, knowledgeable, and wise enough to address global challenges – like sustainable development while addressing global climate change; sufficient clean water without conflict for everyone; balancing population growth and resources; evolvement of genuine democracy emerge from authoritarian regimes; the global convergence of information and communications technologies work for everyone; ethical market economies to help reduce the gap between rich and poor; the threat of new and re-emerging diseases and immune micro-organisms; new security strategies to reduce ethnic conflicts, terrorism, and the use of weapons of mass destruction; meeting growing energy demands safely and efficiently, accelerating scientific and technological development to improve the human condition, and ethical considerations into global decisions. These global issues need to be solved for the benefit of the society. It is expected that the solutions to such global issues come from universities. However, most of the times, university faculties are unable to undertake research that addresses global issues because of funding contingencies. Global universities address global issues.

A global university educates global students. A global university should be able to attract international students coming from different countries with diverse ethnic backgrounds and all students be treated identically.

Cultural openness is a critical requirement. Simply being open to the presence of international faculty members and students does not make a university global. Indeed, if there is no real mixing of students coming from different nations, then the university campus becomes a set of silos. The willingness to adopt attitudes, pedagogies and systems from beyond the national context is necessary. This does not mean setting aside lightly the contributions that a particular location and institutional tradition might provide but it certainly means being comfortable going beyond them.

A global university has global partnerships. A global partnership is to be built on complementarily with the parties gaining mutual advantage each from the other. A global university understands that the world is a big place. It knows that it cannot be globally present, it must make choices about where to focus its efforts. The difference between a global university and a national or regional university is that those choices are made with a view to opening up to global influences and contributing to the global scene rather than a decision driven purely by local financial imperatives. It also understands that international strategy is a long game, with partnerships taking time to cement and presence recognised slowly.

Finally, but most importantly, a global university educates students to be global citizens and for global careers. This is easy to say, and hard to implement. It covers a wide array of challenges from certification and accreditation, at the more straightforward end; through ensuring curricula reflects international problems to the teaching of the much more complex soft or transferrable skills that are called upon in global careers. It cannot be disregarded in the belief that an internationally diverse staff and student body will suffice to make a global educational experience.

The mantle of a global university should not be casually assumed. It imposes significant responsibilities on all members of the university community. Accepting the responsibilities requires knowledge and understanding that implies an educational task in itself.

The realisation of global university dream for any country does not come easily and so also for India. It is beyond that a country makes huge financial investments to push some of its universities to global university status. To support the cause of global university dream, it is essential that support and commitment of federal and local governments, cultural acceptance and tolerance amongst local communities, enormous exposure of faculty members to global challenges, strategies, and educational practices are all necessary. It is all about converting a city like Bengaluru into London or Boston and making members of faculty think like Harvard or Cambridge University professors and converting your people into global citizens.

# 7

# Internationalisation of Higher Education

Internationalisation is not an altogether unknown phenomenon in higher education in India and other developing countries. Students have for many decades gone aboard for higher studies, and professionals have gone out to teach or do research. Foreign faculty have come to our shores for teaching and managing institutions. Foreign books and journals have been an indispensable source of knowledge for our university students and teachers. Thus, teaching and learning, research, and institution building have all been influenced by some form of internationalisation or the other.

Internationalisation of higher education (IHE) is a process of integrating an international, intercultural and global dimension into the purpose, functions (teaching, service, research), and delivery of higher education. International higher education means a series of international activities such as academic mobility for students and teachers, international linkages, partnerships and projects, new international academic programmes, and international initiatives. IHE is the delivery of education to other countries through new types of arrangements such as branch campuses and franchises and using a variety of face-to-face and distance learning techniques. To many it means the integration of an international, intercultural, and global dimension into the curriculum and teaching learning process. Traditionally, higher education has been considered to be a social responsibility, and government and society have both contributed to its development. However, with the expansion of higher education to make it easily available to the masses, there has been a continuously increasing demand for professional programmes, first at the national level, and then increasingly at the international level.

The governments of various countries support higher education programmes by providing scholarships, fellowships, exchange programme support, and chairs. A number of ways exist for collaborating with the international higher education system:

- By promoting international student mobility through exchange and scholarship programmes
- Promoting faculty mobility
- Promoting cultural understanding by way of scholarships, fellowships, and chairs
- Offering offshore distance education programmes

- Establishing academic partnerships with foreign institutions related to teaching
- Promoting research collaboration at individual and institutional levels
- Setting up international branch campuses abroad
- Developing linkages in sports and cultural activities.

International organisations, associations, and the governments of a number of countries support several international programmes/schemes/scholarships, and fellowships for international higher education,

## Favourable Effects of Internationalisation

- Quality of higher education will improve following the close cooperation of universities at a worldwide level
- Students would have greater choices in selecting courses as per their aptitude and interest
- Economies of scale could bring down the cost of education
- International standards of education can be ensured
- ICTs would benefit students, irrespective of their nationality
- Research and development may scale new heights
- Mobility of teachers is likely to enhance homogeneity in teaching quality
- Cultural, specific, and technological integration may lead to more multifaceted development
- Modern system of examination, education, and testing would develop and spread.

Possible Adverse Effects of Internationalisation

- Global education may adversely affect national sovereignty, and lead to domination by the west
- Indigenous arts and culture of a country may face a threat of loss or extinction.

## Earlier Efforts of Internationalisation in India

### *The Mysore Statement*

Perhaps, for the first time the issue of internationalisation was deliberated as a desirable change by the Association of Indian Universities in 2001. The AIU organised a Round table of Vice Chancellors on Internationalisation of Indian Higher Education in February 2001 at the University of Mysore under the leadership and guidance of Prof. K.B. Powar, the then Secretary General, AIU and an expert in the field of internationalisation of higher education. The Round table was attended by senior Indian educationists and planners, international educators, and representatives of developed as well as developing countries. After an in-depth discussion on the global scenario related to the internationalisation of higher education, several recommendations were made for the government, academic institutions, and the AIU to act upon.

Some of the recommendations were:

- Urgent action should be taken in the matter of finalisation of government policies relating to the promotion of Indian education abroad. They proposed that a Committee for the Promotion of Indian Education Abroad (COPIE) be constituted at an early date and its functioning activated.
- The University Grants Commission Act, 1956, and the Acts of other statutory councils, need to be amended to include a specific provision allowing universities to open offshore campuses, and export Indian education through the distance mode. There is also a need to enact legislation that would regulate the operation of foreign institutions, and thereby prevent the gross commercialisation of education. It is also necessary to frame legislation that would regulate the operation of Indian partners of foreign institutions to allow only genuine academic institutions to participate in twinning activities.
- Urgent steps should be taken to strengthen the data and information base so that prospective international students can obtain information related to academic programmes available at different universities, eligibility criteria, admission procedures, and tuition fees.
- Government, statutory bodies, and the University Grants Commission should grant greater autonomy and flexibility to universities in dealing with the process of admission of foreign students and in entering into collaborative arrangements with foreign institutions, especially in the establishment of offshore campuses and centres.
- The government should set up a mechanism for monitoring the standard of education that is imparted by foreign universities. There is also a need to establish a National Quality Framework that would provide for lateral transfer as well as vertical progression both nationally and internationally.
- International education is a two-way process and it is essential that Indian academic institutions, and especially the universities, should establish partnerships and develop networks with foreign universities in both the developed and the developing countries.
- In order to facilitate the internationalisation of Indian higher education, AIU should assume the role of coordinator. It should serve as the nodal agency within the university system, to be responsible for the coordination of activities of universities in the area of international education.

### *Amritsar Declaration*

In the backdrop of the Mysore Statement, the Association of Indian Universities organised the second Round table on Internationalisation of Indian Higher Education in February, 2002. It was attended by representatives of the higher education system of the United States of America, Australia, Germany, France, and India. The Round table discussed the issues related to government policies, student mobility, building institutional links, and marketing of education. Along with other recommendations, it was suggested that AIU should assume the role of coordinator. Some of the recommendations were:

- The Indian government needs to play a pro-active role in order to promote the internationalisation of Indian higher education. The Indian embassies and high commissions should take the initiative in providing information on the Indian higher education system, and about the facilities for higher education available in the country. The formalities related to registration, entry test requirements, issue of 'No Objection Certificate,' and issue (and extension) of visa need to be simplified. There is a need to adopt an open door policy as regards self-financing students. A single-window clearance mechanism should be set up for admitting students to different professional programmes. It is also desirable that a mechanism to monitor the quality of education imparted to foreign students by the Indian institutions be formulated.
- As stated in the World Declaration on Higher Education for the Twenty-first Century, partnership and alliances based on mutual respect and credibility will be a prime matrix for renewal in higher education in the twenty-first century. Indian academic institutions should establish links with foreign institutions (twinning programmes), and if possible, be a part of an international consortium. This will help the institutions to develop and maintain international standards in both teaching and research.
- There is a need to establish a nodal agency that will be responsible for maintenance of databases, networking with other international agencies, coordinating student exchange programmes, developing institutional links for both teaching and research, and possibly marketing Indian higher education abroad. The Association of Indian Universities has already taken the initiative as regards internationalisation of higher education and could be assigned this role by the government, with adequate financial support.

### *AIU Task Force (2004)*

The general body of the Association of Indian Universities in its 78th Annual Meeting held at Sri Venkateshwara University, Tirupati on 21 November 2003 resolved to constitute a Task Force to examine various issues involved in internationalisation of higher education. Following the resolution, a Task force was constituted. The recommendations of the Task Force were:

- Before plunging into any agreement related to higher education with the trade partners of the country, the following measures should urgently be taken: (a) All requests and offers regarding higher education received by the government from the WTO members should be made publicly available with full details, to the public at large; (b) An impact assessment of these proposals should be carried out by several groups of experts having different ideological backgrounds; (c) This impact assessment should particularly focus on the following issues: (i) What will be the impact of GATS, policy of 'progressive liberalisation' and its rule of 'non-discrimination' on Indian higher education? (ii) What kind of short-term and long-term restructuring of higher education would be required as a result of this? (iii) Will it result in reduction or complete elimination of public funding/subsidy of higher education? If so, what will be its effect on the quality of opportunity to access higher education, quality of education, on various types of 'profitable' and 'non-profitable' courses/activities, and on cross-subsidisation? (iv) Will it make international cooperation in the field of higher education more difficult, expensive, and less meaningful? (v) What will be the impact on society of the reduction in the regulatory capability of government, and elimination of policy options available to it in future? (vi) How will it affect the academics? How will it affect their academic freedom? What will be the effect on their employment/service conditions, bargaining capacity etc.? Will it make their life more 'miserable' and less creative/exciting through contractual/ad-hoc/temporary/casual appointments? (vii) What will be its impact on the students? Will the reduction or complete elimination of public funding, fee deregulation along with increased self-financed courses become the norm? Will it affect the access to higher education and make it more dependent on their financial capability, rather than their intellectual worth? Will it lead to widespread indebtedness of students? If so, what will be its effect on the students, their education, and the society at large?

- These impact assessments should be made publicly available, and an exhaustive and widespread public debate based on these impact assessments should be promoted among all the stakeholders of higher education. Moreover, all relevant government departments and ministries such as NGOs, UGC, AIU, MHRD (Now MoE), Commerce Ministry, Finance Ministry, Home Ministry, Youth Welfare Ministry, Foreign Ministry, Defense Ministry, Planning Commission, etc. should be actively and jointly involved in this nationwide debate.
- The Task Force noted a few points which are positively in favour of the liberalisation policy of the GATS, are mentioned here: (a) Innovation development in higher education; (b) Entry to new service providers; (c) Greater student access; (d) Increased economic gains; (e) New hybridisation; and (f) Fusion of culture through mobility of people. At the same time the Task Force desired to put forth the lurking dangers

awaiting us if we jump into the plans laid down by the GATS. These dangers are enumerated below: (a) Sovereignty of the country will be at stake; (b) Government will be forced to reduce subsidies; (c) Only professional courses will find place in the education system; (d) Depriving the poor of developing countries the benefits of higher education and benefiting mainly the upper middle and the rich classes; (e) Development of unrest in students at large; (f) Threat to linguistic diversity, especially through dominance of English; (g) Commoditisation of higher education will erode the autonomy of the universities and the academic freedom of the university teachers; (h) Higher education under GATS may not be in congruence with national policy of education, which will lead to larger socio-political turbulence; and (i) GATS could undermine cooperative internationalisation.

- After having thoroughly examined the strengths and weaknesses of Indian higher education, and also the opportunities and threats to the Indian higher education under the GATS, the Task Force thus came to the conclusion that it is not in the interest of the country at this stage to open up its higher education system for global competition under GATS. It suggested an all-pervasive and exhaustive national debate, involving all the stakeholders in the country on the issue of liberalising higher education, to arrive at a final decision for its acceptance or otherwise.

### *Initiatives by the University Grants Commission*

The recommendations of both the Round Tables organised at Mysore and Amritsar by the Association of Indian Universities culminated in the formation of a Standing Committee of University Grants Commission on Promotion of Indian Higher Education Abroad (PIHEAD). In the tenth Five Year Plan, UGC recognised internationalisation as a thrust area. Hence, it formed an expert committee to encourage free flow of students from other nations to India and vice versa. The PIHEAD committee submitted its report in 2004. PIHEAD has been engaged to ensure speedy implementation of various proposals initiated by the UGC. A provision has been made to obtain the required information from the universities/institutions with regard to their programmes, course content, admission criteria, fee structure, transaction of curricula, evaluation procedures, etc. which would provide support to PIHEAD to promote higher education abroad.

In 2006, UGC formed a study group which came out with the report *'Modalities to Provide Educational Opportunities to Foreign Students and to Generate Resource for Higher Education'* suggesting setting up of 'Consortium for International Education' either at the UGC, AIU, or at any university in Delhi. Further, in 2009 a panel of the UGC prepared a plan on 'Internationalisation of Higher Education,' but a decision on it is pending for want of further action.

### *Initiatives by Ministry of Human Resource Development*

The Government of India made a legislative attempt to regulate the educational system better by putting forth in the parliament the Foreign Education Institutions (Regulation of Entry and Operation, Maintenance of Quality and Prevention of Commercialisation) Bill in 2007. The objective of the bill was to provide an ideal regulatory framework in which reputed institutions are able to enter and operate in terms of India's National Policy, while at the same time check and control substandard operators. However, the bill could not be enacted.

Recently, the Union Cabinet approved a new programme titled Global Initiative of Academic Network (GIAN) in Higher Education aimed at tapping the international talent pool of scientists and entrepreneurs, to encourage their engagement with the institutes of higher education in India, so as to augment the country's existing academic resources, accelerate the pace of quality reform, and elevate India's scientific and technological capacity to global excellence.

Further, an innovative scheme – Connect to India – was launched by the Ministry of HRD on the assumption that this initiative will be a value added programme, under which around 200 U.S. students would be provided opportunities to visit India every year to attend a 4-6-week study programme in one of the 15 select Indian universities. It is expected that the Connect to India programme would be beneficial to both Indian and American students.

### *Stand of the National Institute of Educational Planning and Administration*

The National University of Educational Planning and Administration (NUEPA, now NIEPA), was engaged in taking up a few programmes on internationalisation of higher education in the form of research studies, seminars, conferences. The NUEPA organised a conference on "Internationalisation of Higher Education: Issues and Concerns" in 2004. The issues having implications on domestic regulation, improving competitiveness of higher education, and the issue of foreign direct investment (FDI) in higher education were deliberated. In 2009, NUEPA organised a "Consultation of Foreign Providers in Indian Higher Education: Issues of Entry, Regulation and Models of Engagement." The major recommendations were as follows:

- For degree and non-degree programmes, accredited and reputed foreign universities may be permitted to collaborate for the delivery of joint programmes.
- Such collaboration may take place with government, and government-aided universities and colleges for joint degree provision.
- Such collaboration may also take place with private universities and colleges under strict guidelines from the UGC to prevent commercialisation.
- The UGC may allow the grant of a joint degree for such collaborative partnerships.

- For non-degree programmes in vocational disciplines, all registered private institutions not included in higher education, may be allowed to collaborate with foreign universities/institutions after registration and regulation by appropriate vocation agencies of the government.
- The branch campus of a foreign university through the trust, and under 2f of The UGC Act, with degree conferring right without university status may at present be deferred till the experiment gained from collaboration partnership warrants the need for more liberalisation.

From the above analysis of India's response to the process of internationalisation of higher education it appears that the process of internationalisation has not yet taken off. If India has to benefit from the process of internationalisation, major policy initiatives and concrete programme activities in the area of student and scholar exchanges, as well as educational institutional tie-ups for collaboration in teaching and research, will have to be put in place. Indian universities must increase the entry of international students with whom the local students can interact. Reforms in the higher education system of India are long overdue, and the emphasis on internationalisation must be given a high priority.

In formulating the Twelfth Five Year Plan 2012-17, India has projected a scheme for setting up an India International Education Centre for promoting internationalisation of Indian higher education. Unfortunately, there does not seem to be any political commitment towards going ahead with such a Centre that could help enhancing India's political standing through international education activities. In short, India has so far not shown its political willingness to use the international education route to play a leading role in a world of globalised education players.

The globalised economic scenario offers us a unique opportunity to establish India as an educational destination for international students as we can offer certain unique advantages, including affordable, quality education in supportive atmosphere strengthened by historic, cultural, and political ties. The provisos necessary for internationalisation of higher education are:

- Enhancing capacity and efficiency
- Improving standards and quality
- Competing in the global arena
- Influencing international relations
- Establishing a regional identity
- Enhancing India's international reputation
- Alleviation of faculty-crunch.

It is unfortunate that the Indian universities, barring only a few, have not been able to capitalise on the opportunities of offering their educational programmes to the world population in any significant manner. The reasons are manifold. The universities in India may not have realised the importance of offering their products and services to foreign clientele. The inherent limitations of the system may also be holding the universities back or making their attempts to reach out the foreign clientele less successful. Quite often the restriction of territorial jurisdiction of individual universities is seen as a barrier in their effort to go international. Sometimes the limitations could be the lack of appropriate information about the Indian campuses to the foreign students. Paucity of suitable infrastructure and physical facilities are indeed a deterrent, but more importantly it is the self-imposed rigidity in the teaching, learning, admission, and evaluation processes that discourage foreign students.

Indian higher educational institutions should urgently start marketing their programmes abroad with the twin objectives of generating additional resources and developing strong relationships with other countries of the world. It is high time that the universities develop international orientation to their working and operation, and the agencies responsible for the management of higher education institutions must ensure that the systemic hurdles in the way of internationalisation of Indian higher education are removed without any further delay.

### ICT and Internationalisation of Higher Education

Information and Computing Technology (ICT) can be instrumental in better articulating the internationalisation process and can actually contribute towards a qualitative change in it.

To do so, ICT brings about an inevitable reformulation of the objectives of internationalisation and culture, ICT may offer new educational opportunities at a lower cost and with more flexibility, irrespective of their physical location. ICT enables virtual internationalisation, which can increase access and choice, as well as helping to mitigate brain drain, a critical concern for less developed countries.

However, many institutions are reluctant to use ICT to its fullest, even those institutions strongly committed to internationalisation. This may be because of ignorance of its potential, lack of adequate training, or, possibly, because of internal resistance to the adoption of ICT.

### Why We Must Internationalise our Higher Education?

- Indian youth need to be exposed to the global culture if they are to become 'global citizens'. This can be achieved by meeting more international students either abroad or on home campuses.
- International students will bring national diversity to our university campuses. Over the years the international students will enhance the visibility of India.
- Opening the education system for global research using more international students could lead to greater international collaborations, better publication records and greater visibility amongst the peers who rank the universities.
- More international students in India would bring in additional revenue to the country through tuition fees and living expenses.

- One of the main goals of internationalised higher education is to provide the most relevant education to students, who will be the citizens, entrepreneurs and scientists of tomorrow. Internationalisation is not an end in itself, but a driver for change and improvement it should help generate the skills required in the 21st century, spur on innovation and create alternatives while, ultimately, fostering job creation.

**Obstacles to Studying in India**

- Some of the obstacles include the liberalisation of foreign exchange for those who wish to study abroad, easing of restrictions on foreign investment, and a limited number of collaborative programmes with foreign providers.
- In the context of global skill needs, the curricula need to be restructured in detail to meet world standards.
- Financing is a challenging issue. Even with the private players investing heavily in setting up collaborative institutions, investment in international education needs to be encouraged.
- There is a dissatisfying trend in enrolment of overseas students which needs to be addressed as early as possible.
- Those who have taken advantage of the new policies are from the private universities. Public universities have not been active on this front so far, nor do they have the resources to take such initiatives.
- Lack of effective and coherent strategy of regulatory framework to monitor and assess these activities.
- A consensus on India's policies on internationalisation in higher education is yet to emerge.
- The use of technology in higher education remains limited and standards of research and teaching in Indian universities are far below international standards, with no Indian university featuring consistently in the top 200 institutions globally.
- In global rankings of universities, very few Indian institutions find a place. The Shanghai world rankings of the top 500 universities/institutes include only three Indian Institutes of Technologies (IITs) and one Indian Institute of Management (IIM), and that, too, at the lower end. The Times global rankings of the top 100 also find a mention of just a couple of Indian institutions.
- In terms of published papers (an indicator of research output), India has slipped from the 8th place in 1985 to the 14th in 2006.
- Paucity of resources is another disquieting feature of India's higher education sector.
- Lack of appropriate infrastructure.
- The sector is plagued by a shortage of trained faculty, poor infrastructure and outdated and irrelevant curricula.

## Possible Solutions/Recommendations

As far as India is concerned, we should be looking for the "import" of services and resources that can aid us in this important endeavour. Successful resolution of these problems could eventually pave the way for us to "export" our services to other countries.

At this point, some of the questions that we need to ask ourselves are, what modes of internationalisation are pertinent to the Indian context of higher education? Which modes will help us to improve access and quality so that higher education becomes more equitable through the expansion of its reach? Some of the recommendations include:

1. Scale up the movement of students to foreign countries for higher studies.
2. Facilitate the participation of students in the distance education programmes of foreign universities (online learning).
3. Permit foreign universities to establish branch campuses in India to offer educational programmes.
4. Encourage foreign universities to offer joint programmes in collaboration with Indian institutions on a much larger scale. This could include twinning, franchising and other modes.
5. Award contracts to reputed foreign universities to collaborate in the creation of world-class universities in India.
6. Make our top universities/institutes a destination for foreign students on a large scale.
7. Encourage Indian institutions to set up campuses/collaborations in other countries to meet the growing international demand for higher education.

Top Ten Sources of Internationally Mobile Students Worldwide (2012)

| *Country* | *Number* |
|---|---|
| China | 694365 |
| India | 189472 |
| Republic of Korea | 123674 |
| Germany | 117576 |
| Saudi Arabia | 62535 |
| France | 62416 |
| United States | 58133 |
| Malaysia | 55579 |
| Vietnam | 53802 |
| Iran (Islamic Republic of) | 51549 |
| Total | 4009312 |

Top Ten Destinations of Indian Students (2012)

| *Country* | *Number* |
|---|---|
| United States | 97120 |
| United Kingdom | 29713 |
| Australia | 11684 |
| Canada | 8142 |
| United Arab Emirates | 7310 |
| New Zealand | 7248 |
| Germany | 4312 |
| Russian Federation | 3351 |
| Ukraine | 2516 |
| France | 1955 |
| Worldwide | 189472 |

# 8
# Excellence in Higher Education

## Concept

What is excellence? How is it defined? *Oxford English Dictionary* would define "excellent" as something that is extremely good or outstanding. *Collins Cobuild Advanced Illustrated Dictionary* defines "excellence" as something extremely good. *Macmillan Dictionary* defines excellence or excellent in terms of being extremely good. In other words, excellence or excellent is that which is extremely good or outstanding,

> When translated, "excellence" in higher education would mean the attainment of "A" Grade in NAAC Assessment and Accreditation (in different cycles): the conferment of the status of University/College with Potential for Excellence and in the case of Deemed Universities the bracketing of the assessed university in category "A" by MHRD (now MoE) (Report of Tandon Committee). In the case of individual departments in universities/colleges, the SAP status and the award of DST-FIST grants would certainly make them outstanding units within that institution. The conferment of autonomy on select colleges would also be interpreted as a mark of excellence.

Put differently, IISc, IITs, IIMs, IISERS, Central Universities and institutions with an "A" Grade by NAAC and similar accreditation by AICTE (NBA) are considered the best or excellent institutions in the country. These institutions are deemed superior to other institutions in terms of their well-qualified and well-trained faculty. Many of whom have PhDs and/or Post-Doctoral Fellows (PDFs) from institutions like MIT, Harvard and Yale universities, with outstanding publications with a high h-index, excellent infrastructure, especially high-end labs and state-of-the-art facilities for carrying out cutting edge research, brilliant students who have cleared national eligibility tests and are head and shoulders above their peers, and other such parameters. In these institutions, the placement record is enviable and potential employers vie with one another to grab these students.

### *Excellence - A Hallmark*

Excellence is the hallmark of all higher educational institutions. It is the express mandate of all institutions to strive for excellence and achieve it in good measure. But what needs to be underlined is the fact that the term "excellence" needs to be reconceptualised in inclusive terms so that all institutions, irrespective of their location and their student population are given an opportunity to excel in their own terms and not necessarily forced to conform to a straight jacketed framework of excellence which defines excellence narrowly in terms of possession of research degrees with good publications, high marks and enviable placement record. Let us strive consciously to expand the perimeter of the concept of "excellence" so that quite a few good institutions that may not otherwise be graded "excellent" and get due recognition.

### Indicators of Excellence

Prime indicator of excellence in higher education is the quality of research. No doubt there is no dearth of potential in this area in our country. The available talent has not however been harnessed judiciously to reach the optimum. Reasons are many and not far to seek. First is the infrastructure. Our universities are nowhere near the quantum of investment made in building the right research ambience and the funding support available for high end research elsewhere in the competitive zone. Private philanthropy and corporate support being minimal, the institutions fall back upon mostly on state sponsorship, which has obvious limitations. As a result, our better talents always look forward to joining institutions abroad which provide improved facilities in their respective field of research.

Secondly, barring a handful of institutions solely concentrating on research, it is our universities which cater to the research needs of our country. Pressed as they are with the demands of taught programmes in undergraduate and graduate level, research for the most has to be the second priority, both from academic and administrative points of view.

Thirdly, one of the handicaps in India to optimise funded research outcome is the funding pattern itself. There is an element of adhocism in the matter of release of money on time. If the funds flow is disturbed, not only the future progress of research is stalled, but the possible outcome of the work already done is seriously jeopardised. The constraints in this regard are to be eliminated by the fund providers at the time of granting any project.

Finally, our universities seem to be concentrating bargaining larger number of mediocre research output. Unfortunately, bulk of this research is oriented towards getting a research degree, which serves as qualification in the job market. Research programmes in many of our universities are but extension of masters' programme; not contributing much to the knowledge domain. This is no means to acquire excellence.

### Centres of Excellence

The world is changing rapidly. That is why achieving excellence challenges, the Higher Education sector needs to transform to meet the expectations of today and build the vibrant, prosperous province of tomorrow. Enhancing educational quality and excellence is a multilevel effort and a continuous process. Nowadays, one of the mechanisms for stimulating excellence in teaching and learning and increasing the status of education in Higher Education has been the establishment of national programmes of 'Centres of Excellence' and 'University with Potential for Excellence'. Attaining excellence in the entire activity of Higher Educational Institutions is the only factor, which can place it among the first, at an international level, implicitly leading to acknowledgement of the excellence of its faculty and students both.

To help all students to learn in this changing environment, academics need to update their knowledge and have a better understanding of teaching and learning issues as well as to advance their pedagogic competencies. Many current methods, such as widespread lecturing to students relegate students to passivity, tend to focus narrowly on subject knowledge, and, thus, are inadequate. Instead, excellent teaching needs to put student's effective learning at the centre of the teaching process. If teachers and the universities adopt a more student-centred view of teaching, then their students will learn more deeply, and they are more likely to be intellectually and morally transformed by their university experience. However, the Higher Education sector needs to be willing to promote this kind of significant learning and help teachers learn how to achieve those aims. It must create environments in which student learning of this kind can take place and in which teachers are rewarded for engaging in such practices. It will not happen by itself. Some steps that should be taken are (Floud, 2010):

- Redefine professional standards for Higher Education teachers.
- Provide 'Teaching Excellence Awards' to deserving teachers.
- Strive for 'Quality' and then 'Excellence' rather than 'Quantity' in Higher Education.
- Measure teaching effectiveness objectively and provide constructive feedback to academics.
- Establish the institutional support base for educational development locally.
- Recognise 'teaching excellence' in hiring and promotion decisions on priority basis.
- Recognise the teacher researcher and provide due incentives.
- Promote researches on teaching and learning, and implementation of their relevant findings;
- Allocate enough funding for educational development and educational researches, and
- Establish an 'excellence forum' within each HEI that pools and shares resources and existing expertise on educational development in general and teaching pedagogy development in particular across borders.

## Parameters of Excellence

The plea is for an inclusive conceptualisation of excellence, where several other parameters, which do not normally fall within the ambit of standardised assessment and accreditation, are given some consideration. Some of these parameters are discussed here. The first parameter would talk of student diversity. What percentage of an institution's students are first generation learners? How many of them are drawn from rural areas? Educating rural and/or disadvantaged learners and preparing them for life is certainly a mark of excellence. Institutions that educate and empower rural, dalit and tribal learners should be deemed excellent institutions. The second parameter would raise questions about the location of the institution. Institutions that are located in remote rural areas and cater predominantly to rural learners are rarely in the limelight. But some of these institutions that empower rural learners despite all odds stake a reasonable claim to be adjudged excellent. The third parameter would take into account the extension and outreach activities of the institution. Rural exposure and immersion programmes occupy an important slot here. Higher educational institutions cannot confine themselves to teaching and undertaking research. In addition to these two domains, they have to focus on the third dimension, namely, extension. Institutions that promote a suitable pedagogy of the oppressed and work for integrated rural development deserve to be called excellent. The fourth parameter would look into the institution's contribution to national development. How well does the institution integrate national policies into its curriculum and what efforts does it take to translate the nation's vision into concrete realities? Institutions that are committed to promoting national integration and inter-religious faith and harmony deserve to be graded excellent.

The fifth parameter would look into the spiritual/value formation of the students. The term spiritual here does not have any religious connotations. How does the institution chisel and sculpt its students and transform them into men and women of character with values? Institutions that mentor students and orient them to lead meaningful lives deserve to be called excellent. The sixth parameter would highlight the provision of holistic education. Those institutions that pay a good deal of attention to good teaching, quality research and at the same time are committed to action based research leading to integrated rural development, dissemination of Gandhian values, especially Gandhi's Nai Talim system of education, and are working for societal transformation leading to the establishment of an egalitarian society deserve to be called excellent institutions. Such institutions are truly excellent for they harmonise the mandate of higher education in general and their specific vision and mission. It has to be pointed out that accrediting agencies, NAAC in particular, has already taken note of some of these parameters. But there is ample space for a good debate on this issue.

### National Initiatives

Apex bodies of Higher Education have taken various innovative steps from time to time. The innovative initiatives taken by UGC to enhance quality and excellence across the country to be facilitated in the 12th Five Year Plan are as follows (George, 2011):

- Making Institutional and Programme Accreditation mandatory
- Attracting Quality Faculty, Promoting Faculty Mobility and Continuous Faculty Development Programmes

- Reforming the Academic Staff College (ASC) System as Faculty Talent Promotion system by rejuvenating ASCs as Faculty Development Centres
- Establishing New Faculty Development Centres
- Increasing the Faculty Development Centres (currently ASCs) from the present 66 to 100
- Faculty Mobility
- Student Mobility
- Evaluation of Teachers by Students and Peer Assessment
- Leveraging Technology for Curriculum Models, Courseware Development and Participatory Teaching-Learning
- A Structural Orientation to Establish Schools in Specific knowledge Domains to Facilitate Holistic Academic Reforms in all universities
- Networking of Universities and Colleges through Setting up a National Educational Resource Portal
- Strengthening the E-Initiatives
- Expand E-Resource Availability
- Priority initiative to implement automation of administration and examination to achieve e-governance
- Structural and Systemic Reforms for Good Governance
- Promotion of Autonomous Colleges
- Reforming the Self-financed Teaching Programmes
- Infusing Culture of Collaboration and Co-operation
- Research Facilities for Science Teachers in State Universities and Colleges
- Improved Funding Pattern for UGC-SAP
- Research Fellowships
- Curbing Plagiarism
- Maximising the Utilisation of Research Facilities of National Institutes/ Laboratories, and
- Establishment of Navratna Universities.

Union Ministry of Human Resource Development (now MoE) has launched its ambitious programme to revamp the Higher Education sector in the country, Rashtriya Uchchatar Shiksha Abhiyan (RUSA) in 2013. The amount of funding from Central Government will be 65% of the total grants, and 35% will be contributed by the State/UT as matching share. For northeastern states, Sikkim, Jammu and Kashmir, and Uttarakhand the matching share is waived to 10%. Through RUSA, it aims to cover 316 state public universities and 13,024 colleges across the country. As per the RUSA document, greater emphasis would be laid on the improvement of the quality of teaching-learning processes in order to produce employable and competitive graduates, post-graduates, and PhDs. RUSA will have a completely new approach towards funding higher education in state universities; it is based on key principles of performance-based funding. Incentivising well performing institutions and decision-making through clearly defined norms.

# 9

# Research Promotion Scenario

Research is actually a journey of discovery. But for that the purpose of the research should be clearly and distinctly defined. Perhaps the most important dimension of a researcher is the ability to synthesise and integrate the subject matter. Until such integration is internalised and finds expression in the performance of researcher, it will not be accepted. So, James Harold Fox has indicated some criteria of good research work:

- The research procedure used should be described in sufficient detail to permit another researcher to repeat the research for further advancement, on keeping the continuity of what has already been attained.
- The aim of the research should be clear and common concept be used.
- The procedure design of the research should be carefully planned to yield results that are as objective as possible.
- The researcher should report with complete frankness, flow in procedural design and estimate their effects upon the findings.
- The analysis of data should be sufficiently adequate to reveal its significance and the methods of analysis used should be appropriate. The validity and reliability of the data should be checked carefully.
- Conclusions should be confined to those justified by the data of the research and limited to those for which the data provide an adequate basis.

So, to design the research work, the anticipation of the subject matter is to be presented in a particular format. For designing the research work, good planning and proper execution are required. The research may be of any field, the framework of the research helps researcher to fulfil the necessary as well as sufficient conditions to carry out the research in the right direction. Therefore, the research work is considered as the subject matter of objectivity. It means, objective 'entertainability' is the most important criteria of the research work. Better conception, planning well and proper execution help in producing an accurately designed research work.

The researcher uses a number of methods in advancement of knowledge, making discoveries and in developing theories. These methods include:

i. Scientific Method
ii. Statistical Method

iii. Historical Method
iv. Research in the Humanities
v. Artistic Method
vi. Analytic Method
vii. Deductive Method
viii. Inductive Method
ix. Synthetic Method.

The research problem involves exhaustive thinking and rethinking process which should be realistic one. Naturally that paves the way for the development of hypothesis and smooth functioning of the research. To define the problem systematically, the steps mentioned below can be undertaken as:

- Identification of research problem
- Review of literature
- Purpose of research work
- Formation of hypothesis (Proposed explanation)
- Classifying data
- Analysing and interpreting the data
- Using logic
- Evaluation of research work for further research.

The methodology used in the research work gives a distinct feature to the subject-matter. The reason is that the methodology employed in research has many implications. The most important implication of the methodology is to give a particular framework to the particular field through a proper process. It makes the researcher to follow the valid procedure which may lead to the systematic conclusion.

### Sensitising Students on Sound Ethical Research Practices

Research should be original, intellectually stimulating, personally satisfying and socially relevant. Good research should be based on sound ethical norms. Against this backdrop, the UGC has introduced a two credit course titled "Research and Publication Ethics" for MPhil and PhD students. This course will not only sensitise students to sound ethical research practices and protocols but will also highlight the ramifications of unethical research practices. In addition to sensitisation of research scholars to sound research practices and protocols, they should also be made aware of the downside of unethical and dishonest research practices. Stringent punishment, including cancellation of registration in extreme cases, will deter research scholars from adopting unethical practices. Indian universities should raise the bar by promoting genuine, productive and socially relevant research founded on sound ethical principles and should deal with any research misconduct sternly.

Seven cardinal ethical practices which need to be followed for achieving excellence in research

1. Plagiarism avoidance
2. Data fabrication and manipulation stoppage
3. Regard for research participants' privacy
4. Avoidance of unhealthy practice of piecemeal publication of data and findings with a view to padding up the publication profile of the researcher
5. Avoidance of publishing the same data in different forms
6. Avoidance of publishing in predatory journals.

### Promoting Research Culture

Mariamma Varghese, Former Vice Chancellor of SNDT Women's University suggests the following ways to promote research culture by the university authorities:

- Facilitating faculty participation
- Providing budget for research (budgetary provision for research, seed money, etc.)
- Research Fellowships for students
- Initiating linkages for research
- Advanced research facilities for different kinds of research
- Introduction of research methodology in curriculum and teaching
- Inculcate critical thinking and spirit of enquiry through participative learning
- Exposure to eminent research scientists through extra-mural lectures
- Contribution to knowledge creation, dissemination and application
- Use of IT in research
- Encourage innovation in research
- Provide latest information and information sources
- Research orientation to students and faculty
- Research Training as part of staff development
- Provide adequate infrastructure facilities
- Have a Research Committee to guide the research agenda
- Information dissemination about major and minor research projects sponsored by different agencies
- Special opportunities for students and staff for enhancement of research activities
- Ensure there are enough research scholars and JRFs
- Ensure there are adequate PhD scholars
- Ensure the institution gets adequate major and minor research projects
- Total outlays for research and development should be adequate
- All patents have to be registered
- Encourage Departments to get UGC/SAP

- Encourage linkage with national research organisations, international universities and research organisations
- Industry linkage for research
- Encourage publication of research findings in national and international referred journals, and of research papers published in international referred journals
- Citation Index/Impact Factor
- Number of books published by the faculty
- Collaborative work with Government and NGOs
- National and international linkages
- Membership in professional organisations
- Enhancing Library resources for research and Networking.

## Research Promotion in Universities

It is an undeniable fact that the Indian Universities are giving added impetus to research and innovation for developing and taking the nation in all its fields to the next level. As a sequel researches are encouraged to discover and invent new technologies in every sphere; and getting funds is not a problem today for serious researchers. The Ministry of Human Resource Development (MHRD) has allocated enormous funds for research projects and is helping the universities to enhance and improve the quality in the areas of teaching and research that should ultimately benefit the society at large.

In the recent years, towards achieving this goal, the University Grants Commission (UGC) has initiated a number of new schemes like SWAYAM (Digital Learning), SMART and SWACHH Campus, Smart India Hackathon (Start-Ups), National Apprenticeship Promotion Scheme (NAPS), Unnat Bharat Abhiyaan (Socio-Economic Betterment of the Community) and Learning Outcome Based Curriculum Framework (LOCF), etc. SMART and SWACHH Campus programmes have been implemented in all universities to equip them with smart and digital classrooms i.e., to offer digital learning in an aesthetically appealing green and clean environment. Every campus is evaluated and ranked by the Ministry of Education (MoE) for its quality and standard of maintaining cleanliness and hygiene. Digital learning is encouraged through SWAYAM which offers free online courses to students with a view to making them employable in the job market on completion of their courses or study.

In the era of global competition for world rankings, higher education sector is increasingly becoming important in India's growth strategy. Some of the other significant initiatives of Ministry of Education (MoE) have to be noted here. The IMPRESS Scheme (Impactful Policy Research in Social Sciences) aims to identify and fund research proposals in Social Sciences with impact on the governance and society. The SERB-STAR Scheme (Science and Engineering Research Board's Science and Technology Award) has been supporting basic research in frontier areas of science and engineering.

The STRIDE (Scheme for Trans-disciplinary Research for India's Developing Economy) aims to build multi-sectoral linkages between University, Government, Community and Industry for national development. The SPARC (Scheme for Promotion of Academic Research Collaboration) has the objective of promoting joint research projects between Indian institutions and the best of the global Universities from 25 selected countries. It provides funds for visits and long term stay of international faculty and researchers in Indian institutions and also gives funds for training Indian students in premier international laboratories. The LEAP (Leadership for Academicians Programme) aims to equip senior faculty members to take up leadership roles in future at various levels in higher educational institutions.

### PhD Work in Universities

PhD is not a degree offered to, rather it is conferred upon an individual. It symbolises a high level of intellectual pursuit. It must remain the pinnacle of formal academic programme. PhD course work must develop research competence among aspirants to carry out future research and build, expand or modify a theory. The candidates should be made aware that the decision to do PhD is not everybody's cup of tea. The five P's, i.e., Passion, Patience, Perseverance, Perspective and Purpose for doing a course work cannot be compromised with its three D's, i.e., Degree, Designation and Dough (money) as enunciated by Goel.

UGC Regulations, 2016 is common for all universities, but its observance in letter and spirit is institution specific. If the academic community including the members of Department Research Committee, Research Advisory Committees, Board of Studies, School Board and Research Board at university level fail to address the quality concerns of PhD course work, then PhD degree may even lose its traditionally established credibility like many other academic and professional degrees. The academic community's responsive responses to the following queries may substantially address some of the concerns of PhD course work for promoting quality research:

- How can course work develop research skills among PhD aspirants to work as independent investigators?
- Should not the course work aim at to develop mastery of a discipline and training of mind?
- Should vigour, authority and efficiency be the criteria of a PhD course work or should it remain feeble preparation for undertaking a just research work?
- Should the existing PhD apprenticeship intend to prepare persons merely to serve as academics?
- Should not the PhD course work aim at preparing persons for high level position outside the academia like industries?

- How can the academic PhD course work fulfil the requirements of and needs for the industries?
- Can the PhD course work at university level be collaborative one involving experts from institutions of higher learning, industries, and NGOs? How much should industry collaborate with the PhD education course work?
- Should the candidates live in an atmosphere of complacency with reference to quality PhD coursework at university level?
- Should the course work preparation for academic PhDs be different than industry-oriented PhDs?
- Should not the present course work oriented for academic PhDs be reoriented for competence-based PhDs: professional PhDs and industrial PhDs?
- Should the course work as research training process prepare the candidates how quickly to earn the degree and increase the number of PhDs?
- Should the course work result in the quality PhDs which seek employment offer from industries and universities and other institutions, or create employment opportunities for undergraduates and graduates?

Select Approaches to Qualitative Research as Applicable to Educational Research Context

1. Semi-structured interviews
2. Participant observation
3. Grounded theory
4. Phenomenological method
5. Case study
6. Discourse analysis
7. Action research.

## Quality in Qualitative Research

Overall concern of qualitative research is with meaning in context and it involves the interpretation of data. Thus, as averred by Carla Willig (2010), the role of qualitative researcher requires an active engagement with data which presupposes a stand point or point out departure. This implies that qualitative research acknowledges a subjective element in the research process. Several authors have tried to identify the criteria for judging the quality of qualitative research. For example, Henwood and Pidgeon (1992) indicated seven characteristics of good qualitative research such as the importance of fit, integration of theory, reflexivity, documentation, theoretical sampling and negative case analysis, sensitivity to negotiated realities and transferability which means applicability beyond the specific context within which the data were generated.

Elliott et al (1999) have developed some specific guidelines for qualitative research reports. Some of these are: Owning one's perspectives, situating the sample, grounding in examples, provides credibility checks, coherence, accomplishing general versus specific research tasks and resonating with readers. To conclude, it may be pertinent to quote Madill et al (2000) that, "qualitative researchers have a responsibility to make their epistemological position clear, conduct their research in a manner consistent with that position and present their findings in a way that allows them to be evaluated approximately."

In the Indian context, research focus is called for to impart an epistemological perspective to qualitative research particularly being undertaken in the field of education and psychology. It will be worthwhile to mention that training in qualitative research methodology and the potential for its intelligent and appropriate use need a special concern by the universities and funding organisations which the recently introduced NPE 2020 aptly reinforces. Sooner this is done, the better it will be in a bid to shift our emphasis from hypothetico-deductive paradigm to empirico-inductive paradigms in educational research. It will be better to recall the words of Benjamin Franklin, "We must indeed all hang together, or, most assuredly, we shall all hang separately". Further, to quote Howard Gardner, 2005, the world of the future with its ubiquitous search engines, robots and other computational devices will demand capacities that until now have been mere options. To meet this new world on its own terms, we should begin to cultivate these capacities now.

## Council of Scientific and Industrial Research

Council of Scientific and Industrial Research (CSIR), established in 1942, is an autonomous body and India's largest research and development (R&D) organisation, with 37 laboratories and 39 field stations or extension centres spread across the nation, with a collective staff of over 17,000 people. Although CSIR is mainly funded by the Ministry of Science and Technology, it operates as an autonomous body registered under the Registration of Societies Act of 1860.

The research and development activities of CSIR include various fields such as aerospace engineering, structural engineering, ocean sciences, life sciences, metallurgy, chemicals, mining, food, petroleum, leather, and environment.

### *CSIR Achievements*

- Developed first Indian tractor Swaraj in 1967 completely based on indigenous know-how.
- Achieved the first breakthrough of flowering of bamboo within weeks as against 20 years in nature.
- First to analyse genetic diversity of the indigenous Andamanese tribes, and to establish their origin out of Africa 60,000 years ago.

- Developed the first transgenic Drosophila model for drug screening for cancer in humans.
- First to introduce DNA fingerprinting in India.
- Helped India to be the pioneer investor under the United Nations Convention on the Law of the Sea.
- Invented once a week non-steroidal family planning pill Saheli, and non-steroidal herbal pill for asthma called Asmon.
- Designed India's first ever parallel processing computer Flosolver.
- Partnered more than 50,000 companies with turnover of more than ₹5 lakhs.
- Rejuvenated India's 100-year old refinery at Digboi using the most modern molecular distillation technology.
- Provided the critical technology for the NMP Lube Extraction Plant of capacity of 2,50,000 tonnes per year.
- With TCS, developed versatile portable PC-based software 'Bio-Suite' for bioinformatics.
- Designed 14-seater plane SARAS.
- Established the traditional knowledge digital library, the first of its kind in the world, accessible in five international languages, English, German, French, Japanese, and Spanish.
- Remained in top three in the list of PCT patent applications amongst all developing countries.
- Topped list of holders of U.S. patents.
- Successfully challenged the grant of patent in the USA for use of haldi (turmeric) for wound healing, and neem as insecticide.
- In 2009, completed the sequencing of the Human Genome.
- In 2011, successfully tested India's First indigenous civilian aircraft, NAL NM5 made in association with National Aerospace Laboratories and Mahindra Aerospace.

*Shanti Swarup Bhatnagar Prize for Science and Technology*

The Shanti Swarup Bhatnagar (SSB) Prizes are awarded annually by the Council of Scientific and Industrial Research (CSIR) for notable and outstanding research, applied or fundamental, in biological, chemical, earth, atmosphere, ocean and planetary, engineering, mathematical, medical, and physical sciences. The prize comprises a citation, a plaque, and a cash award of ₹500,000. In addition, recipients also get ₹15,000 per month up to the age of 65 years.

### Research Funding Agencies in India

India has various funding agencies that strive to promote research in emerging areas like humanities, social sciences, languages, literature, pure sciences, engineering and technology, pharmacy, medical, agricultural sciences, and defence studies etc. They fall under the different ministries of the government. Some of the funding agencies at the national level include the University Grants Commission (UGC), Indian Council of Social Science Research (ICSSR), National Council for Educational Research and Training (NCERT), All India Council for Technical Education (AICTE), Department of Science and Technology (DST), Department of Biotechnology (DBT), Council of Scientific and Industrial Research (CSIR), Defence Research and Development Organisation (DRDO), Aeronautics Research and Development Board, Department of Atomic Energy (DAE), Department of Coal (DOC), Department of Ocean Development (DOD), Department of Scientific and Industrial Research (DSIR), Indian Council of Medical Research (ICMR), India Meteorological Department (IMD), Indian Space Research Organisation (ISRO), Department of Space, Ministry of Communications and Information Technology (MoCIT), Ministry of Environment and Forests (MoEF), Ministry of Food Processing Industries (MFPI), Ministry of Non-Conventional Energy Sources (MNES), Ministry of Water Resources (MoWR), Ministry of Power, Central Power Research Institute (CPRI), Indian National Science Academy (INSA), Science and Technology for Weaker Sections (STAWS), Science and Technology Application for Rural Development (STARD).

### *Indian Council of Social Science Research*

The Indian Council of Social Science Research (ICSSR) was established in 1969 by the Government of India to promote research in social sciences in the country. It supports a network of 27 ICSSR research institutions.

The Council is meant to:

- Review the progress of social science research and give advice to its users;
- Sponsor social science research programmes and projects, and administer grants to institutions and individuals for research in social sciences;
- Institute and administer scholarships and fellowships for research in social sciences;
- Indicate areas in which social science research is to be promoted, and adopt special measures for development of research in neglected or new areas;
- Give financial support to institutions, associations, and journals engaged in social science research;
- Arrange technical training in research methodology and provide guidance for research;
- Coordinate research activities and encourage programmes for interdisciplinary research;
- Develop and support centres for documentation service and supply of data;
- Organise, sponsor, and finance seminars, workshops, and study groups;

- Undertake publication, and assist publication of journals and books in social sciences;
- Advise the Government of India on all matters pertaining to social science research as may be referred to it from time to time; and take such measures generally as may be necessary from time to time to promote social science research and its utilisation.

### *National Social Science Documentation Centre (NASSDOC)*

India's National Social Science Documentation Centre (NASSDOC) was established in 1969 as a Division of the ICSSR with the objective to provide library and information support services to researchers in social sciences, those working in academic institutions, autonomous research organisations, policy making, planning and research units of government departments, business, and industry etc. NASSDOC also provides guidance to libraries of ICSSR Regional Centres and ICSSR supported research institutions.

Facilities Available at NASSDOC

1. Documentation, library, and reference services;
2. Collection of unpublished doctoral dissertations, research project reports, current and old volumes of social science journals of Indian and foreign origin;
3. Literature search service from printed and digital databases, i.e.CD-ROMs, floppies, online database etc;
4. Compilation of short bibliographies on request;
5. Study grant to doctoral students for collection of research material from various libraries located in different parts of India;
6. Financial assistance for taking up bibliographical and documentation projects;
7. Document delivery service by procuring books and journals through inter-library loans, or by photocopying the documents;
8. Short-term training courses for research scholars, social scientists, librarians, and IT professionals to acquaint them with the latest information and communication technology, and
9. Cyber café to facilitate access to Internet resources on social sciences.

### Do's and Don'ts of Social Research

There has been a continuous debate over social research, its results, its objectivity, validity, and human interference, which still prevails among scholars. Why do people have problems with conducting social research?

In a broader sense, social researchers claim that they study social realities. Their units of study are people, their interests, protests, notions, opinions, and subjective experiences. There is great need of such researches because of rampant inequalities and discriminations within and between social groups, based on a wider range of purposes.

But some unresolved questions remain like, what is reality? How can it be checked? How is it to be measured? Reality is not static; it is dynamic and changing in nature. Then, how does a social researcher study a unit of society which is continuously changing? The real problem people have in social research is with operational definition of variables, and measuring such variables. Social researchers are trying and struggling to do it. On many occasions they have succeeded by creating matrixes, indices, scales, and established indicators, etc. We must appreciate that.

### Doctoral Research Programme

Some observations on doctoral research programmes.

- Research is not the prime focus in majority of the institutions of higher education till date. Orientation and creation of awareness towards research in these institutions is very rare. Rather they are busy in generating educated young unemployed workers who run after governmental jobs, and the public services like postal, railway, land surveys, etc.
- Though research has been a part of mandate of any university, a critical look reveals that most of the Indian universities are not paying adequate attention to it.
- Very few students engage themselves in the pursuit of quality research, where as many of them are trying to get a degree.
- Not only the researchers, but also very few research supervisors pay adequate attention, or give sufficient time to their research scholars.
- Lack of research-minded students in the campus undermines the quality of research as it is a collaborative, cooperative activity which requires rigorous discussion, interactions, etc.
- The traditional mindset of senior faculty members seldom allow a student to seek inter-faculty interaction, or undertake inter-disciplinary research.
- Misconceptions about information and communication technology and its utility undermine its usage in research.
- Lack of autonomy, and accountability are primarily responsible for poor research.
- Time and freedom to the researcher is another important factor.

It is a common observation that the demand and production for PhD degree has exponentially increased over the last few decades, because PhD degree is now linked with appointment and promotion (career advancement scheme - CAS) in the institutions of higher education. In response to the general demand, many universities increased their PhD production without being sufficiently ambitious about the quality benchmarks. There was a time when rarest of the rare used to pursue a PhD Degree even if the procedure for getting admissions was not as complicated as it is now. In the meantime, UGC regulation made either NET/SLET/SET or PhD as the minimum eligibility condition for appointment as teachers/lecturers, especially in the colleges and universities. Again, a new resolution was passed by the UGC in 2009 wherein those who pursue PhD as per UGC PhD Regulation-2009 are exempt from the said examination.

### Kakodkar Committee — 10,000 PhD Scholars a Year

The Kakodkar Committee, set up by the then MHRD to suggest ways of enhancing the contribution of the IITs to the nation, recommended that the number of engineering PhD scholars being produced per year should be increased to 10,000 over the course of the next decade.

The IITs are presently producing around 1,000 PhD scholars per year in engineering and technology. "This figure is not adequate for a country of our size. The USA and China are producing around 8,000 to 9,000 PhD scholars each in engineering and technology, each year.

"Without sufficient numbers of persons trained in research, we will not have a firm foothold in the higher technologies that are key to our future development," observed Union Minister for HRD.

The Committee observed that as PhD scholars would have first completed a master's degree, it is imperative that the intake in the MTec and MSc programmes in the IITs also be increased proportionally.

The Committee suggested that over the next decade, India should add another five IITs. India should also scale the IIT system to 16,000 faculty members, and 1,60,000 total student strength with 40,000 at the PhD level, 40,000 at the masters level and 80,000 UG students.

The steps needed to make this a reality, are given below.

1. *Rejuvenate doctoral programmes across disciplines*: While the above recommendations are aimed at attracting potential doctoral students and enabling a research environment, it is vital that prospective doctoral students are chosen with sufficient care. The following measures are proposed with this objective in mind:
   - A review of the whole selection procedure and monitoring process for graduate students.
   - Multiple pathways for entry to a PhD programme, while maintaining entry standards.
   - Support for quality research in arts, humanities, and other areas.
   - Support and promotion of cross-disciplinary teaching and research programmes.
   - Greater exposure of undergraduate and postgraduate students to cutting edge research.
2. *Ensure quality of doctoral work and academic research in institutions:* At the same time while striving for greater influx of people to a research career, institutions must ensure that the research undertaken matches global quality in the relevant field. In addition, the graduate programmes should

be continually reviewed so as to make them vibrant, challenging, and internationally relevant. Here are some steps to be taken in this regard:

- A preliminary vetting of the synopses of the thesis followed by rigorous external examination of doctoral thesis.
- Broad funding for the organisation of and participation in workshops, seminars, and symposia in India and overseas.
- Encouraging doctoral students to teach, with remuneration provided via teaching assistantships.
- Wider dissemination of research work, especially through current digital media in universities and research institutions.

3. *Enable vigorous industry-academic interaction:* In the modern context, there is a crying need for a healthy and enlightened cooperation between private industry and academia, which replaces the existing feeling of doubt and mistrust. While industry should recognise that support for education is beneficial; universities should take cognizance of the changing needs of private enterprise in planning new courses. This could be achieved by taking the following measures:
    - A policy framework for meaningful public-private partnership in universities, and concerted efforts to nurture industry-academic interaction.
    - Encouraging private investment in education, research, and innovation, backed by appropriate taxation measures.
    - Promoting collaboration between research and development units within industry and universities.
4. Foster global outlook in research: Research is increasingly becoming a collective global endeavour. It is thus necessary to harness global talent and expertise to develop capacity within the country. This is also essential if the nation is to remain a participant in global cutting edge research. With this in view, the NKC recommended the following:
    - Encouraging NR/PIO scientists to establish meaningful links with Indian institutions, and participate in the academic development of the nation.
    - Creating joint PhD programmes between universities, both within and outside the country.
    - Financial and administrative support for international research collaboration.
    - Identifying important areas of research where national expertise needs to be developed, and initiating steps for funding and capacity building by way of collaborations, guest faculty, pro-active hiring, etc.

In conclusion, it must be recognised that investment in education and research produces a broad range of dividends, both tangible and intangible. Our existing base in research needs to be urgently strengthened to arrest any further erosion. While the NKC welcomed the augmented allocation for education in the Eleventh Five Year Plan, it is important that these funds are effectively utilised to make a visible difference to our academic landscape. As a first step, we urge the government to set itself a target of tripling the existing research base within the next dozen years, and meaningfully work towards it. We strongly feel that a mission-oriented approach is necessary for creating the required research ecosystem in the country.

Theses in Social Sciences

| *S. No.* | *Year* | *No. of Theses in Social Sciences* |
|---|---|---|
| 1 | 2000 | 926 |
| 2 | 2001 | 793 |
| 3 | 2002 | 1267 |
| 4 | 2003 | 1519 |
| 5 | 2004 | 1269 |
| 6 | 2005 | 1239 |
| 7 | 2006 | 1632 |
| 8 | 2007 | 1501 |
| 9 | 2008 | 1922 |
| 10 | 2009 | 1319 |
| 11 | 2010 | 1639 |
| 12 | 2011 | 1349 |
| 13 | 2012 | 1428 |
| 14 | 2013 | 827 |
| 15 | 2014 | 938 |
| 16 | 2015 | 703 |
| | Total | 20271 |

Faculty-wise Number of Doctorate Degrees (PhD) Awarded during 2007-2011

| *S. No.* | *Faculty* | *2007-08* | *2008-09* | *2009-10* | *2010-2011* |
|---|---|---|---|---|---|
| 1 | Arts | 4405 | 3496 | 4862 | 5037 |
| 2 | Science | 4514 | 3603 | 4619 | 5232 |
| 3 | Commerce/Management | 873 | 724 | 980 | 1259 |
| 4 | Education | 425 | 403 | 588 | 645 |
| 5 | Engineering, Technology | 1427 | 1141 | 1449 | 1682 |
| 6 | Medicine | 277 | 298 | 386 | 601 |
| 7 | Agriculture | 664 | 427 | 652 | 586 |
| 8 | Veterinary Science | 123 | 93 | 162 | 165 |
| 9 | Law | 127 | 152 | 146 | 220 |
| 10 | Others | 402 | 444 | 633 | 666 |
| | Total | 13237 | 10781 | 14477 | 16093 |

## Improving Quality of Research

In order to improve the quality of research, the following points need to be considered.

- Higher education institutions should generate adequate infrastructure which can meet the needs of researchers in emerging disciplines.
- Higher education institutions should create Information Resource Centre (IRC), which facilitates the researchers to give various information regarding ongoing researches.
- Higher education institutions should have a central instrumentation centre, as a result of which researchers of various departments can avail the opportunities to carry out their researches.
- Individual computers with high speed Internet facilities should be provided to each researcher.
- Research scholars should be encouraged for carrying out independent, collaborative and interdisciplinary researches.
- There should be a research committee and concrete research policy for guiding the research scholars of various disciplines.
- Seminars/training programmes/workshops on research methodology in general, and concerned areas in particular, should be organised in order to motivate and enhance the knowledge of researchers.
- Extension lectures should be organised at regular intervals.
- There should be proper budget allocation to carry out/promote the research.
- Incentives and rewards/awards should be given for quality research papers.
- Higher education institutions should publish high quality research papers in appropriate journals.
- Each institution should publish a research bulletin mentioning the research work being carried out in various fields, the number of research papers published in online and offline journals etc., as well as research awards received by the research scholars.
- Library should be digitalised, and ongoing research work should be uploaded for dissemination of knowledge in the specific field.
- Higher education institutions should promote the participation of research scholars in research and extension activities.
- Higher education institutions should move ahead to strengthen the research culture by signing MOUs with national/international institutions of higher learning, and generating institution-industry linkages.
- More focus should be given to research aptitude tests at the time of selection of research scholars.
- Transparency should be maintained in research by disseminating of information on a regular basis.

# 10

# Accreditation

## *Assessment of Quality Education*

The reasons for the concern for quality in higher education vary from country to country. Factors like history, culture, state of economic development, awareness, and approach for growth of higher education play a significant role in the evolution of quality assurance and controlling system in a particular country. However, it is becoming clear that self-regulation coupled with peer review carried out by an independent agency could bring in an era of quality in higher education. But in the changing context of globalisation of economic activities, education has become an international service, and there is a need to withstand the pressure of this changing context. Countries have been pressurised to ensure and assure quality at an international level. Consequently, many countries have initiated quality assurance mechanisms.

In recent years, the creation of national system for the assessment of quality in higher education has been a major feature of development in many countries. There are now over 70 quality assessment agencies around the world which have responsibility of undertaking a review of the quality of higher education provision in their respective countries. Concern for quality in higher education has become the prime agenda world over. In countries like India though, the explicit focus on quality assurance in higher education is relatively new.

Within Europe, both the European Commission and the Association of European Rectors have initiated development work in the field. The Organisation for Economic Cooperation and Development, through its programme on Institutional Management in Higher Education, has a project which extends from Europe to America and Australia. In addition, UNESCO has supported activity in this field at its European Centre for Higher Education, and various national quality agencies have formed an international body, the International Network for Quality Assurance in Higher Education.

The United States has had a diverse system of mass higher education for many decades. This new economic and social reality has brought fresh attention to its quality assurance practices by both state and federal policy makers. At the state level, growing concerns about the quality of college graduates entering the work force first led to policies in the 1980s on student assessment designed to improve the quality of undergraduate education.

### Accreditation

Accreditation is a type of quality assurance process under which academic programmes and student and staff related services offered by a higher education institution are evaluated by an external body, known as accreditation body or accreditation agency which determines whether the higher education institution meets applicable standards. Accredited status is granted to the institution by the accreditation body or agency.

During the last fifteen years there has been a sharp increase in awareness, amongst all connected with higher education regarding the need to maintain quality in university-level institutions, and the desirability of adopting formalised quality assurance procedures. Concern for quality of education is being expressed by society (represented by the government and the tax-payers); the institutions of higher learning (represented by its management and faculty); and their clients (students and prospective employers).

It is true that higher education in India is heavily dependent on government support and as such as it can hardly generate private funds to maintain its independent status and expansion. Governmental funding on such a large scale also has resulted in lowering of the quality, getting higher degrees and diplomas easily, thereby compromising the academic merit and competence. A change in this pattern is needed. The University Grants Commission has been given the primary mandate to monitor and maintain the standard of teaching examination and research. According to the UGC, the objectives of assessment and accreditation are:

- To accord recognition to the quality and excellence of education imparted by higher educational institutions, and thereby to advance academic quality;
- To enable students and other stakeholders to make informed choice with regard to higher educational institutions;
- To enable students, teachers, and other stakeholders to provide inputs concerning the quality of education imparted by the higher educational institutions;
- To facilitate higher educational institutions to gain international recognition, cross-border and trans-national collaborations; and
- To facilitate effective teaching-learning processes, and access to quality teaching-learning material in all the languages permitted by the higher educational institution as medium of instruction or examination.

The National Policy on Education 1986) and the Programme of Action (PoA, 1992) that spelt out strategic plans for the policies, advocated the establishment of an independent national accreditation agency. Consequently, the National Assessment and Accreditation Council (NAAC) was established in 1994 as an autonomous institution of the University Grants Commission (UGC).

The mandate of NAAC as reflected in its vision statement is in making quality assurance an integral part of the functioning of higher education institutions (HEIs).

### Vision and Mission of NACC

The vision of NAAC is:

> To make quality the defining element of higher education in India through a combination of self and external quality evaluation, promotion, and sustenance initiatives.

The mission statement of the NAAC aims at translating the NAAC's vision into action plans, and define specific tasks of NAAC engagement and endeavour as given below:

- To arrange for periodic assessment and accreditation of institutions of higher education or units thereof, of specific academic programmes or projects;
- To stimulate the academic environment for promotion of quality in teaching-learning, and research in higher education institutions;
- To encourage self-evaluation, accountability, autonomy, and innovations in higher education;
- To undertake quality-related research studies, consultancy, and training programmes, and
- To collaborate with other stakeholders of higher education for quality evaluation, promotion, and sustenance.

Striving to achieve its goals as guided by its vision and mission statements, NAAC primarily focuses on assessment of the quality of higher education institutions in the country. The NAAC methodology for assessment and accreditation is very similar to that followed by quality assurance (QA) agencies across the world, and consists of self-assessment by the institution, and external peer assessment by NAAC.

The accreditation framework of NAAC is based on the following core values:

- Contributing to national development;
- Fostering global competencies among students;
- Inculcating a value system among students;
- Quest for excellence.

#### *Process of Accreditation followed by NAAC*

Once an institution is ready for accreditation, the process involves completion of a self-study report followed by a NAAC peer team visit to the institution in order to validate the self-study report. These factors form the basis of the final grade assigned to the institution as well as its certification and accreditation status. As of now, NAAC functions in a voluntary manner, meaning that the institutions who are interested in getting their systems validated by accreditation are accredited and the rest are left alone. While this defines the highest order of quality assessed by a government body that has experts in the panel, the voluntary nature of the process does not satisfy the very idea of uniform quality set throughout the country. In order to correct this lacuna, the process needs to be made compulsory for recognised institutions.

### *Benefits of NAAC Accreditation*

- Grading of higher education institutions (HEIs) and their programmes. Further promote and enhance the academic environment and quality of teaching and research in these institutions. Help the institutions through workshops about the academic objectives, and how to achieve the standards set.
- Expected to promote needed changes, innovations, and changes that need to be attained in all aspects of the institution that is being accredited.
- Encourage innovations, self-evaluation, accountability in higher education, overall assessment of the quality aspects of the departments and programmes, and ensure the quality is sustained over period of time. Help establish internal quality assurance cell (IQAC) to ensure that the quality attained is continued and sustained.
- The grade clearly shows the quality level of the institute, but at the same time informs the various quality measures that need to be put in place, and thus improve the system. The improved quality helps teachers to work towards raising teaching and learning capabilities and be on a par with the quality standards laid by regulatory bodies.

### *Milestones in the Journey of NAAC*

The following are a few milestones of the past decade in the NAAC's journey of promoting quality-related initiatives in higher education:

- A significant achievement of the NAAC is the partnership with stakeholders for proactive measures to promote assessment and accreditation.
- Many states have established quality cells to promote assessment. The NAAC's efforts to promote usage of the assessment outcome as reliable information for decision-making have been very successful.
- The NAAC accreditation has been made a prerequisite for the granting, and continuation of autonomous status, and deemed-to-be university status for institutions.
- The level of funding under the UGC scheme for "Colleges with potential for excellence", consideration for expansion in terms of courses and student intake in teacher education institutions by NCTE, granting of permanent affiliation, etc. are now linked to the accreditation status.

- Due to stakeholder usage of assessment outcome, a large number of institutions are volunteering for assessment. The training programmes of the NAAC for the peers who are involved in the assessment-related activities have ensured the professionalism of the NAAC's process for the large volume of assessment. In fact, NAAC is building a collegium of assessors.
- Action plans for quality evaluation, quality sustenance, and quality upgradation have been developed by the NAAC with the participation of a cross-section of academics in the country.
- The Ministry of Human Resource Development (MHRD) has accepted the NAAC's action plans. In September 2001, during the meeting of State Higher Education Secretaries organised by the MHRD, the year 2002 was declared as the year of "Quality in Higher Education".
- In 2002, about 300 institutions got accredited, and in 2003 about 600 institutions have been accredited by the NAAC. This is a remarkable achievement in the history of assessment and accreditation all over the world.
- Moving beyond accreditation, the NAAC has expanded its scope by strengthening its advisory role. State-wise analysis of accreditation reports has been initiated for policy initiatives – this exercise is for states where at least 15 per cent of higher education institutions have been accredited.
- Collaboration with other national professional bodies for accreditation of specialised subjects have been initiated. The NAAC and Distance Education Council have jointly laid down the guidelines for accreditation of open universities and distance education units.
- The National Council for Teacher Education has a MoU with the NAAC for assessment and accreditation of teacher education institutions.
- The NAAC is active in international forum too. As a member of the International Network for Quality Assurance Agencies in Higher Education (INQAAHE), which is the largest such network in the world, the NAAC organised the sixth biennial meet of the member agencies in 2001 at Bengaluru.
- The NAAC is actively collaborating on many quality assurance initiatives of other countries, especially in the Asia-Pacific region. In 2002, with the support of the UNESCO, it organised the Expert Meet on Indicators of Quality and Facilitating Academic Mobility in the Asia-Pacific Region.

## Efforts of Government to Enhance the Strength of Accreditation

The Government of India through National Accreditation Authority Bill, 2010, attempted to enhance the strength of accreditation through mandatory accreditation. The bill envisaged the establishment of National Accreditation

Authority. The Authority will grant license to accreditation agencies in India to accredit higher education institutions. It was intended to create competitiveness among accreditation agencies in India. The National Accreditation Authority Bill was an attempt to make a complete paradigm shift with respect to the accreditation regime in India.

### *Major Changes*

G. Srinivas, Joint Secretary of the UGC narrated six major changes in improvising the process of Assessment and Accreditation.

1. Visible change is the shift from voluntary to mandatory accreditation NAAC was instrumental in spreading the quality consciousness in majority of the colleges and universities in India through a variety of awareness programmes. The UGC has projected NAAC assessment and accreditation as a tool for quality measurement enhancement and communication among different stake stakeholders. Till 2012 it was continued as a voluntary activity to include willing institutions in the orbit of accreditation. Currently, accreditation is mandatory for all higher education institutions and is also a necessary condition for funding from the Government of India.
2. The measurement and representation of accreditation status has been evolving in the last two decades. Initial method was a dichotomous one with two categories viz. accredited and unaccredited. This was later changed to graded star system like five Star, four star etc. which further evolved into alphabetical model of grading, like A, B, C, and D, subsequently accreditation from a four point mode of grading to nine point grade with letter grade A ++, A +, A, B ++, B +, B and C ++, C +, C were adopted to bring more precision, clarity and differentiation across accredited institutions.
3. The role acquisition information is getting increasingly important in policy planning, as accreditation becomes more visible and has attracted attention from Civic Society as an indicator of quality, the UGC has initiated two important measures related to accreditation. As a part of its policy mandate, 1) make the accreditation mandatory for all institutions of higher education in India, 2) linking the acquisition outcomes to financial incentives as well as making it a prerequisite for the recognition under certain schemes.
4. The movement from a single accreditation agency like NAAC to multiple Accreditation Agencies.

   So far, NAAC and NBA are the two central agencies engaged in accrediting the higher education institutions in India. While NAAC is conducting institutional accreditation, the NBA or AICTE has taken up programme accreditation in Technical Education.

Currently, about 25% of Higher Educational Institutions are accredited by NAAC. As it is felt that current pace of progress in the accreditation process is inadequate to reach the targets, the UGC has recently brought out regulations permitting multiple accreditation agencies in addition to NAAC and NBA. Following are the positive impacts.

- Faster rate of accreditation.
- More innovation into accreditation space.
- Competition among accreditation agencies.
- Wider accreditation choices for HELs.

5. Significant shift happened is in relation to the accreditation framework. The Revised Accreditation Framework (RAF) of NAAC, operational since 2017, is more data centric, ICT intensive and transparent compared to the earlier mode which was entirely resting on the visiting experts and their allegedly possible subjectivity in assessment.
6. The recent Quality Mandate of the UGC stipulates that every institution shall get NAAC accreditation with a minimum score of 2.5 by 2022 as one of the five objectives.

NAAC has been improvising the process of assessment and activation of changes of summarised in the following table:

**Significant Changes in Accreditation**
*(Last Quarter Century)*

| *From* | *To* |
|---|---|
| Voluntary accreditation | Mandatory accreditation |
| Dichotomous category outcome | Nine-point gradient outcome |
| Outcome used mainly for institutional governance | Accreditation outcomes into policy planning |
| Absence of formal internal quality structures | Compulsory internal quality assurance through IQAC |
| Implementation of accreditation framework rests solely on peer-team report | Revised accreditation framework is more data-centric and multistage, considered as robust |
| Single accreditation agency | Multiple accreditation agencies |
| Generic mandate of UGC | Specific quality mandate of UGC |

## Future Orientation

What differentiates the years ahead is the increased use of data points are the levels of institutions as well as regulators. By now, most institutions, states, and policymakers have accumulated huge educational and financial data regarding accredited institutions on different parameters. A seamless conversion of this information to more usable form for decision-making will be seen in future. Some of these are future orientations being summarised in the following table:

| *Present* | *Future* |
|---|---|
| Compliance driven | Excellence driven |
| Limited choice of accreditation bodies for institutions | More number and types of accrediting bodies |
| More commonality among parameters | Differentiated parameters |
| Relatively similar emphasis on many factors | More emphasis on student outcome, skills and employability |
| Institution's initiative | Data driven with more possibilities of mentoring driven approach |
| Parameters like change orientation, risk tolerance of the institution and degree of social connect are measured with limited categories | More precise longitudinal measurement of such factors |
| ICT enabled at the institutions. ICT intensive at the accreditation agency | ICT intensive on both ends, reducing the conventional documentation and paper clutter |
| Innovation as one of the themes | Innovation and different type of innovations (R & D and Non R & D based) as major themes in different areas of educational practices |

## National Education Policy 2020 on Accreditation

The National Education Policy (NEP) 2020 is the first education policy of this century and aims to address the many growing developmental imperatives of our country. This Policy proposes the revision and revamping of all aspects of the education structure, including its regulation and governance, to create a new system that is aligned with the aspirational goals of 21st century education, including Sustainable Development Goal 4 (SDG 4), while building upon India's traditions and value systems (Government of India, 2020: p.3).

While talking about the fundamental principles that will guide both the educational system at large and the individual institutions within it, the NEP 2020 indicates "light but tight" regulation by a single regulator for higher education. This policy envisions a complete overhaul and re-energising of the higher education system to overcome these challenges and thereby deliver high-quality higher education, with equity and inclusion (Government of India, 2020).

### *Transforming the Regulatory System of Higher Education*

Regulation of higher education has been too heavy-handed for decades; too much has been attempted to be regulated with too little effect. The mechanistic and disempowering nature of the regulatory system has been rife with very basic problems, such as heavy concentrations of power within a few bodies, conflicts of interest among these bodies, and a resulting lack of accountability. The regulatory system is in need of a complete overhaul in order to re-energise the higher education sector and enable it to thrive, hence, the regulatory system of higher education will ensure that the distinct functions of regulation, accreditation, funding, and academic standard setting will be performed by distinct, independent, and empowered bodies. This is considered essential to create checks-and-balances in the system, minimise conflicts of interest, and eliminate concentrations of power. These four structures will be set up as four independent verticals within one umbrella institution, the Higher Education Commission of India (HECI).

The first vertical of HECI will be the National Higher Education Regulatory Council (NHERC). The second vertical of HECI will, therefore, be a 'meta-accrediting body', called the National Accreditation Council (NAC). The third vertical of HECI will be the Higher Education Grants Council (HEGC) and the fourth vertical of HECI will be the General Education Council (GEC).

Accreditation of institutions will be based primarily on basic norms, public self-disclosure, good governance, and outcomes, and it will be carried out by an independent ecosystem of accrediting institutions supervised and overseen by NAC. The task to function as a recognised accreditor shall be awarded to an appropriate number of institutions by NAC. In the short term, a robust system of graded accreditation shall be established, which will specify phased benchmarks for all HEIs to achieve set levels of quality, self-governance, and autonomy. In turn, all HEIs will aim, through their Institutional Development Plans (IDPs), to attain the highest level of accreditation over the next 15 years, and thereby eventually aim to function as self-governing degree-granting institutions/clusters. In the long run, accreditation will become a binary process, as per the extant global practice.

Strict compliance measures with stringent action, including penalties for false disclosure of mandated information, will be ensured so that Higher Education Institutions are conforming to the basic minimum norms and standards. There will be transparent public disclosure of all the financial matters with recourse to grievance-handling mechanisms to the general public. The accreditation system developed by NAC will provide a complimentary check on this system, and NHERC will consider this as one of the key dimensions of its regulatory objective.

Transparent mechanisms for fixing fees with an upper limit, for different types of institutions depending on their accreditation, will be developed so that individual institutions are not adversely affected. "Through a suitable system of graded accreditation and graded autonomy, and in a phased manner over a period of 15 years, all HEIs in India will aim to become independent self-governing institutions pursuing innovate and excellence" (Government of India, 2020, pp. 46-49).

***Salient Points on Accreditation in NEP 2020***

1. National Accreditation Council (NAC), envisioned as the second vertical of HECI will be a meta-accrediting body.
2. The accreditation system developed by NAC will provide a complimentary check on the regulatory system, and NHERC will consider this as one of the key dimensions of its regulatory objective.
3. Through a suitable system of graded accreditation and graded autonomy, and in a phased manner over a period of 15 years, all HEIs in India will aim to become independent self-governing institutions pursuing innovation and excellence.
4. The task to function as a recognised accreditor shall be awarded to an appropriate number of institutions by NAC.
5. Accreditation of institutions will be based primarily on basic norms, public self-disclosure, good governance, and outcomes, and it will be carried out by an independent ecosystem of accrediting institutions supervised and overseen by NAC.
6. Every HEI will aim, through its Institutional Development Plans (IDPs), to attain the highest level of accreditation over the next 15 years, and thereby eventually aim to function as self- governing degree-granting institutions/clusters. In the long run, accreditation will become a binary 10 process, as per the extant global practice.
7. Transparent Public Disclosure system: The underlying principle will be that of a faceless and transparent regulatory intervention using technology. There will be transparent public disclosure of financial matters with recourse to grievance-handling mechanisms to the general public.
8. Accreditation System would strive towards ensuring uniformity in high quality of education, and teaching-learning, across all HEIs.
9. Fostering the culture of autonomy to innovate and empowerment by gradually phasing out the system of 'affiliated colleges' over fifteen years through an ecosystem of graded autonomy.
10. Four Year integrated B.Ed degree to be minimum degree qualification for teaching by 2030: The 4-year degree course shall have a strong practical component for student-teaching at local schools.
11. B.Ed degrees would be offered only by accredited multidisciplinary higher education institutions offering 4-year integrated B.Ed programmes.
12. Multidisciplinary higher education institutions are offering the 4-year in-class integrated B.Ed programme and having accreditation for ODL

may also offer high-quality B.Ed programmes in blended or ODL mode to students in remote or difficult-to-access locations and also to in- service teachers who are aiming to enhance their qualification, with suitable robust arrangements for mentoring and for the practicum training and student-teaching components of the programme.

13. All colleges currently affiliated to a university shall attain the required benchmarks overtime to secure the prescribed accreditation benchmarks and eventually become autonomous degree- granting colleges.
14. ODL will be renewed through concerted, evidence-based efforts towards expansion while ensuring adherence to articulated standards of quality. ODL programmes will aim to be equivalent to the highest quality in-class programmes available.
15. A framework for quality of ODL that will be recommendatory for all HEIs to be developed.
16. A Board of Governors (BoG) shall be established consisting of a group of highly qualified, competent, and dedicated individuals who have proven capabilities and a strong sense of commitment to the institution. The BoG of an institution will be empowered to govern the institution free of any external interference, make all appointments including that of the head of the institution, and make all governance decisions.
17. It is envisaged that all HEIs will be incentivized, supported, and mentored during this process, and shall aim to become autonomous.

## Strategies for Implementation

### *Constitution of National Accreditation Council (NAC) and Graded Accreditation*

As the first step in this direction, it is proposed that the NAAC should be upgraded to the 'meta- accrediting body' and renamed as the 'National Accreditation Council' (NAC), considered to be one of the verticals of the Higher Education Commission of India (HECI).

Presently, the existing HEIs namely colleges functioning under universities and different types of universities having various disciplines are being accredited by NAAC. The NAAC has developed various parameters for the assessment and accreditation of different types of universities and colleges offering programmes in specific disciplines and specialisations. With its long experience and knowledge base, NAAC is most suited to perform this major role in the future.

The NEP proposes (Government of India, 2020b): three broad types of HEIs, namely (i) Colleges; (ii) Autonomous Degree-granting Colleges; and (iii) Research/Teaching Intensive Universities. HEIs will be categorised under these three categories and placed in this proposed continuum. HEIs will have the autonomy and freedom to move gradually from one category to another as depicted below in Figure 2. The vision of NEP is that in the next 15 years all HEIs in India will aim to become independent self-governing institutions pursuing innovation and excellence

The role of NAC shall be:

- Identification and empanelment of Recognised Accreditors;
- The orientation of Recognised Accreditors;
- Development of benchmarks for the proposed range of HEIs to facilitate their upgradation and movement from one category to the next;
- Allocation of HEIs to Recognised Accreditors;
- Overseeing the functioning of Recognised Accreditors;
- Renewal of contract of Recognised Accreditors;
- The final assessment of Reports of HEIs submitted by the Recognised Accreditors;
- Award of grades to HEIs valid for three years; and
- Attending appeals received from HEIs and resolving the disputes that may arise.

As far as graded accreditation as proposed in NEP 2020 (Government of India, 2020b) is concerned, there is a need for a robust system that not only works as an accrediting body but also plays a key role as a member to encourage, support, and incentivize the HEIs to gradually attain the minimum benchmarks. To gradually phase out the system of affiliated colleges over fifteen years through a system of graded autonomy, the digital form of the Annual Quality Assessment Report of each HEI may be submitted to the NAC every year within a stipulated time frame and the same may be evaluated by the Recognised Accreditors empaneled by the NAC. A year-wise evaluation report of each HEI may be maintained at the NAC level. NAC would also develop and decide on the qualifying scores to be achieved to move from one category to the next level. After every three years, a consolidated report of each HEI may be shared with these Recognised Accreditors to evaluate the incremental growth of the HEI towards attaining autonomy over the years. In this way, the consolidated progress of every HEI during 15 years would additionally be monitored and if required, these Recognised Accreditors may work as mentors for the HEIs to guide them on how to achieve the benchmark quality parameters. Accordingly, the HEIs would be assessed for graded autonomy (Government of India, 2020).

## Top Accreditation Council

### *1. University Grants Commission (UGC)*

University Grants Commission (India) is statutory body set up by the Union government in accordance with the UGC Act, 1956 under Ministry of Human Resource Development (now MoE) and is charged with coordination, determination, and maintenance of standards of higher education. It provides recognition to universities in India and disburses funds to such recognised universities and colleges. It also advises the Central and State Governments on the measures which are necessary for the development of Higher Education. UGC was modeled after University Grants Committee of UK that was an advisory Committee of the British government and advised on the distribution of grant funding amongst the British universities. Currently, UGC conducts NET (National Eligibility Test) for appointments of teachers in colleges and universities along with CSIR. Since 2009, NET qualification is mandatory for teaching at Graduation and Post-Graduation level.

### 2. All India Council for Technical Education (AICTE)

All India Council for Technical Education is the statutory body and a national level council for technical education under Department of Higher Education, Ministry of Human Resource Development that was first established in November 1945 as an advisory body. AICTE is responsible for proper planning and coordinated development of the technical education and management education system in India and also accredits postgraduate and graduate programmes under specific categories. It grants approval for starting new technical institutions, the introduction of new courses and variation in intake capacity in technical institutions. Every year as per the direction of Ministry of Human Resource Development (now Ministry of Education), Government of India, AICTE conducts a national level entrance examination called CMAT (Common Management Admission Test). A score of CMAT is accepted by all AICTE-Approved institutions, University Department/Constituent Colleges/ Affiliated Colleges.

### 3. Association of Indian Universities (AIU)

Association of Indian Universities was formed in 1925 with an idea of bringing together all the universities on a common platform emerged from the deliberations of a Conference of the Vice Chancellors of Universities convened by Lord Reading, the then Viceroy of India at Shimla. It is an organisation and association of major universities that is based in Delhi that evaluates the courses, syllabi, standards and credits of foreign Universities pursued abroad and equates them in relation to various courses offered by Indian Universities. The AIU is mainly concerned with the recognition of Degrees/Diplomas awarded by the Universities in India which are recognised by the University Grants Commission, New Delhi, and abroad for the purpose of admission to higher degree courses in Indian Universities. It is also a registered society under the Societies Registration Act, 1860 with the membership of Indian Universities. It acts as a bureau of information exchange in higher education and brings out a number of useful publications, including the Universities Handbook, research papers and a weekly journal titled *University News.* It is also empowered to grant Associate Membership to universities of the neighboring countries of India.

### *4. Institute of Chartered Accountants of India (ICAI)*

The Institute of Chartered Accounts of India is the national professional accounting body of India established on July 1, 1949. It was formed under the Chartered Accountants Act, 1949 to regulate the profession of Chartered accountancy in India. ICAI is the only licensing cum regulating body in India of financial audit and accountancy profession. It is also the second largest professional Accounting and Finance body in the world in terms of membership after American Institute of Certified Public Accountants. Any member wanting to engage in public practice has to first apply for and obtain a Certificate of Practice from the Council of ICAI as only these candidates can act as auditors or certify documents required by various tax and financial regulatory authorities in India.

### *5. Institute of Company Secretaries of India (ICSI)*

The Institute of Company Secretaries of India is the only recognised professional body in India to develop and regulate the profession of Company Secretaries that was constituted under the Company Secretaries Act, 1980. It awards the certificate of bestowing the designation of Company Secretary (CS) to a candidate qualifying for the membership of the Institute. The ICSI functions under the jurisdiction of Ministry of Corporate Affairs. It registers students with 10+2 and graduate qualifications for Foundation and Executive Programme of Company Secretaryship, respectively with course contents in Corporate and Economic Laws, Management, Accounting, Taxation and Finance disciplines.

### *6. Film and Television Institute of India (FTII)*

The Film and Television Institute of India is an autonomous institute under the Ministry of Information and Broadcasting of the Government of India that is aided by the Central Government of India. It is also a member of the leading schools of film and television in the world known as the International Liaison Centre of Schools of Cinema and Television (CILECT). The FTII is registered under Societies' Registration Act of 1860. It also conducts FTII Entrance Examination for the candidates who wish to pursue their career in film and television industry.

### *7. National Assessment and Accreditation Council (NAAC)*

National Assessment and Accreditation Council is an autonomous body established by the University Grant Commission of India (UGC) to assess and accredit institutions of higher education in the country. It lays special emphasis on evaluating the quality of higher education in India. NAAC has introduced a new methodology to assess and accredit the higher education institutions in India. In the first step, the institution is required to seek Institutional Eligibility for Quality Assessment (IEQA) and the second step is the assessment and accreditation of the institute under the grades A, B, C for accredited institutions:

and D for those which are not accredited. NAAC has identified seven criteria for assessment procedure: Curricular aspects, Teaching-learning and evaluation, Research, Consultancy and extension, Infrastructure and learning resources, Student support and progression, Governance and leadership and Innovative practices.

### 8. National Board of Accreditation (NBA)

National Board of Accreditation, India was established by AICTE as an autonomous body under section 10(u) of AICTE Act, 1994 for periodic evaluations of technical institutions and programmes basis according to specified norms and standards as recommended by AICTE council. It is the only authorised body in India entrusted with the task of undertaking accreditation of technical education programmes from 7 January 2010. NBA came into existence as an autonomous body with the objective of assurance of quality and relevance of education, especially of the programmes and professional and technical disciplines, i.e., engineering and technology, management, architecture, pharmacy and hospitality through the mechanism of accreditation of programmes offered by technical institutions. It has received two awards: Golden Peacock Eco Innovation Award 2013, for eNBA project and Best Education Project – Silver award.

### 9. National Institutional Ranking Framework (NIRF)

National Institutional Ranking Framework is a methodology adopted by the Ministry of Human Resource Development (MHRD), the Government of India to rank all institutions of higher education in India. NIRF was set up to identify the broad parameters for ranking various universities and institutions that are teaching, learning and resources research and professional practices, graduation outcomes, outreach and inclusivity and perception.

### 10. All India Management Association (AIMA)

With the active support of Government of India and Industry, All India Management Association was created in 1957 as an apex body of professional management. It is a non lobbying organisation working closely with industry, government, academia and students to further the cause of the management profession in India. It is the federation of Local Management Associations (LMAs). AIMA also brings to the Indian managers the best management practices and techniques through numerous foreign collaborations with professional bodies and institutions.

### 11. Bar Council of India (BCI)

The Bar Council of India is a statutory body established under the Section 4 of Advocates Act, 1961 that regulates the legal practice and legal education in India. It also grants recognition to universities whose degree in law will serve as qualification for enrolment as an advocate, it performs certain representative functions by protecting the rights, privileges and interests of advocates and through the creation of funds for providing financial assistance to organise welfare schemes for them. It prescribes standards of professional conduct, etiquette, and exercises disciplinary jurisdiction over the bar. To practice law, it is mandatory to pass All India Bar examination that is conducted by BCI since April 10, 2010. The entrance examination is held biannually, in which a candidate can appear any number of times after clearing this entrance examination. Every advocate is entitled to a certificate practice of law throughout India.

### *12. Dental Council of India (DCI)*

The Dental Council of India is a statutory body incorporated under the Dentist Act, 1948, to regulate dental education on the profession throughout India that is financed by the Ministry of Health and Family Welfare. And through the local state dental councils. Main objective of DCI is to maintain uniform standards of dental education in India and regulate the curriculum in the training of dentists, dental hygienists, and dental mechanics and to regulate the level of examinations and qualifications. As per the bill introduced in the Parliament of India, Medical regulatory bodies like The Dental Council of India, Nursing Council of India and Pharmacy Council of India are proposed to dissolve and replaced with a common statutory body known as National Commission for Human Resources for Health.

### *13. Distance Education Council (DEC)*

Distance Education Council is responsible for the promotion and coordination of the Open University and distance education system and for determination of its standards based in New Delhi, India. It was constituted under the Indira Gandhi National Open University Act, 1985. It tries to promote an innovative system of university level education that has flexible and open methods and pace of learning, combination of courses, eligibility for enrolment and age of entry. It also advises the State Governments, universities, and other concerned agencies on their proposals to set up open universities or to introduce programmes of distance education. It appoints Review Committees periodically, which study and assess the performance of the open universities/ distance education institutions in its network. But in June, 2013, DEC was taken over by the University Grants Commission by establishing Distance Education Bureau (DEB) to govern the distance education programmes in India.

### *14. National Institute of Electronics and Information Technology (NIELIT) aka Department of Electronics and Accreditation of Computer Courses (DOEACC)*

National Institute of Electronics and Information Technology (NIELIT), earlier known as the DOEACC Society, is an autonomous scientific society under the administrative control of Ministry of Electronics and Information Technology of the Government of India. It is also a National Examination Body, which accredits institutes/organisations for conducting courses in IT in the non-formal sector. At present, it has 35 offices with its headquarters in New Delhi. It has acquired very good expertise in IT training through its wide repertoire of courses, ranging from O Level (Foundation), A Level (Advance Diploma), B Level (MCA equivalent), C Level (M-Tech level), IT literacy courses such as CCC (Course on Computer Concept), BCC (Basic Computer Course) and other such long term and short term courses in the non-formal sector like courses on Information Security, ITS-BPO (Customer Care/Banking), Computer Hardware Maintenance (CHM-OIA level), Bio-Informatics (BI-OIA/B level), ESDM etc., besides high end courses offered by NIELIT Centres at Post-Graduate level (M.Tech) in Electronics Design and Technology, Embedded Systems etc. which are not normally offered by Universities/Institutions in the formal sector, in association with the respective state universities.

### *15. Indian Nursing Council (INC)*

The Indian Nursing Council is a national regulatory body for nurses and nurse education in India formed by the Central Government under section 3 (1) of the Indian Nursing Council Act, 1947 of the Indian parliament. Its function is to establish and monitor a uniform standard of nursing education for nurse, midwife, Auxiliary Nurse-Midwives and health visitors by doing an inspection of the institutions, promote research in nursing and to improve the quality of nursing education. As per a bill introduced in the Parliament of India, medical regulatory bodies like the Dental Council of India, Nursing Council of India and Pharmacy Council of India are proposed to be dissolved and replaced with a common statutory body known as the National Commission for Human Resources for Health.

### *16. Medical Council of India (MCI)*

The Medical Council of India is a statutory body for establishing uniform and high standards of medical education in India. It grants recognition of medical qualifications, gives accreditation to medical schools, grants registration to medical practitioners, and monitors medical practice in India. But recently states have approved the proposal of NITI (National Institution for Transforming India) Aayog to replace Medical Council of India (MCI) with a statutory body known as the National Medical Commission. As per a bill introduced in the Parliament of India, medical regulatory bodies like the Dental Council of India, Nursing Council of India and Pharmacy Council of India are proposed to be dissolved and replaced with a common statutory body known as the National Commission for Human Resources for health.

### *17. National Council for Teacher Education (NCTE)*

National Council for Teacher Education is a statutory body of Indian government set up under the National Council for Teacher Education Act in

1995 to formally oversee standards, procedures and processes in the Indian education system. The main objective of the NCTE is to achieve planned and coordinated development of the teacher education system throughout the country, the regulation and proper maintenance of norms and standards in a teacher education system and for matters connected therewith.

### *18. Pharmacy Council of India (PCI)*

Pharmacy Council of India is a statutory body of Government of India constituted under the pharmacy Act, 1948 on 4th March 1948. The objectives of the PCI is to regulate the pharmacy education in the country for the purpose of registration as a pharmacist under the Pharmacy Act and regulate the profession and practice of Pharmacy. Recently as per the bill introduced in the Parliament of India, medical regulatory bodies like the Dental Council of India, Nursing council of India and Pharmacy Council of India or proposed to be dissolved and replaced with a common statutory body known as the National Commission for Human Resource for Health.

### *19. Veterinary Council of India (VCI)*

Established under the Ministry of Agriculture of the Government of India in 1984, the Veterinary Council of India is a statutory body which regulates veterinary practices in India. The Council is governed by the Indian Veterinary Council Act, 1984 and receives 100% grant in aid from the Department of Animal Husbandry and Dairying, Ministry of Agriculture of Government of India under a Plan Scheme namely Professional Eficiency Development for undertaking the activities of the Council.

### *20. National Council for Human Resource in Health (NCHRH)*

To regulate health education there will be a new regulatory agency in India by enforcement of a new bill being the tabled in the Parliament of India. The Ministry of Health and Family Welfare has approved the revised draft for the proposed NCHRH bill which will be an overarching body for the health sector. There will be a common MBBS entrance test (single PMT) National eligibility for entrance test UG replacing the overall India pre medical tests (PMTs) conducted all over the country for over 35,000 undergraduate seats. As per the bill introduced in the Parliament of India, medical regulatory bodies like the Dental Council of India, Nursing council of India and Pharmacy Council of India are proposed to be dissolved and replaced with a common statutory body known as a National Commission for Human Resources for health.

# 11

# Institutional Ranking

## Academic Ranking of Higher Education Institutions

There is an increasing interest worldwide in university rankings, as can be witnessed by the growing number of annual rankings being published across the world. Higher education institutions use these rankings as a promotion tool that shows their educational, research or business excellence and many candidate students use them as a guide to help them make a choice about the institutions to which they will apply. Marketing based on rankings may facilitate increased options for funding and may assist an institution in attracting high quality scholars which in turn can further enhance a university's reputation. Institutions can also employ ranking criteria for strategic planning and quality improvement purposes as well as to stimulate a culture of quality.

## Purpose of Academic Ranking of Higher Education Institutions

Ranking is done for a variety of reasons, the most frequent being:

- to provide the public with information (whatever the specifics of the ranking format) on the standing of higher education institutions for individual or group decision-making (potential students, parents, politicians, foundations, funding agencies, research councils, employers, international organisations, etc.);
- to foster healthy competition among higher education institutions;
- to provide additional evidence about performance of particular higher education institutions and/or study programmes;
- to stimulate the evolution of centres of excellence; and to provide additional rationale for allocation of funds;
- To provide additional rationale for allocation of funds.

## Sources of Academic Ranking of Higher Education Institutions

There are, generally speaking, four sources of data and information that are collected for the conduct of rankings:

- surveys that allow the receipt of opinions from various stakeholders (there is a clear preference for peer-review) in order to obtain a set of comparable data on quality and prestige for different institutions, study programmes and/or other activities;

- generally available (public domain) data and information collected by government agencies and other various agencies involved in higher education and research;
- data and information collected by institutions of higher education, which can be of two types – data on governance and management that is usually collected by institutions, and/or data and information exclusively requested and provided to those drawing up the rankings; and
- hibliometric/scientometric databases, such as those run by Thomson Reuters (IS! Web of Knowledge) and Elsevier (Scopus), which facilitate a multidisciplinary and research performance assessment.

### *Ranking Criteria of Top World Ranking Organisations*

The rankings criteria of five Top World Ranking Organisations are given below.

*The Academic Ranking of World Universities (ARWU) — Shanghai Jiao Tong University, China (http://www.arwu.org/)*

The Academic Ranking of World Universities (ARWU) founded and compiled by the Centre for World Class Universities of Shanghai Jiao Tong University was the first multi-indicator ranking of global universities commencing in 2003. Although the initial purpose of ARWU was to find the global standing of the top universities in China, it has attracted a great deal of attention from universities, governments and public media worldwide.

*The QS World University Rankings Quacquarelli Symonds (United — (http://www.topuniversities.com/home/)*

The QS World University Rankings is a ranking of the world's top 500 universities by Quacquarelli Symonds using a methodology that has been published annually since 2004. It is originally published in collaboration with Times Higher Education and known as the Times Higher Education-QS World University Rankings (THE-QS World University Rankings). Quacquarelli Symonds (QS) assumed sole publication of the existing methodology when Times Higher Education split in order to create a new ranking methodology that it first published in 2010. These rankings are the second longest-running global effort of their type.

*The Times Higher Education World University Rankings (http://www.timeshighereducation.co.uk/)*

The Times Higher Education World University Rankings is an international ranking of the world's top universities published by London-based Times Higher Education (THE). A publisher of international Quaequarelli Symonds between 2004 and 2009 under the name "Times Higher Education-QS World University Rankings', have been cited as one of the two most prominent world university rankings, along with the Academic Ranking of World Universities compiled by Shanghai Jiao Tong University.

*The "Webometrics Ranking of World Universities" — Cybermetrics Lab (Research Group), Spain (http://www.webometrics.info/)*

The Webometrics Ranking of World Universities is an initiative of the Cybermetrics Lab, a research group belonging to the Consejo Superior de.

**Features of Different Ranking Systems**

Shanghai Jiao Tong University publish the ARWU Ranking System since 2003. It is thought to be the leading ranking system. The universities included in its sample are those which have Nobel laureates and have highly cited research papers in journals like Science and Nature.

The Times Higher Education (THE) Ranking System is published since 2004. Firstly, it has used top 500 universities of the world in terms of impact of research but later on opinion of scientists and international employers started to play a crucial role in ranking (Saisana et al., 2001).

The CWTS Leiden ranking system at present focuses on around 1000 universities all over the world. It takes bibliographic data from the Web of Science database of Clarivate Analytics, Philadelphia, PA, USA. The Leiden ranking system offers three perspectives – List view, Chart view and the Map view. List view is supposed to be the best. It is based on selected indicators. Chart view shows scatter plot of universities while in map view, universities are shown in a world map which provides their geographical perspective and performance (leiden ranking.com).

The QS system provides subject as well as global ranking. It also provides five independent region-wise tables i.e., Asia, Latin America, Europe and Central Asia, Arab region and BRICS. The QS system is the only ranking system of the world which has received the approval of International Ranking Expert Group (IREG). However, it is criticised for its over dependence on subjective indicators and reputation surveys.

U-Multirank is a multidimensional ranking system which uses five dimensions i.e. teaching- learning, research, knowledge transfer, international orientation and regional engagement (umultirank.org).

In these different criteria of ranking, one of the most well-known ranking is to evaluate the quality of institutes on the basis of research products in the form of number and impact of publications in peer-reviewed journals or the procedure of admission in the institutes. But such type of criteria downgrades the quality of those institutions emphasis paid by ranking systems on institutional resources and reputation may not truly represent university quality. They found that the indicators used for ranking are neither sufficient to promote policy decisions nor for consumer choice. Usher and Savino (2006) in their study have reviewed 19 league tables and different university ranking systems used around the world and concluded that different ranking systems have different purposes and notions for university quality.

Johns (1988) said that ranking is quantitative because it indicates the position of a scholar, university or country relative to others. On the other hand, quality can be considered the essence of scientific research.

Altbach (2006) states in his research that the weakness of education system to measure the quality of teaching and its effect on students should be taken care and must be included in ranking the institutions. This finding is in line with the findings of Brook (2005) who says that Raters did not know about 33.33% of the programmes which they rate.

Moed (2017) in his paper had tried to compare and evaluate five world ranking systems: ARWU, Leiden, THE, QS and U-Multirank. He had presented the institutional overlap between each pair of ranking systems.

## Rankings for Higher Education Institutions in India

The institutions of higher education in India are in need of infusion of quality and clarity on the approach of building world class educational institutions in the Indian context and environment, new benchmarks of quality need to be defined to help overall system to move up on the quality spectrum. Research assessment and the national ranking of Indian educational institutions can play an important role in improving performance and quality of academic institutions.

## National Institutional Ranking Framework (NIRF)

National Institutional Ranking Framework (NIRF) is the methodology adopted by the Ministry of Human Resource Development (MHRD), Government of India, to rank all institutions of higher education in India. The framework was approved by MHRD and was launched by Minister of Human Resources Development on 29 September 2015. There are separate rankings for different types of institutions depending on their areas of operation, like universities and colleges, engineering institutions, management institutions, pharmacy institutions, and architecture institutions. The framework uses several parameters for ranking purposes like resources, research and stakeholder perception. The parameters have been grouped into five clusters, and those clusters were assigned certain weightages. The weightages depend on the type of institution.

### *Methodology of National Institutional Ranking Framework (NIRF)*

The NIRF provides for ranking of institutions under five broad generic parameters, namely

#### *i. Teaching, Learning and Resources (TLR)*

These parameters are related to the core activities of any place of learning. These lay emphasis on measuring numbers and quality of faculty, library and lab resources and general facilities for development of young persons. These are organised into the following sub-parameters:

- Faculty Student Ratio with Emphasis on Permanent Faculty (FSR)
- Faculty Student Ratio with Emphasis on Eminent Visiting Faculty (FSR)

- Metric for Faculty with PhD and Experience (FQE)
- Metric for Library, Studio and Laboratory Facilities (LL)
- Metric for Sports and Extra Curricular Facilities (SEC)
- Metric for Teaching and Innovation (TI).

*ii. Research, Professional Practice and Collaborative Performance (RPC)*

Excellence in teaching and learning is closely associated with the scholarship of the faculty and students. Equally, faculty members are expected to make their knowledge and expertise available to benefit the society and industry. These parameters, therefore, attempt to measure the quantity and quality of research output as seen through international databases, IPR generation and interface with industry and fellow professionals. These are organised as follows:

- Combined Metric for Publications (PU)
- Combined Metric for Citations (CI)
- Intellectual Property Rights (IPR)
- % of Collaborative Publications and Patents (CP)
- Footprint of Projects and Professional Practice (FPPP).

*iii. Graduation Outcomes (GO)*

This parameter forms the ultimate test of the effectiveness of the core teaching/learning activity, and measures the student graduation rate and their success in finding appropriate placement in industry and Government or taking up higher studies. There are organised as follows:

- Combined Performance in Public and University Examinations (PUE)
- Performance in Placement, Higher Studies and Entrepreneurship (PHE)
- Mean Salary for Employment (MS).

*iv. Outreach and Inclusivity (OT)*

The Ranking framework lays special emphasis on representation of women and socially challenged persons in student and/or faculty populations, and also on outreach activities of the institution. These are detailed below:

- Outreach Footprint (Continuing Education, Service) (CES)
- Percentage of Students from other States/Countries: Region Diversity
- Percentage of Women Students and Faculty (WS)
- Percentage of Economically and Socially Disadvantaged Students
- Facilities for Differently Abled Persons (DAP).

*v. Perception (PR)*

The ranking methodology gives a significant importance to the perception of the institution by its stakeholders. This will be accomplished through Stakeholder Surveys.

- Process for Peer Rating in Category (PR)
- Application to Seat Ratio (SR).

## Types of Ranking Framework for Higher Education Institutions

The framework is primarily divided into two categories: Category A will cover institutions with academic autonomy and greater focus on research and category B will comprise colleges and centres affiliated to a university and more focused on teaching.

### *Five Parameters and 20 Sub-parameters of National Institutional Ranking Framework*

1. Teaching, Learning and Resources (TLR)
   - Faculty Student Ratio with Emphasis on Permanent Faculty (FSR)
   - Faculty-Student Ratio with Emphasis on Eminent Visiting Faculty (FSR)
   - Metric for Faculty with PhD and Experience (FQE)
   - Metric for Library, Studio and Laboratory Facilities (LL)
   - Metric for Sports and Extra Curricular Facilities (SEC)
   - Metric for Teaching and Innovation (TI)
2. Research, Professional Practice and Collaborative Performance (RPC)
   - Combined Metric for Publications (PU)
   - Combined Metric for Citations (CI)
   - Intellectual Property Right and Patents (IPR)
   - % of Collaborative Publications and Patents (CP)
   - Footprint of Projects and Professional Practice (FPPP).
3. Graduation Outcome (GO)
   - Performance in University Examinations (PUE)
   - Performance in Placement, Higher Studies and Entrepreneurship (PHE)
   - Mean Salary for Employment (MS).
4. Outreach and Inclusivity (OT)
   - Outreach Footprint (Continuing Education, Services) (CES)
   - Percentage of Students from Other States/Countries (RD)
   - Percentage of Women Students and Faculty (WS)
   - Percentage of Economically and Socially Disadvantaged Students (ESDS)
   - Facilities for Physically Challenged/Differently Abled Persons (DAP).
5. Perception (PR)
   - Process for Peer Rating in Category (PR) and
   - Applications to Seat Ratio (SR).

### *National Institutional Ranking (NIR)-2016*

About 3500 institutions of India voluntarily participated in the first round of rankings. The ranked lists were released by MHRD on 4 April 2016.

### *University Ranking*

In the Ranking of University, Indian Institute of Science (IISc), Bangalore has been ranked best with a score of 91.81 followed by Institute of Chemical

Technology, Mumbai with a score of 87.58. The Jawaharlal Nehru University has been ranked 3rd with a score of 86.45, University of Hyderabad is at fourth

Top 5 Category-wise HEIs Institutions of India

| *Institution Category* | *Rank 1* | *Rank 2* | *Rank 3* | *Rank 4* | *Rank 5* |
|---|---|---|---|---|---|
| University | Indian Institute of Science Bangalore | Institute of Chemical Technology | Jawaharlal Nehru University | University of Hyderabad | Tezpur University |
| Engineering | IIT Madras | IIT Bombay | IIT Kharagpur | IIT Delhi | IIT Kanpur |
| Management | IIM Bangalore | IIM Ahmedabad | IIM Calcutta | IIM Lucknow | IIM Udaipur |
| Pharmacy | Manipal College of Pharmaceutical Sciences | University Institute of Pharmaceutical Sciences, Chandigarh | Jamia Hamdard | Poona College of Pharmacy, Erandwane, Pune | Institute of Pharmacy, Nirma University |

National Institutional Ranking (2016)

| *Name* | *Est* | *City* | *State* | *Score* | *Rank* |
|---|---|---|---|---|---|
| Indian Institute of Science, Bangalore | 1909 | Bengaluru | Karnataka | 91.81 | 1 |
| Institute of Chemical Technology | 1933 | Mumbai | Maharashtra | 87.58 | 2 |
| Jawaharlal Nehru University | 1969 | New Delhi | Delhi | 86.45 | 3 |
| University of Hyderabad | 1974 | Hyderabad | Telangana | 85.45 | 4 |
| Tezpur University | 1994 | Tezpur | Assam | 84.31 | 5 |
| University of Delhi | 1922 | Delhi | Delhi | 83.19 | 6 |
| Banaras Hindu University | 1916 | Varanasi | Uttar Pradesh | 81.22 | 7 |
| Indian Institute of Space | 2007 | Thiruvananthapuram | Kerala | 78.82 | 8 |
| Birla Institute of Technology & Science | 1964 | Pilani | Rajasthan | 76.85 | 9 |
| Aligarh Muslim University | 1920 | Aligarh | Uttar Pradesh | 76.62 | 10 |
| Visva Bharati | 1922 | Kolkata | West Bengal | 76.11 | 11 |
| Punjab University | 1882 | Chandigarh | Chandigarh | 76.02 | 12 |
| Pondicherry University | 1985 | Coimbatore | Pondicherry | 74.44 | 13 |
| Bharathiar University | 1982 | Puducherry | Tamil Nadu | 74.31 | 14 |
| North Eastern Hill University | 1973 | Shillong | Meghalaya | 72.41 | 15 |
| King Georges Medical University | 1905 | Lucknow | Uttar Pradesh | 72.24 | 16 |

| *Name* | *Est* | *City* | *State* | *Score* | *Rank* |
|---|---|---|---|---|---|
| Homi Bhabha National Institute | 2005 | Mumbai | Maharashtra | 72.06 | 17 |
| Jamia Hamdard | 1989 | New Delhi | Delhi | 71.44 | 18 |
| Amrita Vishwa Vidyapeetham | 2003 | Coimbatore | Tamil Nadu | 71.03 | 19 |
| Goa University | 1985 | Goa | Goa | 69.90 | 20 |
| Guru Gobind Singh Indraprastha Vishwavidyalaya | 1998 | New Delhi | Delhi | 69.65 | 21 |
| Gauhati University | 1948 | Guwahati | Assam | 68.58 | 22 |
| International Institute of Information Technology | 1998 | Hyderabad | Telangana | 68.38 | 23 |
| Guru Jambheshwar University of Science and Technology | 1995 | Hissar | Haryana | 67.46 | 24 |
| Guru Nanak Dev University. | 1969 | Amritsar | Punjab | 67.32 | 25 |

## Conclusion

To conclude, although the academic institutions have a responsibility that resources must be managed efficiently through research and their outcomes, it is also true that currently there does not exist any standardised evaluation mechanism for research performance of institutions so that they can be compared. Hence, there is an urgent requirement of such indicators.

If we conclude that ranking will lose its importance in the future, then that would be an immature assumption about the ranking. However, if we want that ranking must stay then we must be aware of their shortcomings, intended or unintended biases and convenience-based usage by institutions.

At the end, it can be said that any effort made at creating an academic quality ranking system must grapple with the difficulty of trying to quantify the intangibles of a set of complex teaching, learning, resource and research phenomena. It is evident that the choice of indicators is a non-arbitrary process that should be guided by, among other things, knowledge of the strengths and weaknesses or limitations of the indicators being considered as well as their validity, reliability and comparability for the higher education institutions to be ranked. The choice of a method for presenting this information in ranked format must be guided by, among other things, an understanding of the nature of quality in higher education institutions being ranked as well as the relationships among the quality indicators that are to be used (Clarke, 2002).

# 12

# ICT in Use

India is known as one of the world's top education destinations in the global education. With some of the best universities and colleges, India has been successful in attracting bright talent from all over the world. Indian education system is robust and built on strong foundations. According to Indian Brand Equity Foundation, Indian education market is currently pegged at a $100 billion with higher education contributing to 59.7%, school education at 38.1%, preschool at 1.6%, and the remainder 0.6% consists of technology and multimedia-based education.

India is not to be early adopter of technology in the education sector but with access to high speed broadband Internet and low-cost computers and mobile devices there has been growth in the use of technology for learning. Today India is one of the finest growing markets for e-learning based products and services. There are different ways technology can be used to bring about a reformation in the Indian education system. Even government aims to increase digital literacy of the country to 50% from current 15% by bringing out favourable policies to give impetus to technology-based learning. Many entrepreneurs and start-ups have grabbed this opportunity to develop technology based educational products for private and government-based schools, colleges and universities.

## Use of Technology in the Education Sector

1. *Distance education*: Distance education is a way of learning where the students as working professionals can learn the courses remotely through online access and interact with faculty via online classroom. It helps students to interact with their mentors or tutors directly through chat, email, or phone call. India is a developing country and for many students, who are living in remote places or villages, getting a degree for higher education is still a distant dream. In such instances technology enabled distance education can help them to complete their studies, upgrade their skills and get degrees. This gives the students or working professionals the flexibility to learn at their own time without the compulsion of going to classes.

According to a report released by All India Survey on higher education 2014-2015 by Ministry of Human Resource Development (now MoE), the total enrollment of students for distance education constitutes 11.7 % out of which 46% are female students. Availability of broadband and high-speed Internet along with low cost computers in tier 2 and tier 3 cities has made learning seamless without any glitches.

2. *Classroom based education learning*: Nowadays technology has become integral part of classroom-based teaching. Today in many schools, colleges and universities in India, instead of blackboard, projector screens are used for teaching. Handwriting of teachers are replaced by PowerPoint presentation. Students experience a different kind of set-up in today's technology-based classroom. Gadgets like tablets and laptops are used to take down notes.

3. *Online learning management system*: Many colleges and universities in India are integrating Online Learning Management Systems or LMS platform into their web portal. Students can remotely log in to access course material and also attend live classes with teachers.

Pre-recorded lecture videos can be uploaded on the LMS platform making it easy for students to go through it multiple times. LMS adoption is still poor in many parts of India where students do not have the access to computers or broadband Internet. However, government is providing computers to remote areas and creating content that consumes less data and can be easily accessed on Internet.

4. *Learning through mobile app*: India has become the second biggest smartphone market in the world after China with more than 220 million active users. This presents a huge opportunity for delivering e-learning content through mobile apps. Today educational mobile apps are available on popular platforms like Android and iOS develops developers or creating educational apps based on particular subjects. They are simplifying complex concepts with easy-to-understand illustrations and animations, puzzles, games, etc.

There are also certain websites like Khan Academy and various YouTube channels that offer video lectures by eminent scholars and teachers on various subjects.

Even though some of the educational institutions in India rank on par with world's best universities and colleges, the use of technology is still limited in Indian education sector. With the rising cost of education, technology-based learning can come to the rescue of those who want to go for higher degree but cannot afford it. Government needs to play an active role in encouraging educational institutions in adopting latest technology for teaching and delivering course content with its population of 1.2 billion people. The scope for technology-based learning can surpass that of many developed and developing nations.

### EduTech—The Future

The advent of Internet has shrunk the entire world into a global village. With everything available digitally, it is very easy for a person from Patna to know the latest research being conducted at Columbia University. Also, PM Narendra

Modi's digitisation initiative and even demonetisation has paved the way for the growth of digital education medium in the country.

In the past, education system in India was restricted to the archaic simple classrooms with blackboards and quarterly exams to measure the students' progress. But all that has changed in the past couple of years with the Internet boom at least in cities. Covid 19 pandemic has further changed the current scenario. Today, India ranks second only to China with 348 million Internet users which is expected to reach about 555.3 million users by end of 2021. This exploration of technology has further led to the influx and rise of EduTech companies in India. These firms brought to the fun back into learning through their innovative concepts and novel teaching methods.

The availability of low cost and high-speed Internet has made it possible for EduTech to teach a wider and vast section of the Indian population. While there are many remote parts in India where students still have to travel for an hour or more to reach their schools/colleges, EduTech has brought classroom into one's living room. An online classroom is not restricted by location or geography and has removed all boundaries imposed by the traditional education system. In the past when one missed a school or college lecture, it was difficult to catch up with the syllabus. But now through online tutoring it is possible to not only catch up with the studies but even stay ahead of the game.

Moreover, as the entire nation is shifting towards digitisation where people are encouraged to pay their milk vendor through Paytm, learning through technology has become easier and more interactive. Learning through Tata Sky or online tutors has become simpler in this fast-moving world where everything is so competitive and chaotic. In cities like Delhi, where there is a huge traffic problem and going from a place to another consumes majority of time, an online class helps you save valuable time. With the help of EduTech mediums, one can learn from the comfort of their home, rather than spending hours in commuting from one location to another. This precious time can further be used productively to sharpen their skills.

EduTech offers teachers/educational institutions practical and smart ways to evaluate a student's progress rather than waiting for quarterly exam results to know a student's progress in a subject. One can use EduTech tools to monitor their performance daily. It offers you ways to track a student's performance by going through his scores, classroom attendance, participation and then come up with a plan to work on their weak areas.

### EduTech—The Future of Indian Education

Unlike the limited knowledge offered by boring textbooks, EduTech offers you a plethora of options to learn. This combined with easy availability of smart phones and Internet, has given students an option to grasp concepts which were earlier learned through traditional methods. Since all students do not have the same learning capability, one can personalise their EduTech tools according to one's needs. A student can learn through concepts taught by Byjus, Khan Academy or opt for online tutoring provided by GuruQ etc.

EduTech offers parents and children stress-free environment to learn subjects and upgrade their knowledge. In a changing world, India needs to move towards technology because that is the way forward.

### Technology – A Way Forward for Indian Education

India's education system is in crisis. It is a crisis that technology can play a critical role in solving. The 2014 Annual Status of Education Report (ASER) showed that nearly 75% children in Class V cannot solve a Class III division problem. Alongside low student learning levels, such as these, India also faces a shortage of 1.4 million teachers, meaning many children face even more difficult access to quality instruction.

So, what can be done? One piece of the puzzle stood to think about what types of learning can be made available through technology that can both help augment child's experience in a classroom and also give access to those in rural areas.

EduTech allows students to study at their own pace which means that gaps in learning are addressed quickly and easily. Self-learning modules enable anywhere anytime learning by reaching directly to students.

The power of technology can also connect students to high quality resources, regardless of their location. Personalised learning using adaptive tools and allowing teachers to differentiate instruction to meet varying student interests is the best way to think of the classroom of the future.

EduTech can help to promote a higher order skills, such as critical thinking, problem solving and creativity by encouraging students to participate in project based work and allowing teachers a time to engage actively with students in such areas. When class time is freed up by using technology, teachers are enabled to spend it with students or in small workgroup situations, enabling learning in many different ways. This can be achieved through blended learning models that combine one to one learning on computers with the teacher instruction. The Nalanda project by the Motivation for Excellence Foundation in Mumbai explores the potential of learning mathematics using a blend of teacher instructions and self-learning through an offline digital learning tool.

We need to recognise that a large number of low-income children in the Indian education system calls for the creation of open educational resources that can be made available free or at a low cost to the students. The cost of proprietary digital content ranging from ₹1,000 to 2,000 per year per subject, is often too high for students, whether they are studying in government or private schools. Moreover, we need to create products in local languages that cater to students studying in vernacular medium schools, and especially to first generation learners.

With the Internet and mobile infrastructure becoming widely available, the government pushing for the adoption of digital technology, and entrepreneurs and funders collaborating to create innovative solutions there is tremendous potential for technology to continue to improve the quality of education and students learning level in India. This is special time in history, when we actually have a chance to help all our students have access to world-class education.

ICT has changed the face of education over the last few decades. "It has proved to be a boon to both the teachers and the learners. Looking for matter beyond the textbooks is no longer a challenge with respect to time and resources anymore."

Assisting in the growth of ICT learning in the country, several brands are ensuring to create a options for educational institutions. Recognising the importance of digital literacy in rural India, Samsung India launched a smart class initiative in collaboration with Navodaya Vidyalaya Samiti in 2013. The initiative is available across 500 Jawahar Navodaya Vidyalaya schools benefiting over 2.5 lakh students. The brand has imparted training to over 8000 teachers on interacting technology.

Gopal Singh Tomar, Principal, Jawahar Navodya Vidyalaya, Dadri, Uttar Pradesh feels, "60% of the students in our school are the first-time users of technology or smart class."

Stating that students are now confident and the use of technology is helping our teaching also to a great extent. He said: "Our results have improved post ICT. Smart classes have helped one of our students Akash Karan in developing a mobile application. This app helps the user in calling his or her dear or near ones in case of any emergency just by using the app and that too by a single touch."

## Technology is Evolving

Indian education system is evolving in many ways owing to the advancement of technology as well as rapid change of mentality of the people of all segments of society. Government intervention in emerging technology with paedagogy system of education has taken Indian education to a new avenue, opening new doors of opportunities for both the educator as well as student.

There are two segments in every education system, teacher and learner. In a traditional education system, the teacher narrates a topic to the students, holds demonstration of the topic occasionally, and then assesses the students. However, not every student has the same grasping capabilities, due to which traditional models of education are gradually paving way for newer innovative methods supported by technology. Government of India has acknowledged the limitations of existing paedagogy systems and taken initiative of incorporating ICT in the education system.

With the help of ICT, teachers can easily explain the complex situations to the students and the students, too, retain information better, remembering the visual explanation of the particular situation for a longer time.

India is emerging as a superpower and it cannot function without the support of ICT. The gap between demand and supply of higher education has urged the government and institutions of the country to formulate policies and initiatives so that education can easily integrate with ICT.

The central and state governments have taken various initiatives for integration of ICT with education system. Since the past two or three decades, the Indian education system has been plagued by many challenges, such as lack of students, poor infrastructure, lack of quality teachers, and a standard curriculum, to name a few. With the integration of ICT in schools, education in India is poised for a paradigm shift, where the education system will be compatible with international education standards.

However, there are many hurdles for this successful integration. ICT requires Internet, computer-based infrastructure and also satellite support and the process of installation is expensive. Moreover, teachers need to be efficiently trained to understand ICT and how they can utilise its numerous benefits best to successfully impart knowledge to the students.

In the current digital day and age, it is imperative that schools and institutes integrate ICT and stay attuned to the modern needs and requirements of students. The use of ICT in learning not only results in the cognitive, social and emotional development of a child, but also has a major motivational influence on his/her learning capabilities.

### IT and ICT Initiatives by Indian Government

1. National digital literary mission
2. Vidyanjali
3. Bharatavani
    - Paathyapustaka Kosh
    - Jnana Kosh
    - Shabda Kosh
    - Bhasha Kosh
    - Suchanaa Pradyogikii Kosh
    - Bahamaadhyama Kosh
4. Web based school GIS
5. Sarva Shiksha Abhiyan
6. Rashtriya Madhyamik Shiksha Abhiyan
7. Shala Darpan
8. e-Pathshala
9. Swayam
10. Image courtesy
11. Experiential learning
12. Unfolding multiple intelligences in the classroom
13. Integrity and ethics
14. Early childhood care and education

15. Creating the happiest learning spaces
16. Early childhood development milestones
17. Read aloud
18. Dance their way to fitter India
19. New ways to teach signs in the early childhood classroom
20. A global idea of Montessori.

## Technology in Schools

The Information and Communication Technology (ICT) in schools have been subsumed in the Rastriya Madhyamik Shiksha Abhiyan (RMSA). Now ICT in schools is a component of the RMSA. The Information and Communication Technology (ICT) in schools was launched in December 2004 and revised in 2010 to provide opportunities to secondary stage students to mainly build their capacity on ICT skills and make them learn through computer aided learning process. The scheme is a major catalyst to bridge the digital divide amongst students of various socio-economic and other geographical barriers. The scheme provides support to States/UTs to establish computer labs on sustainable basis.

The scheme has essentially four components:

- the first one is a partnership with state government and union territories administrations for providing computer-aided education to secondary and higher secondary government and government-aided schools.
- the second is the establishment of smart schools which shall be technology demonstrators.
- the third component is teacher related interventions, such as provision for engagement of an exclusive teacher, capacity enhancement of all teachers in ICT and a scheme for national ICT award as a means of motivation
- fourth one relates to the development of e-content, mainly through Central Institute of Education Technologies (CIET), six State Institutes of Education Technologies (SIETs) and five Regional Institutes of Education (RIEs) as also through outsourcing.

The scheme currently covers both government and government-aided secondary and higher secondary schools. Financial assistance is provided for procurement of computers and peripherals, educational software, training of teachers, development of e-content, Internet connectivity and set up of smart schools. So far 87,033 government and government-aided secondary and higher secondary schools have been approved for coverage under ICT in school scheme.

## Government Support to ICT in Education

Worldwide research has shown that ICT can lead to improved student learning and better teaching methods. A report made by the National Institute of Multimedia Education in Japan, proved that an increase in student exposure to educational ICT through curriculum integration has a significant and positive impact on student achievement, especially in terms of "Knowledge Comprehension". "Practical skills" and "Presentation skills" in subject areas, such as mathematics, science, and social studies.

In India, student strength is increasing day by day due to growth of population, awareness about advances of education and government policies and facilities to promote education. Indian government is providing free education, free books, free dress, free midday meal and scholarship, etc. It is not easy to do all these because of the geographical structure, infrastructure and economic problems of our country. ICT can play an important role in achieving them.

India has the third largest system of education in the world, next only to the USA and China with more than 700 universities and around 30,000 colleges. To introduce ICT enabled education in such a large system one needs to have high quality multimedia enriched content in different disciplines for various courses including its multilingual conversions, capacity building of teachers and students in ICT skills and state of the art infrastructure along with networking and Internet connectivity via Virtual Private Network (VPN) broadband connectivity for disseminating the content and affordable access devices so that it reaches the doorsteps of the learners. The ongoing National Mission on Education through ICT (NMEICT) is a major initiative of the Government of India in this direction with an aim to leverage the potential of ICT in providing high quality personalised and interactive content free of cost to all the learners.

In order to use technology to help achieve the goals of education in a better and more effective way, one has to be first of all clear about what our expectations are from the education system, what and how do we want our students to learn and what type of individuals our classrooms should produce: rote learners or those with an analytical mind having an in-depth understanding of the subject.

### Barriers in Technology Use

*Avoiding nature of people*: In general, the attitude of people is not of acceptance of ICT. People are ignoring the importance on the need of ICT. When people are having problems with themselves mentally or technically, they put the blame on technology.

People think technology means solution for all problems in the magic way, which is not practically possible. People have to develop themselves.

*Economic problems*: Developing countries like India and other Asian countries have financial problems. Economic positions of common people are not good so it is difficult to afford for computer, tab, and android phones.

*Lack of good quality infra support*: In developing countries like India, electricity, network, and other facilities are not available. People are not getting proper power supply, if they are getting that not in proper standard. It is same with the network, telecommunication companies. They are just making money, not providing proper network.

*Gadgets' maintenance problems*: In developing countries, all gadgets like laptop, tab, and android mobile have their maintenance problems. Technology is changing very fast, next morning we can see new model in market and there is no service facility for old models. Government does not have any clear cut policy on service part or customers education for proper use of gadgets.

*Social and cultural scenario*: Social and cultural structure of India and Asian countries is different from western culture. Using technology among the common people is not easily accessible. Society raises a voice even against the use of mobile by girls.

Browsing Internet is not safe. This is one of the reasons that society is concerned with cultural and social laws for children. It is very difficult to safeguard the children from porn sites.

*Computer skill and education English language problem*: Even now computer and English is not common among the common people in India. Still 70% of rural schools do not have facility of computer; English is also a problem to students and both are necessary for education with ICT.

## Initiatives for Quality Improvement

Indian higher education sector is suffering from lack of qualified faculties even in premier institutes like IITs and NITs. Therefore, Indian ministries and premier education institutions have taken many ICT based initiatives to improve access to quality education by every individual of India sitting anywhere between Kashmir to Kanyakumari. Article highlights major ICT based programmes started recently in India.

In order to improve GER in higher education by 5% during Eleventh Five-year Plan, Indian government commenced NME-ICT project and allotted a budget of ₹5 billion. The major focus of this scheme was to fulfil three key cardinal principles of education policy, viz. access, equity and quality. Therefore, the project targeted to provide high bandwidth availability with low-cost computing devices Aakash tablet to most of the institutes in a phase wise manner. Another major goal of the project was to generate good quality study material and relevant content. Some of the key objectives of the mission are as follows:

- effective utilisation of intellectual resources and anytime availability of desired knowledge at appropriate levels to self-paced learners.
- platform for sharing ideas techniques and knowledge resources to support learners and scholars.
- utilise the full potential of developments in the field of ICT to take the resources at the doorstep of the learner.
- emphasis on e-learning, content generation, evaluation, and mentoring.
- develop repository of e-books, e-journals and provide easy access to the learners.

- encourage teachers to participate in the digital era of learning and be available on the Internet to guide learners.
- foster multilingual content generation for the diversified Indian population and motivate indigenous open-source software development.
- utilisation of satellites to broadcast study channels via direct to home service.
- online certification-based courses for self-paced learners by reputed institutes of India.

Under the banner of NME-ICT a project called National Programme on Technology Enhancement Learning (NPTEL) like Massachusetts Institute of Technology's open courseware is started to provide video lectures of well known professors of Indian Institute of Technologies and Indian Institute of Sciences in almost all the engineering courses. Presently NPTEL provides India's largest repository of free video lectures for engineering students with certification facility after course completion.

IIT Kharagpur and IIT Bombay together working on the project called the T10KT (Train 10,000 teachers). It is a major initiative under the NME-ICT to improve the teaching skill of skills of engineering college teachers of the country in core engineering and science subjects. IIT Madras started quality enhancement in engineering education (QEEE) that offers live classes and virtual life lab environment as a supplement material to the colleges lacking basic pedagogical resources, viz. qualified teachers, well equipped labs, and quality content. Under NME-ICT project, IIT Bombay started spoken tutorial programme that provides audio video tutorial of only open-source software in various Indian regional languages. IIT Bombay also executed the project of India's first low-cost tablet named Aakash and distributed it to around 1,00,000 students as its remote centre. In the future, it has planned to distribute every institute at least a single Aakash tablet.

## Other Quality Improvement Initiatives

University Grants Commission of India set up a Consortium for Educational Commission (CSE) as one of the Inter University Centre to cater the needs of Higher Education through the use of television along with ICT. Many other initiatives in this connection to use ICT to deliver free, easily accessible and good quality education are also being taken, viz. e-PG Pathshala for postgraduate students, Shiksha for students of Central Board of Secondary Education, E-Gyankosh – a digital content repository, Vidyavahini for school kids, National Digital Library containing six million books ranging from primary to PG level etc.

It is certain that realisation of most of the ICT based projects is dependent upon good Internet and Wi-Fi, therefore HRD ministry recently announced to launch a campus connect programme to make 21,000 colleges and 4,20,000 classrooms Wi-Fi enabled under the programme, all the buildings of 700 universities having one (1) GBPS bandwidth will be made Wi-Fi enabled.

# 13
# Employability of Educands

In simple words, employability is the quality in an individual to attract job-givers to her/him. It is the ability to be equipped with needed skills, competencies and attitudes in order to be worthy of a job. Hillage and Polard (1998) opined that employability refers to a person's capability of gaining initial employment, maintaining employment and obtaining employment, if required. A widely accepted definition of employability given by Enhancing Student Employability Coordination Team (ESECT) 2014 held that employability is a set of achievements, skills, understanding and personal attributes that make graduates more likely to gain employment and be successful in their occupation which benefits them, the workforce, the community and the economy.

## Employability Skills

Employability skills refer to ones that are required to acquiring and retaining a job. In the past, employability skills were thought to include only the academic skills or subject-knowledge. Current thinking, however, has broadened the definition of employability skills to include not only the foundational academic skills, but also a variety of attitudes. These include the ability to solve complex, multidisciplinary problems, work successfully in teams, exhibit effective oral and written communication skills, and practise good interpersonal skills" (Robinson, Garton and Vaughn, 2007). These are actually a blend of technical and soft skills. The first ones make the incumbent technically and the second ones behaviourally sound. The Future of Jobs Report (2018) remarked: "Proficiency in new technologies is only one part of the 2022 skill equation, however, as 'humane' skills such as creativity, originality and innovative, critical thinking, persuasion and negotiation will likewise retain or increase their value, as will attention to detail resilience, flexibility and complex problem solving. Emotional intelligence, leadership and social influence as well as service organization also see an outsized increase in demand relative to their current prominence." Some of the oft-discussed employability skills (Anonymous, 2019) are:

- *Communication Skill*: Ability to explain what one means in a clear and concise way through written and spoken means.
- *Problem-solving Skill:* Ability to understand a problem by breaking it down into relevant smaller parts, and identifying the key issues, implications and identifying solutions.

- *Creativity, Initiative and Self-motivation:* Having new ideas which can be transformed into a reality, showing a strong personal drive and not waiting to be told to do things.
- *Planning, Organisation, and Time Management*: Being organised and methodical; able to plan work to meet deadlines.
- *Inter-personal Relationship and Teamwork:* Ability to work with other people from different disciplines, backgrounds, and expertise to accomplish a task as a member of a team.
- *Negotiation and Persuasion:* To take on board other people's feelings and express one's own requirements in an unemotional and objective fashion to achieve a desired outcome.
- *Flexibility*: Adapting successfully to changing situations and environments.
- *Leadership Skill*: Ability to motivate, take responsibility and lead other people in order to achieve set goals.
- *Technological Skill*: Ability to use a range of computer packages and software, including email, word-processing, databases, spreadsheets, and Internet, etc.
- *Numeracy Skill*: Ability to handle data to support evidence or demonstrate a point.

Besides the above-mentioned skills, some other such qualities that the employers generally look for in a job-seeker are:

- Fundamental knowledge of the discipline studied
- Decision-making ability
- Critical analytical thinking
- Integrity
- Willingness to learn, unlearn and relearn
- Trustworthiness
- Risk-taking ability
- Discipline
- Respect for diversity.

At the time of Independence, agricultural sector used to contribute over 60 per cent and the service sector just 24 per cent of India's Gross Domestic Product (GDP). However, at present service sector is the largest contributor to our GDP. In 2018-19, this sector accounted for 54.40 per cent, and industrial sector contributed 29.73 per cent, while agriculture and allied sectors shared only 15.87 per cent of our GDP (*Statistics Times*, February 8, 2019). These data indicate the emergence of a knowledge-driven economy in India. Given the unprecedented development in information and communication technology, a changing pattern of employability skills could be noticed at present. The executive summary of Higher Education in India: Moving towards Global Relevance and Competitiveness (FICCI Higher Education Summit Report, 2014) observed: "By 2020, 90 per cent of India's GDP and 75 per cent of employment is expected to be contributed by the services and manufacturing sectors... structural shift in employment will increase demand for sophisticated workers, innovators, and thinkers who can thrive in a globally-connected and dynamic economy." At present, with around 600 million people under the age of 25, there is seen a surge of enrolment in higher education sector, and the pass-outs are in search of opportunities in the globalised economy. The working age population (15-59 years old) in India is growing rapidly. Most of the developed countries are suffering from reducing working age population while India will add around 200 million to its workforce in next 20 to 30 years (Aiyar, 2018). Higher education is generally believed to help in developing knowledge-based economy and provide skilled manpower and training to execute specific tasks and jobs (CRISIL, 2010; Rahaman and Ramabrahmam, 2015). From the data, already given, it is true that we have enough degree-holders in our country, but they are not skilled, and hence, are not readily employable.

## Scenario of Unemployment

Unemployment rate is highest among diploma-holders (37 per cent), graduates (36 per cent) and postgraduates and above (36 per cent) (Quartz Creative, June 10, 2019). Technical programmes, on the other hand, are popular, as public think that pass-outs of these programmes find job more easily. However, there has been a decline in employability of people passing out with B. Tech., other engineering streams, MCA, technical and computer-related courses. Aspiring Minds (2019) reported that 80 per cent of Indian engineers are unfit for a job in the knowledge-economy. According to ASSOCHAM Education Committee (*India Today*, February 6, 2018), only 7 per cent of management graduates are employable in India, other than the top 20 B-schools, including IIMs. AISHE, 2019 reported that, except for the IITs, some of the NITs and private engineering colleges could not make the candidates job-ready.

The organised sector, which most graduates expect to enter, makes up only 15 per cent of the job market (Ministry of Labour, 2018). However, no job-skill training is given in these general UG programmes. Traditionally, graduates from these programmes apply for government jobs (Mehrotra, 2015). However, since the growth in enrolment has out-numbered the vacancy in government jobs, these pass-outs turn to private sectors for employment. Unlike technical colleges, only a few elite colleges have placement cells, leaving graduates ending up working in the unorganised sectors with lesser pay (ibid).

The NSS report (*The Times of India*, February 3, 2019) revealed that now unemployment has reached its highest level in the last 45 years and most of the unemployed are higher educated young people. One or two instances will speak volumes about it. A report by *The Times of India* (July 11, 2017) showed that, among 300-plus applications that Malda Medical College in West Bengal received for two laboratory attendants whose job profile was to handle dead bodies and organs in post-mortem section of anatomy classes, one out of four applicants was either doing a Ph. D. or already had an M. Phil. Some candidates even had double M.A.s and every third candidate was a graduate. More recently, *The Ananda Bazar Patrika* (September 12, 2019) reported that, for the post of 819 facility manager group III posts in Government hospitals in West Bengal, a whopping 3.5 lakh candidates applied. It meant 427.35 applications for a single post! Among the applicants, many were B.Tech. civil engineers and high-scoring candidates of science stream. All these reports are indicators of the huge army of educated youth waiting for any opening.

### Reasons for Low Employability of Higher Educands in India

- Almost no or poor entry-level check for a particular educational programme. As a result, people having no flair for a certain job, undergo degree of that job
- Being fluent in English increases the chance of getting a job. But we have kept our youth deprived from pursuing higher education in English medium
- Curriculum is sadly backdated to meet up the demand of the day
- Less focus on experiential learning
- No connection between industry and academia
- No scope to instill life skills and soft skills into the learners
- Poor communication and inter-personal skills
- Incompetent faculty to teach and train the learners
- Lack of vision on the part of the HEIs
- Ineffective evaluation system.

### Measures to Adopt for Increasing Employability of Higher Educands

The challenge now facing the country is how to make our educated youth job-worthy. The following measures may be adopted to overcome this challenge:

- *Introduce Outcome-based Education***:** It is high time to move towards a more outcome-based education. In such education, students will have chances to demonstrate their competency in given areas – working through content, experiences and assessments.
- *Allow Students Space for Self-exposure:* Focus should be shifted from teacher-talk to student-talk in the classroom. Thus, they can be exposed to presenting themselves before audience.
- *Instill Critical Thinking and Problem-Solving Skill into the Educands:* The aim of learning should be empowering students with the capacity of critical thinking. Techniques that may foster problem-solving need to be stressed while teaching and evaluating their performance.
- *Redesign Curricula:* "Knowledge doubles in every 13 months" (Fuller, 1981). The explosion of knowledge compels us to update curricula on a regular basis. While designing curriculum for any discipline, care should

be taken to provide opportunities for acquiring fundamental knowledge, discipline-related skills and attitude, which the employers expect from a job-seeker. Curricula should focus on promotion of applied research, creativity, and innovation. There is a need to integrate higher education curricula to the issues of various government schemes and missions, like Digital India, Make in India and Skill India.

- *Integrate Employment Skills into Curricula:* It is necessary to integrate the skill components into the curricula. Apart from skill specific short-term certificate/diploma courses, provisions could be made to have direct access to skill development programmes through SWAYAM and MOOCs.
- *Develop Global Competencies in Students:* With globalisation of economy, education and human resource markets, it is important for HEIs to develop global competencies in students. Universities should make modular curricula which will familiarise students with different global cultures and social life to facilitate smooth transition from one culture and temperament to another.
- *Role of Corporate Private Sectors:* In the western countries, the corporate sector "give back to society" by doing some social welfare programmes like save girl child, conversation of environment, animal rights, etc. In India, few corporates have taken initiatives to shoulder social responsibilities. Time is ripe for corporate sectors to come forward to mitigate unemployment. The door to lots of jobs like chefs, waiters, assistants, and drivers in hotel and travel industry, plumbers, fitters, electricians, mechanics, technical assistants, supportive staff in construction industries, personnel in security services and many more may be opened to our educated youth by the corporates. The corporate sector may come forward to remove the mismatch between demand and supply in the labour market.
- *Take Steps for Industrial Growth:* Skill training alone would not solve the issue of unemployment unless there is industrial growth, leading to job creation in our country.
- *Promote Linkage between Higher Education System and Industry:* Colleges, universities and research institutes across the country need to develop strong linkages with industries to ensure that the young workforce is trained on skills, knowledge and attitude.
- *Stress on Communicative English:* Competency in verbal and written English would go a long way in securing employability of our educated youth.
- *Nurture Soft Skills:* It is time to re-orient the system of higher education to incorporate life and soft skills to make it more inclusive and meaningful. Each degree programme can remain domain-specific, but it may be ensured that each student, irrespective of system or degree programme,

must undergo rigorous training of life and skills. In order to do so, universities must allocate sufficient proportion of credit to life and soft skills, such as communication in English, problem-solving, critical thinking, leadership, etc. If in any case, it is not possible for a degree programme to incorporate life and soft skills into it, it may be made mandatory to pursue certificate courses offline or online and make up for it in order to receive the degree.

- *Set up Skill Development Centres in HEIs:* It is high time to open the door of vocational courses along with mainstream ones in the HEIs. To facilitate such large-scale skilling of the youth, it would be necessary to establish skill development centres in the premises of HEIs.
- *Strengthen Quality Assurance Framework:* There is a need to improve the quality of a large number of middling qualities in HEIs. Assessment and accreditation for each HEIs should be made mandatory.

# 14

# Environmental Education

## Concept of Environmental Education

The area of Environmental Education has been discussed thoroughly at several national and international seminars, workshops and conferences. Most of the people have recognised the urgent need of environmental education, but only some have clear idea and understanding about the concept of Environmental Education that need to be taught to the students of education. Environmental education has been defined in different manner by various persons. The definition of environmental education in the draft of US Environmental Education Act is considered to be very authentic and is frequently quoted. It states:

> 'Environmental Education is an integral process which deals with man's interrelationship with his natural and manmade surrounding, including the rate of population growth, pollution resource allocation and depletion, conservation technology and urban and rural planning to the total human environment. Environmental education is a study of the factors influencing eco systems, mental and physical health, living and working conditions, decaying cities and population pressures. Environmental Education is intended to promote among citizens the awareness and understanding of environment, our relation to it and the concern and responsible action necessary to assure our survival and to improve the quality of life.'

*Environmental Education should:*

- Consider the environment in its totality natural and built, technological and social.
- Be a continuous lifelong process, beginning at the pre-school level and continuing through all formal and non-formal states.
- Enable learners to have a role in planning their learning experiences and provide an opportunity for making decisions and accepting their consequences.
- Be interdisciplinary in its approach, drawing on the specific content of each discipline in making possible holistic and balanced perspective. In interdisciplinary model relevant components of many disciplines are drawn to create a unit of Environmental Education.
- Be centred on practical problems related to real life.
- Aim at building up sense of values.

The decade of 1970s saw a growing concern about the deteriorating state of the environment, and a need was felt to do something about conservation and improvement of the situation.

In response to the concern, United Nations Conference on the Human Environment was held in Stockholm (1972). It was for the first-time representatives from 113 countries attended the conference, which focused on the need to work out a practical plan of action for the benefit of all. The Stockholm conference initiated the idea of observing World Environment Day on 15 June every year.

In response to the recommendations of the Stockholm conference, UNESCO and UNEP organised a workshop on International Environmental Education Programme (IEEP) at Belgrade in 1975. The Belgrade Charter stressed that Environment Education should:

- Be a continuous lifelong process.
- Be interdisciplinary in approach.
- Consider the environment in its totality.
- Emphasise active participation in preventing and solving environmental problems.
- Examine major environmental issues from a world point of view giving due importance to regional differences.
- Promote value of local, national and international cooperation in the solution of environmental problems.

In 1977, the first inter-governmental conference on Environment Education was held at Tbilisi, USSR. The Tbilisi conference reinforced the major goals of Environment Education which were to develop awareness and concern among the world population about the ecological, economic, political and social interaction and interdependence in the environment and their problems. The declaration of the conference stated:

> "Environment Education should constitute a comprehensive lifelong education, one responsive to changes in a rapidly changing world. It should prepare the individuals for life through an understanding of the major problems of the contemporary world and the provision of skills needed to play a productive role towards improving life and protecting environment."

> "Environment Education should simultaneously attempt to create awareness, transmit information, teach knowledge, develop habits and skills, promote values, provide criteria and standards and present guidelines to problem solving and decision-making."

This definition stresses that Environment Education is comprehensive, continuing process, rooted in broad interdisciplinary base. Environment Education thus aims to assist individuals in understanding that people are inseparable part of an environmental system. Whatever they do, they alter their surroundings in both harmful and beneficial ways.

Environment Education is multifaceted and touches upon every aspect of life, however, most people take it for granted. But can education and awareness about environment be taken for granted?

Environmental education is a process of providing learning experiences to obtain knowledge understanding, skills and awareness with desirable attitudinal changes about man's relationship with his natural and manmade surroundings which includes the relation of population, pollution, resource allocation, transportation, technology and urban and rural planning to the total human environment. Environmental education must utilise diverse learning environment and a broad array of educational approaches to teaching learning about and from the environment with due stress on practical activities and first hand experiences. It should help learners to discover the symptoms and real causes of environmental problems and thus develop critical thinking and problem-solving skills. Environmental education should be a continuous life-long process, beginning at the pre-school stage level and continuing through all formal and non-formal stages and should be interdisciplinary discipline or making possible a holistic and balanced perspective.

Most of us are aware that the first world-wide initiative into environment education was taken by the "Inter-governmental Conference on Environmental Education" held at Tbilisi in 1977. Environment Education should:

a) be considered in its totality wherein natural and built, technological and social, economic and political, moral and cultural, historical and aesthetic aspects are intertwined.
b) be a continuous lifelong process through all formal and non-formal stages.
c) be interdisciplinary in its approach drawing on the various disciplines to make possible a holistic and balanced perspective.
d) examine major environmental issues from local, national, regional and international points of view and emphasise cooperation as well as active participation at all levels in preventing and solving environmental problems.

Environment Education may be considered from different angles:

- Knowledge: Education about the environment
- Values, Attitudes and Actions: Education for the environment
- Resources: Education in and through the environment.

The Johannesburg Summit in 2002 reaffirmed society, environment and economy as the three pillars of sustainable development. Consequently, Environment Education should not be treated as an isolated subject. To achieve sustainable development, we need to focus on:

- An inter-disciplinary and holistic approach permeating the whole range of curricular activities, both formal and informal
- Value-orientation towards sustainable development
- Critical thinking and problem-solving so as to address the dilemmas and challenges

- Different methods and forms wherein teachers and learners interact through collective decisions and activities to shape the local and larger environment.

### Key Concepts in Environment Education

Environment has been defined as the sum total of all the external conditions and influences affecting organisms. The environment may be divided into man-made and natural environments.

- Man-made environment includes all the social, cultural and religious components of human activities
- The natural environment may be further divided into biotic (living things) and abiotic (non-living things) components.

However, environmental components in the biosphere act as a whole interacting with each other in the sustenance of life.

There are certain principles associated with environment. These are:

i. Principle of dependence and mutual influence: every component depending on and influencing the other directly or indirectly. Interdependence and interaction are key terms.
ii. Principle of balance: due to this interdependence and interaction, environment remains more or less stable, there is ecological balance.
iii. Principle of unity: all living components are made up of the same basic units namely, amino acids and the same structural and functional units namely, cells. This is not so of artificial substances.
iv. Principle of diversity: organisms differ in terms of their morphological, anatomical and physiological characteristics. This diversity gives stability to the environment.
v. Principle of active tendency: organisms can develop resistance against man-made substances.
vi. Principle of continuous production: normal loss in an organism is replaced but nature keeps most population within limits. Any excess is detrimental.

### Environment (Protection) Act

The Environment (Protection) Act was passed by the Parliament on 23rd May 1986. The Act refers to the Stockholm Conference of 1972 and is based on Article 253 of the Constitution. By virtue of this Act, the Union Government has armed itself with considerable powers deemed necessary for the prevention, control and abatement of environmental pollution. The power include coordination of action by states planning and execution of nationwide programmes, laying down environmental quality standards, specially those governing emission or discharge of environmental pollutants, placing restrictions on the location of industries and so on. The powers claimed are indeed comprehensive; the coverage includes handling of hazardous substances, prevention of environmental accidents, research, inspection of polluting units, establishment of laboratories, dissemination of information, etc.

A whole set of administrative procedures and structures are envisaged under the act. If implemented in letter and spirit the act will convert the Ministry of Environment and Forests into a super ministry controlling the entire gamut of industrial and other developmental activities.

## Status of Environmental Education in India

The importance of environment has been recognised in India since long. This is also reflected in the Constitution, wherein it states:

It shall be the duty of every citizen to protect and improve the natural environment, including forests, lakes, rivers and wildlife and to have compassion for living creatures [Article 51 A (g)].

The importance of Environmental Education is reflected in National Policy on Education (NPE 1986 and 1992) in the following words:

8.15. There is paramount need to create a consciousness of the environment. It must permeate all ages and all sections of the society: beginning with the child environmental consciousness should inform teaching in school and colleges. This aspect be integrated in entire educational process.

### *Formal Education*

Environmental Education has percolated to all aspects of education including primary, secondary and tertiary education through formal and informal systems of education.

Environmental Education has the target population that includes students, teachers, doctors, engineers, and common man. For this reason, one has to use both formal and informal system of education. The objective of Environmental Education includes opportunities to acquire the knowledge, values, skills, attitudes, commitment and improve the environment and to create new patterns of behaviour of individual group and society as a whole towards society. It, therefore, requires that appropriate action takes place in the behaviour to protect and improve the environment. Since the basic objective of Environmental Education is not environment itself but concern environmental problems, the successful Environmental Education programme includes development of correct values and attitudes towards environment.

### *School Education*

In this method of incorporation of Environmental Education in the school curricula, the environment concepts are infused in already existing curriculum. National curriculum for elementary and secondary education starting two general objectives related to Environmental Education along with other objectives, these are:

i. Understanding of environment and its limited resources and the need for conservation of natural resources and energy.
ii. Appreciation of various consequences of large families and over population and need of checking population growth.

In 1985, Ministry of HRD launched the scheme of Environment orientation of school education. This scheme is implemented in states and union territories through education department and voluntary agencies having expertise and interest in Environmental Education.

At senior secondary level, there is also a vocational course in India. It contains general foundation course which is allotted 15% of time. Out of this 1/3 has been given to Environmental Education and Rural development.

### *University Education*

There are about 10 universities for teaching environment sciences. University education has three major components: Teaching, Research and Extension. At post graduate level four major areas are recognised.

### *Environment Engineering*

It includes subjects like architecture, civil engineering, town and country planning including human settlements, slum improvement.

### *Conservation and Management*

Includes fields like land use, forestry, agriculture, energy, waste management, etc.

### *Environment Health*

Environment Health deals with public health and hygiene, sanitary and chemical engineering nutrition and drug use etc.

### *Social Ecology*

It includes subjects like ecology, sociology, social planning etc.

There are several government and non-governmental organisations to educate people and to create awareness of environment. A department of environment has been set up in 1982 on environment information system for this purpose. There is a Centre for Environmental Education (CEE) at Ahmedabad. There are more than 200 private organisation working for Environmental Education.

A large variety of approaches have been used for EE. These include legislative efforts, curriculum-based approach that goes with formal education system and informal approaches through camps, seminars, mass media. In formal system also, there is variety. The co-curricular activities of education are the most appropriate means for action, the teacher is the main means for implementing the programmes and realising the objectives of EE and organisation of co-curricular activities in school and outside the school. There are two main programmes recommended by educational commission and policy i.e. NSS and SUPW. Many organisation and institutions both government and private play the role of Env. Educators. NCERT, CEE, forest departments, MHRD play a leading role in this. Some conferences and seminars are organised for this purpose. One such conference organised in India was international conference on Environmental Education, 1981 it touched upon almost every aspect of Environmental Education.

# 15

# Vocational Education and Training

## Bases for Vocational Selection

There are several courses and subjects available for students in Vocational Education, which play instrumental role in deciding the profession of the student. Subjects should be selected after analysing individual qualities and desired qualities for the profession.

Following must be kept in a mind while choosing a profession:

- Nature of work which includes the kind of work, charge, responsibility, duty, and interest
- Working conditions
- Necessary personality traits – nature, adapts in behaviour, power of leadership
- Level of intelligence
- Mental abilities
- Interest and aptitudes
- Necessary education and training
- Income, chances of promotion and permanency
- Social prestige, and
- Demand of the job.

Higher education must play a key role in preparing individuals for the world of work. The 12th Five-Year Plan (2012-2017) estimated that less than 5% of the Indian workforce in the age group of 19-24 received formal vocational education; in comparison, the USA has 52%, Germany has 75%, and South Korea has 96%.

Vocational education distinguishes itself from academic education in the close linking of knowledge and skills to specific practical challenges and work situations in the economy. Therefore, integrating vocational education into all educational institutions – schools, colleges and universities and providing access to vocational education to at least 50% of all learners by 2025 is taken as main objective in the draft of National Educational policy 2020.

Vocational education integrates a complex of knowledge, attitudes and skills, for particular occupations. Thus, skills are a part of vocational education.

## Problems of Vocational Education in the Present Education System

- *Lack of Institutions*: The Institutions related to Vocational Education introduced after 15 August 1947 are not adequate. The youngsters of

India with aims of getting technical education can hope for a bright future but such institutions are very short in numbers in consideration to such a large population. There are 10,426 institutes for vocational training (AICTE 2018-19).

- *Attitude of the People:* In the present scenario, more importance and respect has been given to the activities related to the intellect than physical activities. On the basis of physical labour, caste system had been introduced long ago in the country. The bases of diversification of labour, based on thousands of years of caste system, have gone deep into our social system. The people engaged in physical work and handicrafts for earning their livelihood are not looked with respect.
- *Short Curriculum:* In the vocational streams, only technical subjects are provided. There is no provision of liberal education. So, with the technical knowledge, the youngsters are not able to acquire knowledge of social objectives and human relations.
- *Medium of Instruction:* Medium of instruction in the vocational courses is also a big challenge. In almost all technical institutions of modern India, English is the medium of instruction. The students who have passed through medium of Hindi or some other regional language find it very difficult to receive technical and Vocational Education in English. Such students are disappointed and leave vocational and technical institutions after a term of stagnation. So this sort of frustration also brings about a loss of money, time and energy
- *Lack of Good Teachers:* Meritorious and able persons having received Technical and Vocational Education are always after good salaries and other material gains. They hesitate to go in teaching profession. Consequently, such institutions are deprived of able and talented persons.
- *Shortage of Practical:* The practical knowledge is not sufficient for the students. They should also be provided industrial training, internship and hands-on experience.
- *Shortage of Continuous Education:* Young people compete for the Technical and Vocational Education and get employed. In the beginning, they are with full of knowledge, but in course of time they forget many things. This brings lack of efficiency in their work.

### What Needs to be Done?

- Set up more institutions for imparting Vocational Education and Technical Education at all stages.
- Emphasis should be given on education to the youth force, to change attitude towards physical work and labour. High earning potentiality of different vocations can also give assistance in changing attitude of the youths.

- Curriculum of Technical and Vocational Education should be broadened with liberal and general education.
- Talented resource persons should be attracted to be teachers in Technical and Vocational Education. Teachers should be given decent pay packages and the society should respect these builders of the youth.
- Regular practical training sessions and workshops should be effectively organised. Young enterprises need to be given practical knowledge of starting industries and setting up business firms.
- Part time instructions should be provided to persons employed in jobs in order to improve quality of work. Refresher courses may be organised with a view to acquaint the people in service with the recent development of knowledge in the field of science and technology.
- Collaborate with NGOs, industries to provide practical skills to the students.
- Work with The National Council of Educational Research and Training (NCERT) and/or State Councils of Educational Research and Training (SCERTS) to create supplementary educational materials for vocational education.
- Appropriate training modules for the teachers should be developed.
- Conduct assessment of all vocational education courses, jointly with the partners that are providing the practical skills training to the students.
- Recognition of prior learning of the students to reduce dropouts.

## National Education Policy 2020 — A Fresh Approach to Vocational Education

- As the most basic and important step, vocational education must be improved. This must be on all dimensions – teacher development and recruitment, curriculum, and infrastructure.
- Vocational education must not be developed separately from 'mainstream' education.
- There must also be easy mobility across vocational and general academic streams, through clear equivalence of qualifications/certifications and credit structures.
- All school students must receive vocational education in at least one vocation during Grades 9-12.
- Students will choose from among a selection of courses that their schools will offer, on the basis of the availability of hands-on training facilities and job opportunities in the region.
- HEIs will also offer vocational courses that are integrated into the undergraduate education programmes.
- A separate National Committee for the Integration of Vocational Education (NCIVE) will need to be set up, consisting of members from across ministries, to review the long term goals outlined here and to work out the steps that need to be taken towards achieving them.

- The NCIVE will work out the modalities for the disbursement of these funds and the processes for monitoring progress.
- Skill gap analysis and mapping of local opportunities.
- Data gathering, MIS and technology support for the rollout of vocational education.

***Areas of Special Focus***

- Production, development and management of various goods and services;
- Textiles and embroidery to the grand architecture of historic buildings;
- Enhancing the work of local crafts persons and artisans;
- Development of local knowledge systems in medicine to myriad varieties of art and handicrafts; and
- Water conservation.

In order to operationalise the fresh approach to Vocational Education, the National Education Policy 2020 envisages the following:

- Relevant and meaningful integration of vocational education into school and higher education through skills analysis and mapping of local opportunities, along with efforts to formalise the capabilities of youth already in the workforce through mechanisms like RPL, adult education, online learning, etc.
- Network of ministries, bodies/agencies and situations as well as local industries and individuals in an effort to optimise the learning and T-exposure of students at all stages.
- Adequate investment in developing infrastructure, as well as recruiting, preparing and supporting individuals to transact vocational education effectively.
- Maintenance of databases and study of possible models of vocational education which can be applied in our context.
- Ensuring mobility of learners across institutions and streams, through alignment with international standards, and curricula and assessment aligned to NSQE.
- Enhanced capacity of vocational education particularly at the higher education stage, and in rural and tribal areas.
- Integration of work of local crafts persons and artisans into the curriculum, along with measures to disseminate their work more widely.

NPE 2020 draft carefully examines the requirement of sustainable and a just society. It highlights the need of liberal education with emotional quotient for successful impact. It emphasises that professional education must seek to develop individuals with a capacity to combine a strong foundation of theoretical knowledge and specific competencies; curriculum for vocational education must be able to connect theory to practice, students must develop an understanding of how their profession impacts the society, students must develop generic competencies such as decision-making, critical thinking, problem-solving and communication skills, and vocational and professional education should be an ethical compass and disposition to be constructive and contributing citizens livestock. Similarly, technical education includes degree and diploma programmes in engineering, technology, management, architecture, town planning, pharmacy, hotel management and catering technology while health care education includes a whole host of allied health staff such as radiologists, laboratory technicians, physiologists, home caregivers for the elderly, and many others that total up to a projected 80 million jobs worldwide by 2030 according to WHO. Many of these sectors are critical to India's wellbeing and overall development, so the very large target of vocational education must be addressed in multiple ways. Government, employers, the respective Sector Skill Councils (SSCs) and all other stakeholders must work together to address a large part of this target. The role of educational institutes providing skill based education will be critical. Thus, NPE should provide amicable solutions to the existing problems and also makes possible efforts towards an employable sustainable society.

### Role of Universities in Imparting Vocational Education and Training

India has one of the largest technical manpower in the world. However, compared to its population it is not significant and there is a tremendous scope of improvement in this area. In India, the emphasis has been on general education, with vocational education at the receiving end. This has resulted in a large number of educated people remaining unemployed. This phenomenon has now been recognised by the planners and hence there is a greater thrust on vocationalisation of education. Another shortcoming in the area of technical and vocational education is that till now, the number of engineers graduating is more than the diploma holders. This is creating an imbalance, as more workers are required at the lower level. India is in transition to a knowledge-based economy and its competitive edge will be determined by the abilities of its people to create, share and use knowledge more effectively. This transition will require India to develop workers into knowledge workers who will be more flexible, analytical, adaptable and multi skilled (Goel, 2000). In the new knowledge economy, the skill sets will include professional, managerial, operational, behavioural, inter personal and inter functional skills. To do this, the workforce of the nation must have education and training that equips them for the labour market. One of the sources of the skilled workforce is the Vocational Education and Training (VET) system.

### Vocational Education and Training in India

In a globalised economy, a large pool of skilled workers is indispensable for attracting foreign direct investment. Developing skilled workers enhances the efficiency and flexibility of the labour market; skill bottlenecks are reduced, skilled workers are more easily absorbed into the economy, and their job mobility is improved. It is crucial to invest in quality secondary and tertiary education and in Vocational Education and Training (VET) if India's economy is to develop and remain competitive in the world markets. For this majority group, access to secondary education and VET is crucial and for most of them secondary education and VET will be the last stage of their formal schooling. An effective school to work transition for these young people, made possible by higher quality secondary and tertiary education and VET, will improve their employment prospects and lifetime earnings (NIOS, 2012).

India lags far behind in imparting skill training as compared to other countries. Only 10% of the total workforce in the country receives some kind of skill training (2% with formal training and eight per cent with informal training). Further, 80% of the entrants into the workforce do not have the opportunity for skill training (ILO, 2011, p.7). The accelerated economic growth has increased the demand for skilled manpower that has highlighted the shortage of skilled manpower in the country. Employees worldwide state a variety of reasons for their inability to fill in jobs. India is one among the top countries in which employers are facing difficulty in filling up the jobs, For India, the difficulty to fill up the jobs is 48%, which is above the global standard of 34% in 2012. The lack of available applicants, shortage of hard skills and shortage of suitable employability, including soft skills, is some of the key reasons in finding a suitable candidate for available jobs in the country (FICCI, 2012, p.3).

According to the National Sample Survey Organisation (NSSO) in 2004-05, only about 26 million (about 6%) of the total workforce (459 million) is in the organised sector and about 433 million (about 94%) is engaged in unorganised sector in India. The World Economic Forum indicates that only 25% of the total Indian professionals are considered employable by the organised sector. The unorganised sector is not supported by any structured skill development and training system of acquiring or upgrading skills. The skill formation takes place through informal channels such as family occupations, on-the-job training under master craftsmen with no linkages to formal education training and certification (FICCI, 2012, p.3).

## Importance of Vocational Education and Training

Vocational Education and Training (VET) is an important element of the nation's education initiative. For Vocational Education to play its part effectively in the changing national context there is an urgent need to redefine the critical elements of imparting vocational education and training to make them flexible, contemporary, relevant, inclusive and creative. The Government is well aware of the important role of vocational education and has already taken a number of important initiatives in this area (Mujumdar, 2011). The Report of the Education Commission (Kothari, 1964-66) set a number of goals to be pursued; one of them was "to vocationalise Secondary Education". Today the training provided in the VET institutions in India is not aligned to the demand for skills from the labour market. Evidence for this mismatch exists in the skill shortages for different sectors of the economy on the one hand, and the high unemployment level of VET graduates on the other. Industry surveys such as the 'Survey on emerging skill shortages in the Indian Industry (2007) conducted by FICCI show that significant skill gaps exist in key sectors where one of them is education (FICCI, 2007). The major weakness of the present education system is the "dysfunctional linkage between education and the world of work" (CRRID, 1985). The introduction of Socially Useful Productive Work (SUPW) as third dimension with a hope "to occupy the central place in the school to curriculum" (CRRID, 1985) has been reduced to a ritual and teachers were unable to tune themselves with the original conceptual basis of the SUPW. Basic of education is regarded by urban middle-class parents as suitable for the rural children and not for their children. Thus, even with the government efforts to strengthen vocational education, the country has huge shortage of skilled people and this is hampering the growth of service and manufacturing sectors (Gore, 1995).

When India is referred to as a 'Young Nation with 28 million population of youth being added every year, only about 2.5 million vocational training seats are available in the country whereas about 12.8 million persons enter the labour market every year. About 90 per cent of employment opportunities require vocational skills, something that is not being imparted on a large scale in schools and colleges. The major reforms proposed for bringing about necessary 'flexibility in the vocational courses offered and development of 'modular competency based curricula' in collaboration with industry to suit the needs of both target groups and the employers (industry) will be useful in reducing the shortage of skilled manpower. It would be beneficial if large number of secondary school children, who have the inclination for vocational education but are compelled to join formal secondary schooling, to be channelised into vocational education. This would lead to a system of education which is more meaningful and relevant in the local context. Gradually the ambit would be expanded to address the needs and aspirations of those engaged in traditional means of livelihoods too. The contribution of such educated youth would boost the state of the Indian economy through the thrust of the Government on universalisation of secondary education, skill development and social justice through inclusive education and training.

### Incorporating Vocational Education and Training within Mainstream by the University (NKC, 2008)

Universities can increase the flexibility of VET within the mainstream education system through the following steps:

- Aspects of general education (such as numeracy skills, etc.) should be retained in VET as far as possible to enable students to return to mainstream education at a later stage.
- Courses in training institutes/polytechnics should have distinct tracks for students of different educational attainments.

- Entry requirements for certain trades should reflect the requirement of the trade (as appropriate, for instance the entry requirement of Class X could be relaxed to Class VIII in some cases).
- Students should be permitted multiple entry and exit options in the vocational education stream.
- Links should be established between the vocational education stream and school education as well as higher education.
- Courses devoted to certain skills training at the primary and secondary level should be introduced in all schools/colleges.
- Vocational training should be made available in various literacy and adult education schemes.
- Schemes for lifelong skill upgradation, through short training programmes, should be introduced.
- There should be a provision for generating a cadre of multi-skilled persons.

## Basics of Vocational Education Training

- Vocational training in India is provided on a fulltime as well as part time basis.
- India is a pioneer in vocational training in Film and Television, and Information Technology.
- Often the curriculum for the courses is prepared after taking suggestions from the local employers.
- These types of courses are mostly certified or diploma courses.
- Vocational education training institutes impart graduation and post-graduation courses to students.
- The best part of these institutes is that even working people can join the course, and even select the timings as per their convenience and nature of job.
- Financial aid is also often provided to students who are economically weak.
- According to the National Skills Development Commission (NSDC) report, India will need 83 million skilled workers across different industry verticals by 2015. Unfortunately, with our current training capacity India will produce only three million!!
- In India, vocational education is imparted through Industrial Training Institutes (ITIs) and polytechnics.
- The skill shortage in the Indian economy today is largely due to neglect of vocational education.

## Major Challenges and Issues in Vocational Education and Training

- Low priority for Vocational Education
- Shortage of trained teachers and trainers

- Inadequate linkages with Industries
- Absence of a National Competency Testing and Accreditation system
- Lack of infrastructure – building, modern equipment and raw materials
- Inadequate or non-coverage of trades in service sector which has higher employment potential
- Lack of equivalence for employment purposes
- Lack of vertical mobility
- Inflexible curriculum
- Lack of convergence between various agencies
- Lack of overall social recognition.

## Problem Areas in Vocational Education and Training System

Through the study of the prevalent Vocational Education System in India, the following problem areas have been identified:

1. There is a high dropout rate at Secondary level. There are 220 million children who go to school in India. Of these only around 12% students reach university. A large part of the 18-24 years age group in India has never been able to reach college. Comparing India to countries with similar income levels – India does not under perform in primary education but has a comparative deficit in secondary education.
2. Vocational Education is presently offered at Grades 11th, 12th – however students reaching this Grade aspire for higher education. Since the present system does not allow vertical mobility – skills obtained are lost. Enrolment in Grades 11th and 12th of vocational education is only three per cent of students at upper secondary level. About 6,800 schools enrol 400,000 students in vocational education schemes utilising only 40% of the available student capacity in these schools.
3. International experience suggests that what employers mostly want are young workers with strong basic academic skills and not just vocational skills. The present system does not emphasise general academic skills. The relative wages of workers with secondary education are increasing.
4. Private and industry participation is lacking. There are no incentives for private players to enter the field of vocational education.
5. Present regulations are very rigid. In-service training is required but not prevalent today. There is no opportunity for continuous skill upgradation,
6. There is a lack of experienced and qualified teachers to train students on vocational skills. In foreign countries, Bachelor of Vocational Education (BVE) is often a mandatory qualification for teachers. However, in India no specific qualifications are being imparted for vocational education teachers.
7. Vocationalisation at all levels has not been successful. Poor quality of training is not in line with industry needs.

8. There is no definite path for vocational students to move from one level/sector to another level/sector. Mobility is not defined and hence students do not have a clear path in vocational education,
9. No clear policy or system of vocational education leading to certification/degrees presently available for the unorganised/informal sector. No credit system has been formulated for the same. Over 90% of employment in India is in the informal sector. JSS offers 255 types of vocational courses to 1.5 million people, Community Polytechnics train about 450,000 people within communities annually and NIOS offers 85 courses through 700 providers. None of these programmes have been rigorously evaluated till date.
10. Expansion of vocational sector is happening without consideration for present problems.

### Government Initiatives: National Vocational Qualification Framework

To stimulate and support reforms in skills development and to facilitate nationally standardised and acceptable, international comparability of qualifications, a "National Vocational Qualifications Framework" is being established by the Central Government. Central Advisory Board of Education (CABE) has resolved to set up an inter-ministerial group which would also include representatives of State Governments to develop guidelines for such a National Framework. The unified system of national qualification will cover schools, vocational education and training institutions and higher education sector. NVQF will be based on nationally recognised occupational standards with a detailed listing of all major activities that a worker must perform in the occupation or competency standards, a detailed listing of the knowledge, skills and attitude that a worker should possess to perform a task written by the particular employment-led sector skills council.

### Recommendations regarding Vocational Education

1. A national level Board for vocational education should be established, called as National Board for Vocational Education.
2. A National Vocational Policy should be formulated. The policy should establish equivalence for degrees, diplomas and certifications in the vocational education sector for lateral and vertical mobility across various learning sectors, that is secondary, vocational and higher education.
3. National Vocational Assessment and Accreditation Council should be established to formulate a regulatory and quality/standards framework.
4. SSC (vocational) or its equivalent 10th grade certification in vocational stream should be created on similar lines as HSC (Vocational) at both national and state levels. Vocational Stream should be introduced at 8th Grade through Bivalent Schools which may provide both conventional

and vocational streams of education at secondary level. Statistics reveal that employers prefer students with some general education skills in addition to vocational skills. Thus, in all schemes related to SSC (Vocational) general education courses should be emphasised, e.g., Problem-solving, English, Soft Skills, Business Management, etc.

5. To ensure vertical mobility, ITIs, MSBVs, Community Colleges and other State Vocational Education Institutions may be granted recognition and accreditation from the respective State Board for Vocational Education to award SSC (Vocational) certification. Vocational Education Providers, Community Colleges, JSS, CP's, Vocational Junior Colleges may also be allowed to award Diplomas and Associate Degrees in addition to HSC (Vocational) certification. Students from Vocational Institutions can be given opportunity for lateral mobility into conventional stream by providing bridge (preparatory) courses.
6. Private Participation from Industry and other players must be encouraged and is critical for the success of the vocational education growth in India. Industry participation must be at all levels especially in Governance, Curriculum Design, Placements and Funding, Monitoring Outcome.
7. Industry participation shall be sought on the Board of Management. Industry representatives will be involved in governance and curriculum design. Production-oriented Research and Innovation Labs will be setup in collaboration with Industry to promote regional economic growth. Industry collaboration shall be sought for funding, placements and apprenticeship for students. Department of In-Service Training shall be set up to encourage industry to send employees for regular skill development and upgradation (this will also gain additional income for teachers).
8. Teachers training will be given special emphasis by the University. The Vocational University shall set up a separate department for Teachers Training and Development in order to build teaching resources and research component. Continuous teacher training programmes shall be emphasised by the University Management. A separate degree called Bachelor in Vocational Education (BVEd) or BEd with specialisation in vocational education is proposed to be introduced. This would be a mandatory requirement for hiring teachers for vocational education and training.

## Benefits of Vocational Training

*Enhances Skills and knowledge*: Vocational education provides job specific skills and contributes to career success. It imparts specialised knowledge, which is the need of the hour today.

*Promotes Entrepreneurship*: In certain cases, the completion of this sort of course provides the learner with a license to allow them to start working immediately. The individual is also equipped enough to start his own business.

*Offers a wide Range of Options*: It prepares the youth for a vocation of their own choice and interest by providing a diverse range of subjects.

*Builds up a Formidable Work Force of International Quality* which would be in demand not only in India but also in all other countries. In India, only IT training is world class. In the manufacturing and service sector, there is worldwide shortage.

*Demand for Skilled Men*: A recent study by global HR consultancy Manpower Inc. says that 41 per cent of employers worldwide are having difficulty filling positions due to lack of suitable talent in their markets. We need millions of trained people in agriculture, floriculture, horticulture, sericulture, fishery, healthcare, tourism and in other manufacturing sectors.

*Easy Employment*: It is often seen that employers prefer to hire a student who has done a vocational course rather than a college pass out, as by doing a vocational course, a student is trained specifically for a particular job. Thus, the student gets a job faster, is able to support and provide for his family and self, becoming a responsible citizen of the society instead of an unproductive burden.

*A Way to Earn Early*: With the changing face of technology, the world requires an individual to be specialised in a particular skill. Only a person who is expert in a particular field can get a good job. Vocational education training helps them to become independent at a particular age. After completing a vocational course, the student already possesses the right temperament, skills, qualities and education for the job.

*Helps to Develop the Economy*: Vocational Training provides an instrument for the promotion of worker employability through the enhancement of human capital and for productivity improvement and competitiveness at the level of the firm or nation. Manpower shortages can cripple economic growth. It can escalate wage rates, thereby reducing the competitiveness of the country.

*Reduces Unemployment* by supplying world-class skilled people. Vocational courses increase the number of small businesses, which further increase employment, thus reducing the stress on the government to provide jobs for the unemployed.

*Serves as an Alternative* to those who cannot afford to take a three-year break to pursue a college degree. The time duration for a vocational course is less and the skills which are imparted to the students are highly adequate

*Lesser Education Costs*: It is the most effective way to gain the right career resources in exchange of minimum amount which costs much less than the regular forms of learning in colleges.

*Flexible Form of Learning*: They are often provided by various community colleges with proper learning infrastructure. Some organisations also use online education system to help students learn at their own convenience. It is suitable for working people also as they can select the timings as per their convenience and nature of job. The vocational institutes allow the students to study online and attend either evening or morning classes.

*Financial Aids*: are also readily available from various public and private sectors for these types of courses. Government funding is also offered to students of vocational training in certain countries.

*Contributes to National Development*: Enhancing the employability of a student is extremely important since it will not only help in youth empowerment, but also contributes to national development.

*More Practical-oriented*: Vocational courses offer the students not just classroom learning but also hands-on practical training in various aspects like customer relationship, people management, personality development etc. are in top demand now.

*Offers a wide Range of Job Opportunities*: Retail, Hospitality and BFSI are the fastest growing sectors and would need 20 million skilled candidates by 2015. Specialised sectors like Auto and Hair and Beauty are projected to need five million resources while the construction sector alone will require over 15 million skilled workers.

## Conclusion

Vocational Training and Education (VET) is a sure way to add a new dimension to the career for a successful future. These courses enhance the employability of a student and are vital as they not only help in youth empowerment, but also contribute to national development. Today, it has become important for employees in every sector. Vocational courses must be seen as a necessary addition to the regular school or graduate education since the college education will only provide knowledge enhancement while the Vocational courses gives training to get a job and start a successful career. Vocational courses can also be incorporated in regular college environment, wherein the student will have easier access to the skills, training, and can complete the course easily along with his graduation. Vocational education is also as good as college education. Vocational training can be considered as a launch pad for a career that can lead to participants becoming masters in their field. Vocational training is a must and should be compulsory as it provides the learner with practical knowledge of the theoretical concepts learned in school. Vocational training should be considered as a stepping-stone to success. This type of knowledge is surely going to be an enabler to help India shine in the future years.

# 16

# Women Education Perspective

Promotion of gender equality in education is essential for human resource development. By educating a woman you educate the whole family. Given that a woman has the responsibility of the whole family on herself, an educated woman is better capable of taking care of the health, nutrition, and education of her children, and be more of an active agent in the social and economic development of the country. It is evident that economic success everywhere is based on educational success. Literacy is the basic building block of education. It is a basic component of social cohesion and national identity. It leads to an improvement in the depth and quality of public opinion. No society has ever liberated itself economically, politically, or socially without a sound base of educated women. Education has a direct impact on women empowerment as it creates in them awareness about their rights, their capabilities, and the choices and opportunities available to them. Studies have indicated that there is a strong correlation between female education and developmental indicators.

## Importance of Women Education

The importance of women's education is manifold:

- Economic development and prosperity: Education will empower women to come forward and contribute towards the development and prosperity of the country.
- Economic empowerment: As long as women remain backward and economically dependent on men, their helpless condition cannot be changed. Economic empowerment and independence will only come through proper education and employment of women.
- Improved life: Education helps us to live a good life. A properly educated woman's identity as an individual would never get lost. She can read and learn about her rights, ensuring that her rights are not trodden on. The life and condition of women would improve a lot, if we take a broad outlook in the field of female education.
- Improved health: Educated girls and women are aware of the importance of health and hygiene. Through health education, they are empowered to lead a healthy lifestyle. An educated mother can take better care of both herself and her baby.
- Dignity and Honour: Educated women are now treated with dignity and honour. They become a source of inspiration for millions of young girls who make them their role models.

- Justice: Educated women are better informed of their rights for justice. Such knowledge is likely to eventually lead to a decline in instances of violence and injustice against women such as dowry, forced prostitution, child marriage, female foeticide, etc.
- Option to choose a profession of her choice: Educated women can be highly successful in various professional fields. A girl child should get equal opportunity for education, so that she can plan to become a successful doctor, engineer, nurse, air-hostess, chef or choose a profession of her choice.
- Alleviate poverty: Women education is prerequisite to alleviate poverty. Women need to take equal burden of the mass of task of eliminating poverty. This would demand massive contribution from educated women. There cannot be much social and economic change unless girls and women are given their rights for education.

## National Policy on Education 1986

National policy on education (NPE), 1986 and its Programme of Action (POA) gave high priority to gender equality and committed the entire educational system to work for women's empowerment. The National Perspective Plan (1988–2000) reiterates this point of view and states that women themselves must overcome their handicaps. Thus, there has been a careful articulation of education for equality for women, which is reflected in the educational policy discourse. Central and state governments attached a lot of significance to actually operationalising the NPE's Programme of Action. In a series of regional meetings with the state governments, consensus emerged that a special review of gender concerns was built into all educational processes. Monitoring committees for women's/girl's education at the Ministry of Human Resource Development level, and also state level were formed to monitor the indicators of gender concerns in all policies and projects.

### *Women Empowerment*

The National Policy on Education (NPE) is a landmark in the approach to women's education when it proclaims: "The education system will play a positive interventionist role in the empowerment of women. It will foster the development of new values through redesign curricula, textbooks, training and orientation of teachers, decision makers, and administrators." The programme implementation document explains women's empowerment through collective reflection and decision-making. For the higher education needs to take responsibility for:

- Cultivation of positive self-image and self-confidence
- Developing capacity for critical thinking
- Achieving group cohesion and fostering decision-making and action
- Providing women's centres in agriculture and home science colleges
- Providing continuing education and correspondence centres for organising vocational and literacy skills

- Revamping the Industrial Training Institutes (ITIs) in terms of diversification of trades and courses, keeping in view the job potential, facilities for vocational counselling, imparting information about credit, banking, entrepreneurial development and, access to women's technical education
- Providing women's studies research centre direction to identify issues, areas of improvement, organise seminars and workshops to discuss and analyse women related issues, disseminate information, and encourage interaction with students and the general public through the media
- Providing classes on legal literacy, programmes for women's socio-economic development delivered via media, adult education, information and training support
- A more relevant and responsive curriculum catering to the cultural and occupational needs of women
- Meeting the expenses of higher education for the rural, backward sections with incentives like scholarships and fee waiver
- Meeting the requirement of achieving full integration of women within the democratic and developmental efforts of the country.

The concept of women empowerment was introduced at the women conference in 1985 at Nairobi. Empowerment is defined as the expansion in women's ability and freedom to make the strategic choices: a process that occurs over time and involves women as agents who have the ability to formulate choices, control resources, and take decisions affecting important life outcomes. The most common explanation of women's empowerment is the ability to exercise full control over one's actions.

The Programme of Action, 1992 has comprehensively given the parameters of empowerment of women mentioned below:

- Enhance self-esteem and self confidence in women
- Build a positive image of women by recognising their contribution to the society, polity and economy
- Develop in them an ability to think critically
- Foster decision-making and action through collective process
- Enable women to make informed choices in areas like education, employment and help especially reproductive health
- Ensuring full participation in the development process
- Provide information, knowledge and skill for economic independence
- Enhance access to legal literacy and information related to their rights and entitlements in society with a view to enhance their participation on unequal flooring in all areas.

Fourth world conference on Women held in Beijing in 1995 recognised that women literacy is a key to empowering women's participation in decision-making in society and improving families' well-being. In addition, the United Nations has articulated the Millennium Development Goals (MDGs) which include goals for improved education, gender equality, and women's empowerment. The MDGs emphasise education's essential role in building democratic societies, and creating a foundation for sustained economic growth. Education is an important tool for promoting gender equality, and advancement of female youth in socio- economic and political development of the nation.

## Factors of Gender Inequality in Higher Education

The following are the dominant factors of gender inequality in enrolment in different levels of higher education and participation in teaching posts of higher education institutes in India:

- The education research literature has focused on the relative contributions of both social background and educational institutional environment to learning and academic achievement. In the United States, the Coleman report from 1966 was among the first to establish the importance of student's family backgrounds to the academic success of children.
- Community and family attitudes regarding the education of girls are embedded in cultural norms and are influenced by marriage and kinship pattens which may lead parents to invest more emotional and financial resources in educating sons rather than daughters.
- In addition, differences in educational investment may result from parents' reliance upon a son's support in old age, leading to a differential investment in the child who would be responsible for the parents' financial security as they grow.
- Several factors influence negative attitudes toward the education of girls. One concern relates to savings for dowry, which may limit the amount of funds that parents have to spend on daughters' education.
- Negative cultural and societal attitudes, different standards – roles for boys and girls, economic reasons like – lack of resources, distance from home, lack of facilities in educational institutes for girls, lack of female teachers, lack of security both in and outside the institutes, curriculum not relevant and flexible, gender stereotyping in curriculum gender, unfriendly classroom environment, early marriage and child bearing, absence of women role models, fear of deterioration of social structure, are the most frequently quoted stumbling blocks to female participation in higher education.

## Blocks to Female Participation in Higher Education

- Socialisation within the family
- Students' family backgrounds to the academic success of children
- Community and family attitudes regarding the education of girls

- Differential investment in child's education results from parents' reliance upon a son's support in old age
- Negative attitudes toward the education of girls are savings for dowry which may limit the amount of funds parents spend on daughters' education
- Negative cultural and social societal attitudes
- Different standard roles for boys and girls
- Economic reasons like lack of resources, distance from home, lack of facilities and educational institutes for girls, lack of female teachers, lack of security both in and outside the institute
- Curriculum not relevant and flexible, gender stereotyping in curriculum, gender unfriendly classroom environment
- Early marriage and childbearing, absence of women role model, fear of deterioration of social structure.

### Towards Gender Equality

Gender mainstreaming is a globally accepted strategy for promoting gender equality. It is a process rather than a goal of creating knowledge and awareness of and responsibility for gender equality among all education professionals engaged in tertiary education. It is not an end in itself but a strategy, an approach, a means to achieve the goal of gender equality in higher education institutions through sensitisation and educating key stakeholders that the costs of women's marginalisation and gender inequalities are borne by all in the education sector as a whole (from pre-primary to tertiary and life-long learning). Mainstreaming involves ensuring that gender perspectives and attention to the goal of gender equality are central to all activities – education policy, curriculum, research, advocacy, resource allocation, facilities and planning, implementation and monitoring of tertiary education programmes.

- Improved health: Educated girls and women are aware of the importance of health and hygiene. Through health education, they are empowered to lead a healthy lifestyle. An educated mother can take better care of both herself and her baby.
- Dignity and honour: Educated women are now treated with dignity and honour. They become a source of inspiration for millions of young girls, who make them their role models.
- Justice: Educated women are better informed of their rights for justice. Such knowledge is likely to eventually lead to a decline in instances of violence and injustice against women such as dowry, forced-prostitution, child-marriage, female foeticide, etc.
- Option to choose a profession of her choice: Educated women can be highly successful in various professional fields. A girl-child should get equal opportunity for education, so that she can plan to become a successful doctor, engineer, nurse, airhostess, cook, or choose a profession of her choice.

- Alleviate poverty: Women education is a pre-requisite to alleviate poverty. Women need to take equal burden of the massive task of eliminating poverty. This would demand massive contribution from educated women. There cannot be much social and economic change unless girls and women are given their rights for education.

## High Priority to Gender Equality in National Policy on Education

National Policy on Education (NPE), 1986 and its Programme of Action (POA) gave high priority to gender equality.

### *Education as Change Agent*

The National Policy on Education, 1986, viewed education as a premier instrument for groups divided by class, caste, and other forms of historic oppression. It regarded education as an agent of basic change in the status of women. It stated that the national education system would play a positive, interventionist role in the empowerment of women. It would also foster the development of new values, through redesigned curricula, textbooks, decision makers and administrators and active involvement of educational institution. It also stated that women's studies would be promoted as a part of various courses and educational institutions would be encouraged to take up active programmes to further women's development.

### *National Commission for Women*

National Commission for Women is a statutory body constituted in 1992 with several functions which include the following:

- to examine all matters relating to the safeguards provided for women in the Constitution and other laws
- to recommend to Government measures for the effective implementation of safeguards for improving the condition of women
- to review all laws and to point out inadequacies and shortcomings in them
- to look into complaints about deprivation of women's rights and non-implementation of policy decisions
- to organise or sponsor special studies or investigations into specific problems, discriminations and atrocities against women and to suggest action for their removal

As agreed, at the 4th World Conference at Beijing, the Government of India evolved National Policy for Empowerment of Women in 2001:

The goal of the Policy was to bring about the advancement, development and empowerment of women. Specifically, the objectives of this Policy included:

- Creating an environment through positive economic and social policies for full development of women to enable them to realise their full potential;

- De jure and de facto enjoyment of all human rights and fundamental freedoms by women on equal basis with men in all spheres – political, economic, social, cultural and civil;
- Equal access to participation and decision-making of women in social, political and economic life of the nation;
- Equal access to women to health care, quality education at all levels, career and vocational guidance, employment, equal remuneration, occupational health and safety, social security and public office etc.;
- Strengthening legal system aimed at elimination of all forms of discrimination against women;
- Changing societal attitudes and community practices by active participation, involvement of both men and women;
- Mainstreaming a gender perspective in the development process;
- Elimination of discrimination and all forms of violence against women and the girl-child; and
- Building and strengthening partnerships with civil society, particularly women's organisations.

Though some efforts have been made to translate policy into action, mostly the Policy remained as Policy on the paper.

### Constitutional Position

The Constitution of India recognises each citizen as equal and guarantees the Right to Equality under the Fundamental Rights. Right to Equality includes equality before the law, prohibition of discrimination on grounds of religion, race, caste, gender or place of birth, equality of opportunity in matters of employment and other socio-economic rights. The makers of the Constitution included the Right to Equality in the Fundamental Rights because they envisaged a society where each will be treated as equal irrespective of their individual identities. Unfortunately, even after 74 years of independence we have a long way to go in terms of achieving the equality that the makers of the Constitution envisaged. We witness rampant poverty, illiteracy, huge urban-rural divide, gender-based discrimination and violence, regional disparities among other forms of deprivation. Under the combined effects of commercialisation, urbanisation, migration and employment, significant changes are taking place in India's process of modernisation. One of the significant changes is the emergence of a population of women in education and in teaching positions as faculty member in education institutes that may influence the ways in which women perceive their identity.

### Literacy Rate — Trends since Independence

India has the dubious distinction of having one of the world's highest rates of adult illiteracy. According to the 2011 Census of India, the overall rate of literacy is 74.04 per cent. But breaking up the national average reveals that while the rate of literacy for men is 82.14 per cent, for women it is 65.46 per cent. This means that more than one-fourth of the country's population is still illiterate, and within that figure, nearly one-fifth of males are illiterate compared with more than one-third of females. That there is a slow rate of growth of female literacy compared with male literacy is a matter of grave concern. An extremely positive development in the decade of 2001-2011 is that the gap of 21.59 percentage points recorded between male and female literacy rates in 2001 Census has reduced to 16.68 percentage points in 2011. Despite the number of efforts made at national and international levels, there exist a significant number of illiterate women in society, a disturbing factor for all development efforts. Female literacy is important as it is a force multiplier for the social development of a country. Illiteracy retards the development of an individual, society and the country.

Literacy plays a significant role in reducing gender inequality.

### *Present Status*

Even after 74 years of independence, women's education has not achieved the desired results despite many efforts. The reasons for this failure are:

- A major section of Indian society does not give importance to girl education, because of their restricted mindset, conservative norms, and underdeveloped mentality.
- Girls are not allowed to take decisions for themselves or step out from their homes, because of social discrimination in a male-dominated society.
- Some girls are unable to go to school as they participate in agricultural and household chores.
- With education getting costlier day by day, people prefer to educate their boys rather than their girls, despite numerous facilities provided by the government.
- Most of the India's population lives in villages. The guardians are hesitant about sending their girls to school due to lack of basic facilities such as non-availability of hygienic water, no arrangement for separate sanitary facility for girls in schools.

Some of the areas of gender studies that need deliberation and have to be addressed are:

- Reduce gender disparities, and all forms of discrimination in education at all levels in rural, semi-urban, and urban contexts.
- Address gender bias and stereotypes in the content and process of education.
- Link knowledge, understanding, skills, and their application to real life situations so that metamorphic social changes are initiated in the society.
- Combat patriarchy by focusing on new and emerging roles taken up by women in different fields.

- Link development agenda with the girl child's life, education, and livelihood.
- Capacity building of girls and women with a judicious mix of new emerging technologies.
- Proactive approach in all sectors of the economy to ensure safety and security of women.
- Undertake regional research studies on barriers to girls' education and empowerment.

## Distance Education

To overcome the rigidities, compulsions, and limitations of the formal system of education, new efforts are made to develop non-formal education system. Women, who mostly remained outside the formal system, are expected to be the major beneficiaries of distance education, which is free from the constraints of time, place, and pace education. Distance education is a home-based and learner-centred form.

In order to assess the impact of distance education on women, their motivation, persistence, and the success rate of distance learners, Mother Teresa Women's University School of Distance Education conducted a study, which revealed the following impact on women learners:

- Gained confidence.
- Improved their career opportunities.
- Achieved greater degree of satisfaction.
- Updated their skills.
- Provided second chance to dropouts.
- Acquired new knowledge.
- Changes occurred in the socialisation pattern of children.
- Acquired better decision-making capacity.
- Increased respect for family and community.
- Gave opportunities for networking and communication.
- Broadened vision.
- Gave freedom and flexibility to learners.
- Assisted in facing challenges in life.
- Increased literacy rate of state and country.

A review of research in distance education recommends the following for the women's wider utility of distance education:

1. Continuous efforts to reduce and eliminate barriers that prevent and restrict women's participation in learning activities.
2. Develop courses that build upon women's diverse experience, but do not impose rigid external expectations, and arbitrary requirements.
3. Recognise that student learning environments comprise the home and local centres from which women study, as well as the educational institutions. This means that "education like technology has to be adapted to local circumstances".

4. Create supportive and safe environments in distance education contexts. Educators need to be sensitive to women's personal and unique circumstances and need to investigate ways to help students develop effective support systems.
5. Increase the number of women's studies courses available via distance learning and ensure that feminist perspectives are incorporated into curriculum in other disciplines.
6. De-emphasise the utility of prescribed materials to promote the assumption that course materials are not the course per se. Women students need opportunities to make real and significant choices regarding their learning goals and activities.
7. Conduct research into the types and levels of interaction essential to feminist learning in distance education contexts. Collect empirical data about actual interactions and breaks that student and tutors experience in distance learning. The nature and prevalence of the social aspects of learning essential to feminist learning also require specific investigation in distance settings.
8. Provide tutors employed for feminist distance courses with useful, appropriate training. Orientation activities need to include skills training in telephone and teleconference technologies, and their applications in such trainings should have as its focus effective use of communication strategies and feminist processes for facilitating adult learning in distance settings.

## National Education Policy 2020 -- Vibrant Bharat

Education is the fundamental right to achieve human potential. There is a need to provide education to all sections of society, irrespective of caste, creed, gender, religion etc. The new National Education Policy 2020 states that gender-based bias often affects an individual's ability to develop and hampers the nation's growth, innovation and progress.

According to the Census, the overall literacy rate in 2011 in India was 73 per cent, but women's literacy rate was only 65 per cent. There exists a gender gap of around 16 per cent between male and female literacy rates. This gender split is higher in rural areas. The rural female literacy rate is only 57 per cent, while the rural male literacy rate is 77 per cent. However, according to the All-India Survey on Higher Education (AISHE) report, 2018-19, the gender gap in the country has narrowed over the past few years, after several new policy interventions by the current government. The female students constitutes almost half (approx. 48.6 per cent) of the total number of enrollments in higher education. Nevertheless, there is a long way to go to bring gender parity. The following should be addressed:

- Gender Disparity in Society
- Gender Disparity in School Curriculum
- Dropouts in Girls

- Gender Disparity in Employability
- Multi-layered Discrimination in Case of Marginalised Communities

To tackle the above subjects and articulate an India-centric educational system, the NEP 2020 policy has prescribed to approach gender as a cross-cutting priority to achieve gender equality in education with the partnership of states and local community organisations. The GOI will constitute a 'Gender Inclusion Fund' to provide quality and equitable education to all girls. The fund will focus on ensuring 100 per cent enrollment of girls in schools and a record participation rate in higher education, decrease gender gaps at all levels, practice gender equity and inclusion in society, and improve the leadership capacity of girls through positive civil dialogues.

The policy will emphasise the number of women on leading positions of the institution, including principals, teachers, wardens, physical instructors and other staff. To decrease the gender imbalance among teachers (especially in some rural areas), alternate pathways for female teacher recruitment will be introduced without compromising on merit and qualification, both educational and professional. NEP 2020 will focus on the safety and security of school-going girls both inside and outside the campus.

Schools have to ensure harassment, discrimination against women, and domineer free campus before enlisting for yearly accreditation. This will increase the attendance of girl children in the classroom. The policy will identify social mores and gender stereotypes that prevent girls from accessing education and cause dropouts. The teachers, Anganwadi workers, and local social entrepreneurs will be trained to deliver proper counselling to families of girl children.

All educational institutions will be mandated to conduct awareness sessions on gender issues to break stereotyped gender roles, on the importance of a harassment-free environment and equal treatment of genders, and on legal protection and entitlement for girls and women under Prohibition of Child Marriage Act, Protection of Children from Sexual Offenses Act (POCSO), the Maternity Benefit Act, and the Sexual Harassment of Women at Workplace Act.

This training will aim to raise awareness of teachers and educational administrators of a gender-sensitive and inclusive classroom management. The policy will specifically concentrate on the educational upliftment of underrepresented socio-economic and socio-cultural groups, and facilitate additional scholarships and fellowships.

The curriculum will be gender-neutral, technology-oriented, and more adjunct to sustainable employment. The NEP has also recommended vocational training inside school campus to acquaint students with first-hand experience of a workplace. In the end, the policy has a clear vision of reconstructing the nation's learning methodology and building a vibrant Bharat.

# 17

# Distance Education

## *Creation of Educational Opportunities*

Soon after Independence, the government realised the important role education plays in the overall national development. They visualised education as a major tool for the regeneration of Indian society, and consequently set before the nation the objectives of notion of democratisation of education and “equal opportunities for access to education”. The authors of the First Five Year Plan realised the need for the creation of educational opportunities outside the formal system.

They envisaged the provision for “facilities of private study through correspondence courses ... and allowing students to take various examinations privately”. However, those in charge of implementation of the Plan did not formulate any policy to translate the idea into action. In 1961, the Central Advisory Board of Education suggested the Government of India to constitute an expert committee headed by Prof. D.S. Kothari to look into the suitability of correspondence courses for expanding educational opportunities.

The Committee recommended the introduction of correspondence courses to expand and equalise educational opportunities. Thus, Open Distance Learning (ODL) in India was introduced by Delhi University in 1962 through the School of Correspondence Courses and Continuing Education to enable those who had the inclination, and the aptitude to acquire further knowledge and improve their qualifications. Subsequently, some other universities started correspondence courses. Rapid expansion of the ODL courses took place in the years to come.

In the eighties, the distance education system expanded further. Not only did more and more universities start opening correspondence course units, but the decade also saw the establishment of single mode distance education institutions (open universities). The Andhra Pradesh Open University, later designated Dr. B.R. Ambedkar Open University (BRAOU), was established in 1982 in Hyderabad by the state of Andhra Pradesh. It was followed by the setting up of the Indira Gandhi National Open University (IGNOU) by the Government of India in 1985 by an Act of Parliament. The establishment of IGNOU is considered to be a landmark development in the country. In our country, the growth of distance education has been exponential over the last five decades beginning in 1962. As of 2016, in addition to IGNOU, 16 State

Open University and about 200 distance education institutions offer diverse programmes in different disciplines.

The journey of distance education in India is through five decades:

- First Decade (1962-63 to 1971-72)
- Second Decade (1972-73 to 1981-82)
- Third Decade (1982-83 to 1991-92)
- Fourth Decade (1992-93 to 2001-02)
- Fifth Decade (2002-03 onwards)

### Who Offer Distance Education

Today distance education in India is offered by the following institutions:

1. National open university
2. State open universities
3. National open school
4. State open schools
5. Correspondence courses/distance education institutions of formal universities
6. Educational radio and TV broadcasts
7. Distance education departments of technological universities
8. Extension education directorates of agricultural universities
9. Central/state government agencies
10. Public and private professional organisations
11. Public and private professional organisation recognised by centre/state governments

### Benefits of Distance Education

Distance education provides benefits for major stakeholders:

#### *For the Student/Learner*

- Increased access and flexibility.
- Ability to combine work and education.
- Reduced travel time and costs.
- More learner-centric approach.
- Relevance to actual learning needs.
- Enrichment, higher quality of education, and use of newer ways of interaction.
- Acquisition of 21st century skills necessary for the workplace.

#### *For Institutions*

- Attracting global underserved populations of potential students.
- Improved teaching quality.
- Support for continuing education.
- Reduced need for bricks and mortar infrastructure.

### *For Employers*

- High quality and usually cost-effective professional development in the workplace.
- Reduced travel time and costs.
- Easy, regular upgrading of skills.
- Increased productivity.
- Development of a new learning culture.
- Sharing of costs and training time.
- Increased portability of training.

### *For Governments, Potential to:*

- Increase capacity and cost-effectiveness of education and training systems.
- Reach target groups with limited access to conventional education and training.
- Reduce gender inequality by allowing women to access higher education through distance learning, while staying at home with their families, and in their own countries and communities.
- Ensure the connection of educational institutions and curricula to the emerging networks and information resources.
- Support and enhance the quality and relevance of existing educational structures and programmes.
- Promote innovation and opportunities for lifelong and worldwide learning.

## Aims and Objectives

The aims and objectives of distance education institutions are as follows:

- Provide an alternative cost-effective non-formal channel for tertiary education.
- Supplement the conventional university system and to reduce the pressure on it.
- Provide 'second chance' education to those who have had to discontinue their formal education, or could not join regular or universities owing to social, economic and other constraints.
- Democratise higher education by providing access to large segments of the population, in particular the disadvantaged groups such as those living in remote and rural areas, working people, women, and other adults who wish to acquire and upgrade their knowledge, and/or skills.
- Strengthen and diversify the degree, diploma, and certificate courses related to employment, which are necessary for building the economy of the country on the basis of its natural and human resources.
- Provide continuing and lifelong education to enrich the lives of the people.

- Provide an innovative system of university level education, which is flexible and open in terms of methods and pace of learning, combination of courses, eligibility of enrolment, age of entry, conduct of examination, and operation of the programmes with a view to promoting learning, and encouraging excellence in new fields of knowledge.

From the charters of various distance teaching universities/open universities the following broad objectives can be identified:

- Expand opportunities for higher education.
- Provide higher education to those who cannot leave their homes and jobs.
- Improve academic and professional qualifications of people engaged in professions.
- Raise the general educational level of society.
- Provide training for teachers. Obtain reduction in education costs.
- Develop a more individualised and student-centred system of teaching and learning.
- Support reforms in education.
- Democratise and revolutionise education.

### Whom do the Distance Education Institutions Serve?

- School leavers who are qualified for traditional university entry but cannot be admitted because of non-availability of seats in traditional universities and colleges.
- Adults who desire to acquire university level qualifications, but cannot choose to apply for entry to a traditional university because they:
  a. lack of education qualifications required for entry;
  b. have family commitments, especially to young children, which tie them to their homes;
  c. prefer to study independently;
  d. live in institutions (e.g. the handicapped) which they are unable to leave;
  e. are in full-time jobs and cannot or choose not to give them up.
- Teachers, professional and manpower groups who require vocational training, professional updating, and increased knowledge levels, but cannot be released from their employment to attend a campus-based university or training college. Adults who wish to pursue lifelong learning opportunities (continuing education) unrelated to the pursuit of a degree level qualification.

### Distance Courses

A distance education institution does not solely duplicate the courses run by other traditional institutions. It has to foster and promote the educational development of a community in which it is located. Different sections of community have different types of educational aspirations and needs. It has to educate people who remain uneducated due to a variety of reasons: economic, social, cultural, and historical.

Many distance education institutions offer academic, vocational, recreational, and literacy programmes. Courses can also be classified as training, awareness, updating, conversion, and academic courses.

A former Vice Chancellor of IGNOU classified the distance courses as: (a) non-conventional courses, (b) job-oriented courses, (c) welfare-oriented courses, (d) continuing education courses, (e) courses for conventional students. The first open university in India in 1982 (Dr. B.R. Ambedkar Open University) aimed:

- to provide educational opportunities to those students who could not take advantage of institutions of higher learning.
- to realise equality of educational opportunities for higher education for a large segment of population including those in employment, women including housewives, and adults, who wish to update their education or acquire knowledge and studies in various fields through distance education.
- to provide flexibility with regard to eligibility for enrolment, age of entry, choice of courses, methods of learning, conduct of exams, and operation of the programmes.
- to provide programmes complementary to those of the existing universities in the state in the field of higher learning, so as to maintain the highest standards on par with those of the best universities in the country.
- to promote integration within the state through its policies and programmes.
- to offer degree courses and non-degree certificate courses for the benefit of the working population in various fields, and for the benefit of those who wish to enrich their lives by studying subjects of cultural and aesthetic value.
- to make provision for research and for the advancement and dissemination of knowledge.

IGNOU offers more than 200 need based academic, professional, vocational, awareness generating, and skill-oriented courses, leading to certificates, diplomas, and degrees. These courses are prepared by 21 academic schools of the university. Significant among them are the School of Law, School of Computer and Information Sciences, School of Engineering and Technology, School of Vocational Education and Training.

### Student Support Services

All institutes of distance education, whether they are divisions of traditional universities or open universities, provide student support services to their students either through their regional centres or through their study centres. They provide varied student support service such as:

- Information support
- Guidance support

- Counselling support
- Tutorial support
- Library support.

Distance education divisions of conventional universities do not provide varied student support service in view of scarcity of funds. This is the major difference between the divisions of distance education of conventional universities and open universities.

Open universities have well prepared manuals along with a student support service. The manuals of IGNOU and BRAOU are well prepared and proved to be very useful to tutorial and counselling staff. The Handbook for Academic Counselors prepared by BRAOU can well be adopted by other state open universities.

The manual for academic counsellors of IGNOU is a well-designed and highly useful document. It suggests several important tasks for academic counsellors in relation to students. The important tasks are: (a) helping students in mastering units of courses; (b) improving study skills in students; (c) expanding knowledge of students through group activities; (d) encouraging student's academic progress; (e) developing independence in students; and (f) improving basic study skills.

### Use of Technology

Of all the distance education institutions in India, IGNOU is using technology to the maximum extent. Instructional system of IGNOU consists of multi-channel, multiple packages. The different components used for teaching-learning include self-instructional print and audio-video materials, radio and television broadcasts, face-to-face tutoring, counselling, laboratory, and hands-on experience, teleconferencing, video conferencing, interactive radio counselling, interactive multimedia CD-ROM, Internet based learning, and the mobile phones for instant messaging for courses in sciences, computer sciences, nursing, medical sciences, education, engineering, and technology. Arrangements are made to enable students to undertake intensive practice classes/practice teaching at select study centres/work centres/programme centres. While the traditional distance education delivers through print, and study centre support is being strengthened, the university is strengthening the development of interactive multimedia content and learner support through video conferencing and web-based platforms.

### Promotion, Coordination, and Maintenance of Standards

Until recently, the ODL system in India was governed by the Distance Education Council (DEC) set up by IGNOU in 1991. DEC was primarily entrusted with the promotion, coordination, and maintenance of standards of ODL system in India, and was expected to create an effective mechanism to monitor implementation and enforcement of its norms. Institutions offering

ODL programmes found the norms prescribed by DEC too rigid and unrealistic lacking the flexibility to meet the diversity of local contexts and emerging concerns.

In August 2010, the HRD Ministry constituted a committee under the Chairmanship of N.R. Madhava Menon to suggest measures to regulate the standards of distance education. The committee questioned the authority of DEC as the apex regulator of ODL system, mainly on the basis of conflict of interest, lack of adequate manpower, and technological support. The committee observed that DEC, UGC, and AICTE do not have the wherewithal to enforce their norms in distance education space.

The committee felt that the ODL system was practically unregulated, and recommended the dissolution of DEC, and the establishment of an independent and effective regulator authority to regulate ODL system. Following this recommendation, the MHRD and IGNOU dissolved DEC in May 2013 and entrusted UGC and AICTE to perform the roles and responsibilities of DEC within their respective jurisdictions.

### Research in Distance Education

A rapid review of research activity in distance education indicates the following:

- Research efforts have been fragmentary and isolated. From the point of view of theoretical value and design, the research activity leaves much to be desired.
- Most of the studies conducted so far have focused on issues at the micro-level
- From the point of view of methodological aspects, most of the studies are of a descriptive type-highlighting the status and functioning of the system after exploring facts and figures related to its different dimensions.
- Maintaining quality in spread of distance education does not seem to be the concern of distance education. With the number of institutions offering distance courses growing day by day, the problem of quality assurance should demand immediate attention.

The research done so far is limited in quantity and quality. The following are some of the broad areas on which further research needs to be promoted intensively:

- Politico-socio-economic factors leading to the establishment of distance education institutions.
- Aims and objects, their fulfillment.
- Organisational structure – reasons for adopting a particular model.
- Role of regional and study centres.
- Course development – approaches-models-significance and problems in course streams.
- Identification of education needs – methods and mechanisms.
- Characteristics of students.

- Problems of dropout and persistence.
- Multimedia instructional system – nature and components.
- Role of communication and information technology.
- Offering science and technology courses problems in providing lab facilities, practical work.
- Student support services – Why? What? How?
- Face to face tuition and correspondence tuition.
- Assessment procedures and methods.
- Evaluation of the system – organisation, methods, procedures results, modification of the system on the results of evaluation.

### Reforms in Distance Education

Various research studies highlight the need for following changes:

- Increase in the number of courses.
- Development of need based and socially useful courses.
- Importance of computer education.
- Organisational accounting and extension education activities.
- Effective provision of student support services.
- Expansion and strengthening of study centres.
- Mobile counselling for the benefit of students in remote areas.
- Transformation of all course materials into self-instructional form.
- Change in timings of television broadcasts. More training for the teaching and non-teaching staff of the university.
- Careful selection and training of academic counsellors.
- Removal of regional imbalances in the provision of student support services.
- Improvement in the infrastructural facilities at study centres.
- Pre-admission counselling to learners.
- Career guidance to learners.
- Provision of special facilities for women learners.
- Collaboration and cooperation of the distance education units of conventional universities in the state in course development, and student support services to avoid duplication and wastage of resources.
- Application of new technologies in the delivery of courses.
- Institutionalisation of research.
- Apex role for promoting and strengthening distance education in the states.
- Continuous research and development activities in all the units of the University.

### Effective Operation

The feasibility of distance education in any country depends on the circumstances in which it operates. Even countries within similar levels of economic development will differ according to geography, local infrastructure, educational structures, and levels of human resources.

However, there is a core set of activities which need to work, if a distance education system or institution is to be effective operationally. These activities include:

- Provide all learners (wherever they are) with specially designed learning materials (whatever the media) in time for learners to make use of them.
- Provide learner with opportunities for interaction with others in a variety of ways.
- Give learners feedback on their learning, in some way, as rapidly as possible.
- Keep accurate records, processed within a given time-scale, and used to manage the system. Monitor key aspects of the operation (whatever the scale) at the centre, and in the field on a regular basis, using the data to assist evaluation and improvement.
- Monitor student progress regularly, for individuals and groups, and modify the materials and the system in response to findings.
- Provide training and support to local support staff and centres, either directly or indirectly (through other agencies) monitor and evaluate their role.
- Evaluate the materials (both in development and in use) and the services offered, in a systematic way. Coordinate the functioning of the sub-systems in the whole operation (production of materials or programmes, support service, administrative functions, and assessment activities) so that conducive conditions for learning are created for the learners.
- Enable learners to complete courses successfully, with results comparable to effective conventional systems, or with demonstrable skills.

| *Open Universities in India* | *Year of Establishment* |
|---|---|
| 1. Dr. B.R. Ambedkar Open University, Hyderabad | 1982 |
| 2. Indira Gandhi National Open University, Delhi | 1985 |
| 3. Vardhman Mahaveer Open University, Kota, Rajasthan | 1987 |
| 4. Nalanda Open University, Patna, Bihar | 1987 |
| 5. Yashwant Chavan Maharashtra Open University, Nashik, Maharashtra | 1989 |
| 6. Madhya Pradesh Bhoj Open University, Bhopal, Madhya Pradesh | 1991 |
| 7. Dr Baba Saheb Ambedkar Open University, Ahmedabad, Gujarat | 1994 |

| *Open Universities in India* | | *Year of Establishment* |
|---|---|---|
| 8. | Karnataka State Open University, Mysore, Karnataka | 1996 |
| 9. | Netaji Subhash Open University, Kolkata, West Bengal | 1997 |
| 10. | Uttar Pradesh Raj Rishi Tandon Open University, Prayagraj, Uttar Pradesh | 1998 |
| 11. | Tamil Nadu Open University, Chennai, Tamil Nadu | 2002 |
| 12. | Pandit Sundarlal Sharma Open University, Raipur | 2005 |
| 13. | The Global Open University, Nagaland | 2006 |
| 14. | K. K. Handique Open University, Guwahati, Assam | 2007 |
| 15. | Uttaranchal Open University, Dehradun, Uttarakhand | 2007 |
| 16. | Venkateshwara Open University, Lekhi, Arunachal Pradesh | 2012 |
| 17. | Odisha State Open University, Sambalpur, Odisha | 2016 |

## Reforming Distance Education

Commonwealth Educational Media Centre for Asia of Commonwealth of Learning prepared a Report on the Status of State Open Universities in India in 2015. The Report provided an overview of the growth of open education in India. It critically examined the recognition of qualifications, standards and regulations and the preparedness of Open Universities in India for the 21st Century. The Report made recommendations for reforming the ODL system in India. The important parts of recommendations are given below.

*Introduction:* To serve the needs of Indian society and growing economy, restructuring of the Open Universities (OUs) on a sound basis is the need of the hour. Most of the OUs have been cast in the mould created more than thirty years ago. They are functioning at a primitive level following the norms of the second and third generations of distance education. They are still catering to an old bygone era – an era when what the country required was a workforce suitable for a production-based economy. Today's knowledge-based economy requires the development and preparation of a differently, but highly, skilled and knowledgeable workforce. Our OUs have to cater to this need of the hour and they have the potential to meet the challenge they need restructuring with this objective at the forefront.

*New Agenda for Open Universities*: India will remain a young nation and also the largest contributor to the global workforce over the next few decades against the rapidly ageing population in the Western countries as well as China. India is expected to enjoy this benefit until 2040. Accordingly, the Government of India, in line with its forecast of a significant requirement of skilled manpower over the next decade, has set the target of imparting the necessary skills to 500 million people by 2022.

This objective, however, cannot be achieved unless the OUs play their role effectively in imparting training and skills to this target group. The OUs, therefore, need to rededicate and energise themselves to achieve this objective.

*India's Economic Goals and ODL:* In the coming years, India needs to become one of the largest, if not the largest, talent pool in the world. To achieve this objective, skill and competency-based education needs to be provided. The OUs seem to be the only available mechanism that, if used effectively and efficiently, can deliver the goals. For the "Make in India" campaign to succeed, there is a need to make our workforce more competent and more skilled. The OUs can give a definitive fillip to this campaign by providing skill-oriented and competency-based courses along with a mechanism for recognising prior learning and certifying it as well.

*Mainstreaming the Ignored Groups*: The rural-urban literacy gap which was 21.2 percentage points in 2001 came down to 16.1 percentage points by 2011. But even a gap of 16 percentage points is alarming and needs to be bridged. The OUs, therefore, need to extend their outreach to the rural populations and bring them into the mainstream.

Significantly, the bulk of the labour force in India, about 93 per cent, works in the unorganised sector largely untouched by any kind of formal training. The OUs should make concerted efforts to tap the vast majority of the labour force and upgrade their skills to help improve their productivity. In the process they will also prepare more people with higher skills needed in the organised/formal sector.

The remodelled OUs should aim at the development of human and knowledge resources as envisioned by the Planning Commission in its "India Vision of 2020" document. In this document, the Planning Commission has envisaged that "by 2020, the people of India will be more numerous, better educated, healthier and more prosperous than at any time in our long history". True it is, today we find healthier and more prosperous people around and larger numbers of educated people who have completed their schooling and are ready for higher education. While on the one hand, however, we are faced with a disparity that population has increased exponentially, on the other, the growth in the number of conventional higher education institutions has remained inadequate. This has left a large proportion of young population outside the reach of higher education. The ODL system, therefore, needs to extend its access and reach far and wide for target groups left ignored and unattended.

*Certification of Prior Learning and Allied Credit Transfer*: The OUs are mandated to cater to the needs of diversified learners who are looking not only for the certification of their learning, but also for their integration with the mainstream of higher education. To achieve this dual objective, the modular approach, that the OUs are already following, needs to be coupled with a lateral entry approach supported by a mechanism for smooth prior learning assessment and recognition (PLAR), which will facilitate the entry of those who have no formal education and training, but have acquired usable and productive skills without obtaining the related certification. Such a mechanism will also benefit those who have discontinued their formal education midway for one or the other reason. The OUs should develop an evaluation framework to assess and recognise competencies gained outside the formal system, assign credit values to such competencies, accommodate (on demand) credits gained at other institutions, and aggregate them or certificates. This appropriately to award relevant degrees, diplomas can very well be achieved through of ICTs-based delivery of education together with the acceptance of certification and qualifications obtained using MOOCs and OER.

There is a need to encourage the development of flexible modular programmes, and uniform and standardised core curricula with elements of flexibility to take care of local and regional contexts across all OUS, so as to make credit transfer easy and operational. A major thrust should be to institute a common credit allocation system for programmes and courses offered through both the distance and the conventional modes. This would smooth out the difficulties being faced by distance learners desirous of migrating from an OU to a conventional university to pursue further studies and vice versa.

*Adoption of New Pedagogies:* The OUs have to cater to three types of learners – digital natives, digital immigrants and digital illiterates. The challenge before them is to deal purposefully with the three groups of learners, whose levels of digital literacy vary significantly. Today learners, rather than simply receiving and memorising information from texts, are demanding education and training through more engaging means, read new technology.

The OUs need to rethink and remodel their operations to provide an enriched learning experience for the present generation of learners. For this, they need to create a learner-friendly environment and adopt the appropriate technology to support it. To ensure their success, besides using the traditional technologies (print, audio and video CDs, television, radio and face-to-face counselling) the OUs should make extensive use of the Internet technology. Each OU should have its own dynamic website with a dedicated LMS and LCMS for each programme offered by it. Further, each OU should have its own e-platform to host all its learning resources on the web and provide online services for its tech- savvy learners.

*Adoption of Economically Relevant Curricula*: The OUs need to envision new approaches to providing instruction. They should provide for "learning on demand" and "learner-centred instruction" by adopting appropriate technologies for transacting the curriculum and also for supporting the learning endeavour of the learners.

There is a need for the curricula to be progressive and application and skills-oriented so that the knowledge and skills gained can actually be applied in the world of work. There is also an enormous gap between the demand and supply that only the OUs can bridge, if permitted to offer degree programmes in professional, technical and skills-oriented areas. The OUs need to revisit all their programmes and modify the curricula in tune with the requirements of the industry and the job market in general.

The OUs should set a new trend that would help in churning out knowledge workers. Instead of emulating the conventional degree awarding universities, they should focus on designing market-oriented and industry-integrated programmes. Employability of the graduates has to be considered as a key factor in curriculum design. Further, curricula can be strengthened by enriching them with purposeful components such as content for a set of skills in the areas of communication, problem-solving, IT, technical and vocational, entrepreneurial capabilities required for employment. Again, the curricula of the new generation programmes should be designed and developed in collaboration with the concerned industry, so that the programmes are not purely theory-based, but practice- and application-oriented and above all, need-based (in terms of the employability of the graduates), with clear cut avenues for the appropriate placement of the graduate in a related industry. These programmes should serve as models of 'work integrated learning' leading to awards that clearly state the skills and competencies acquired. The OUs should adopt the policy of providing stipends to the new apprentices to encourage the learners and facilitate the sharpening of the skills acquired.

*Twenty-Four Seven Support Services*: Learner support services need to be revamped in order to provide them at a scale and a level, which not only promise, but also offer high quality customer services with the objective of complete customer satisfaction and significantly high pass-out rates. The use of technological solutions should be encouraged in all the support services. Such solutions should be driven by the needs of learners together with the range of access they provide and promote. The network of support services should be accessible to all types of learners enrolled in the system. There should be mechanisms for efficient student tracking and improving the retention rates. Apart from the services provided through the network of various Learner Support Centres, namely Regional Centres and Study Centres, all OUs need to move on to technology-based options, so as to provide instant, accurate and timely service to their learners. Further, technology-based solutions should also promote two-way communication. In other words, they should promote learner-teacher interaction which is essential for maintaining motivation, providing feedback, and for diagnosing difficulties and finding solutions for them. Whatever the self- directed learners may do by themselves, whatever the level of their self-motivation and the nature of their interaction with the content provided in the form of SLMs, they remain vulnerable at the point of application. Moreover, interaction among learners themselves is equally important and is recognised as an extremely valuable resource for learning.

In fact, skills of successful teamwork are regarded so essential for functioning in today's work environment. Peer group interaction, whether synchronous or asynchronous, encourages the development of expertise and competencies, and also enhances stimulation and motivation. An active platform for peer interaction is a much required facility, which the usual ODL operations have not been able to activate. ICTs can help the OUs in providing this facility for most of their programmes and learners.

*ICTs in Programme Design and Delivery*: The next logical step would be to convert all the courseware or the major portions of the courseware into e-content. All the existing learning resources, irrespective of the medium they are in, should be converted into e-content, preferably in the form of e-learning modules, which should be Sharable Content Object Reference Model (SCORM) compliant so that they can be reused, revised, remixed, and re-distributed. Further, it is necessary for the OUs to adopt the Creative Commons License and open, standardised end-user-learner oriented architecture through LMS and interactive Web.2 tools. This would ensure pliancy of the learning resources being used and reused as per the design of programme delivery. Also updating and revisions can be affected easily at frequent intervals as per the requirement. Further, this will make it possible for the OUs to allow choices to their learners, who opt to study for a programme fully online, partly online and partly offline, or just offline.

The e-learning modules should not be passive but interactive in design. Each module should be a judicious media mix of text, audio, video and animation. The e-content should be designed in a manner that would allow integration of content with relevant learning activities, so as to enable learners to master the content and develop critical thinking, creativity and decision-making skills. Learners should be engaged in authentic learning through real-life simulations, examples and experiences. The said activities should deepen learners' involvement in the process of learning by engaging them in sound paedagogic activities answering questions, interpreting different cases or situations, or solving relevant problems. This will make the e-content engaging, motivating and enlightening and, as a result, it will promote active learning. Evaluation of learner achievements could be managed through formal or informal tests, or through self-assessment strategies. Talking of evaluation, the methods of evaluation, in use today, are often outdated and are designed to test learners' memory regarding the concepts taught, or supposed to have been learnt, instead of testing their ability to apply the learnt concepts in problem-solving activities. Consequently, most of the concepts learnt during the academic year are forgotten once examinations are over. Evaluation should help the learners to reflect on what they have been doing and derive useful insights as well as skills in relation to the topic or content. In e-learning the modules should demonstrate a balance among the three components of effective instruction, namely content, practice and feedback.

*Creation of an e-Gateway*: The purpose of creating an e-Gateway is in tune with the MHRD's National Mission for Education through ICT. There is a vast body of literature on Open and Distance Education in India, scattered in the form of books, articles published in journals, conference proceedings, newspapers and magazines, mimeos, reports, manuals, etc. The idea behind the e-Gateway is to consolidate all that knowledge, filter it and arrange it systematically, so that it may be used and reused by policy makers, administrators, researchers, teachers and anyone anywhere interested in knowing about the ODL system as it operates in India. Further, the distributed repositories available at all the OUs should be linked to this e-Gateway, so that all knowledge resources as well as the whole range of intellectual resources, created by the OUs, are available to the world. It should be managed by a Central Government Agency, i.e. an independent autonomous body which can serve as a national backbone that provides advanced networking capabilities through high bandwidth connectivity. Further, it should be linked with OER worldwide, which can bring the complete range of intellectual resources available in the world to the Indian population and vice versa. Keeping as view the challenges that the ODL system is facing today, the creation of an e-Gateway will help in making a qualitative change in education, an important social institution. Teachers as well as learners will get wider exposure to develop a world perspective so essential in this age of globalisation and internationalisation of higher education.

*Introduction of OER and MOOCs*: In keeping with the times, the OUs must develop a policy to systematically place e-content as Open Educational Resources (OER). To achieve this objective, they need to develop standards to ensure interoperability, accessibility and reusability of the OER through the adoption of Creative Commons Licence and open, standardised end-user-learner oriented architecture through the adoption of LMS and interactive Web 2.0 tools, as pointed to earlier.

Open sharing and reusing of resources will speed up the development of new learning resources required to serve the needs of the ever-growing diverse groups of learners. This will also reduce and prevent duplication of efforts and indirectly save unnecessary expenditure and effort in reinventing the same or similar type of content that is already available. Further, reuse of learning resources developed using public funds is definitely a better return on investments of tax payers' money. Being in the public domain, OER will promote quality consciousness among the content developers and also bring about qualitative changes in educational offerings at all levels and of all types.

The OUs also need to introduce Massive Open Online Courses (MOOCs). Their policy on MOOCs should be contextualised keeping in mind local needs and requirements. In developing MOOCs, priority needs to be given to extensive use of the local or vernacular languages; their relevance to the cultural milieu needs to be ensured; the quality of knowledge and the accuracy of information contained therein should be unquestionable; and, above all, free and easy access to them needs to be ensured at all costs. Selection of courses to be offered as MOOCs should be done with definite objectives in view, very much on the lines of the Incredible India Campaign, by asking institutions to identify courses that would attract both national and overseas clientele. Secondly, local institutions, state-wise, could be asked to identify such courses as would serve the needs of the rural populations living in the hinterland, or any specific target groups as per their needs and requirements. This would suit the socio-economic needs of each state and its diverse population. Further, the said policy should also display a global perspective by highlighting the need to focus on such areas that have a global market as well.

*Technology Driven Governance*: It should be mandatory for all OUs to go for ICT applications in all their operations. They should each create a separate fully fledged Department of e-Learning with a Director, who should be competent enough to initiate and coordinate the adoption of diverse technological (ICTS based) solutions for the OUs' operations. It will enhance their effectiveness in reaching and serving the diverse and dispersed learner populations, improve the quality of interaction and learner participation in the educational transactions. This will bring about operational transformation in the processes of student registration, support services and learner evaluation.

*Vibrancy of Faculty and Staff:* There is a strong need for a vibrant faculty and staff at all the SOUs. In addition, there should be well defined paths for promotion and career advancement for the teachers, other academics (including the technical staff) and administrative staff working at the SOUs in line with those available in the higher education system of the country. The SOUs also have other academics, who function as academic administrators and technical staff involved in electronic media production and ICT operations. This is a category of personnel which is non-existent in the conventional universities. Their equivalence with the faculty (i.e. the teachers) and the administrative staff should be clearly spelt out so that:

i) they are not deprived of any benefit, and
ii) they do not drag along their jobs indifferently.

It should be mandatory for the faculty and the rest of the staff to periodically undergo training for upgrading their skills and know-how and acquainting them with the latest technological possibilities as well as familiarising them with e-Learning options, not only for purposes of promotions, but also to improve the functioning of the OUs and their services to the learners. Faculty members should be entitled to attend an international conference, a seminar or a workshop once in two years, and a national level conference, seminar or workshop once in a year. Similarly, their visits to regulatory bodies and/ or other ODL institutions at regular intervals should be ensured to promote cross-pollination of ideas and purposeful practices and the consequent growth. The administrative staff, too, should be entitled to attend national conferences, seminars and/or workshops pertaining to e-Governance, Management, Right to Information (RTI) related themes and the like.

Further, the faculty should be encouraged to undertake research activities for which the SOUs should allocate funds annually for teachers as well as for other academics. To make this thrust meaningful, mechanisms should be in place for research-based outcomes to be ploughed back into the system on a regular basis.

*Accreditation of OUs and their Programmes:* The time has come to adopt a transnational approach to quality assurance and accreditation and international benchmarking of standards and practices in the emerging borderless world. The erstwhile DEC did this work and currently the DEB, through its policy regarding the recognition of ODL institutions and their programmes is, in a way, enhancing the quality of the system. The evaluation of quality, as effected under this policy, is more like an external review, which is not enough to ensure quality in all respects. The immediate need to internalise the process of qualitative evaluation is to insist on self-evaluation practices that would account for internal self-audit alongside the external assessment of quality. The creation of a Centre for Internal Quality Assurance (CIQA) at each of the OUs during the Eleventh Plan period (2007-12) was the first step taken in this direction. It was mandated to facilitate the OUs to raise awareness about quality assurance in general and initiate internal review practices that would gradually become embedded in the routine and regular conduct of work. The next logical step is to introduce systematic accreditation of all the ODL providers. It is time to revisit the said first step, ensure that the related operations are in place, and move on to the suggested second step, alongside.

There is an urgent need for a National Accreditation Board specifically for the ODL system in India, as the DEB under the UGC is only an interim arrangement awaiting the creation of an apex body for the purpose by an Act of Parliament. Since the UGC does not have the mandate to accredit institutions other than the universities, all ODL standalone institutions (that are not universities) are outside the ambit of the DEB and have no authorised agency to ask for recognition either of their institutions, or their programmes. All conventional universities apply to NAAC for accreditation, but the OUs have never applied to NAAC, as NAAC has not developed any parameters to accredit the ODL institutions.

Ideally, the MHRD should notify all the accredited programmes and display the related comprehensive list on its website. This will provide the much-needed transparency, so crucial for all stakeholders and particularly for students and for employers. In the process, no distinction should be made between the conventional and the ODL institutions. As a consequence, the awards obtained through the distance/ODL mode will not be discriminated against.

# 18

# Academia-Industry Interaction

In an era of globalisation, industry-academia linkages have become significant to generate industrially relevant knowledge at affordable cost. The current level of linkages between industry-university/academia/R&D institutions in India has to go a long way to work in tandem. There are several institutional bottlenecks in forging such relationships. These obstacles need to be overcome in the larger interest of the nation, and competitiveness of the Indian industry in the global arena.

The need for institution-industry collaboration was foreseen in various policy statements of the Government of India. During the preparation of the National Policy on Education, a document entitled *Challenges of Education – A Policy Perspective* was prepared by the Ministry of Education which noted that the collaboration between industry and technical institutions, which is so crucial for ensuring relevant quality and cost-effectiveness, remains weak despite exhortations for closer cooperation. Subsequently, the National Policy on Education adopted by the Parliament in 1986 emphasised the need for the collaboration by stating that:

> "The curricula of technical and management programmes will be targeted on current as well as the projected needs of the industry or user systems. Active collaboration between technical or management institutions and industry will be promoted in programme planning and implementation, exchange of personnel, training facilities and recourses, research and consultancy and other areas of mutual interest. Networking will have to be established between technical education and industry. R&D organisations, programmes of rural and community development, and with other sectors of education with complementary characteristics."

The technology policy statement, prepared by the Department of Science and Technology in 1993 (DST, 1993), for widespread dissemination emphasised the collaboration between engineering educational institutions and industry through statements such as:

> "Attention will be directed to further enlarge the base of polytechnics, technical, and vocational institutes, and engineering institutions and launch programmes for training and retraining and technical personnel in numbers significantly more than what has been attempted hitherto. Industrial cooperation will be involved in this process of upgrading the human skills....Pursuit of R&D as a career prospect will be deliberately encouraged through further concrete

measures so as to attract scientists and technologists to the challenges of creative science and innovative development with a target of doubling their number in R&D by 2000 AD."

The Technology Policy Statement (DST, 1993) further stated that: "In view of such a predominant role being envisaged for Research, Design and Engineering (R&DE) in the coming years, continual examination and reorienting the work programmes of the R&D institutions are necessary, based upon the emerging needs of the country and the areas where large foreign investments are taking place or substantial foreign technological inputs are needed. The linkages with industry, markets, customers, and feedback and feed-forward research would become important and mechanisms to achieve these would be provided for."

The DST Policy Statement, 1993, further suggested various steps for encouraging collaboration:

- Funding national laboratories and academic institutions through linked projects.
- Promoting university-industry linkages by diverse means, including adjunct positions for necessary personnel.
- Encouraging the use of national laboratory facilities and their expertise by industrial units by way of contract research projects appropriately paid for by the industry.
- Developing the consortium approach involving academic institution, national laboratories, including those of the mission agencies namely, Department of Atomic Energy, Space, and Defence Research and Development, wherever feasible, and the user industry, for goal-oriented programmes, and new product development
- Facilitating easy mobility of personnel among universities, laboratories, industry (including R&D institutions connected with industry), and the ministries.
- Assigning multi-dimensional responsibility to the existing technological institutions.

State governments have been assigned a special role in encouraging R&D and in providing linkages at the local levels. The DST Policy Statement, 1993 further stated, "R&D institutions including academic institutions would be encouraged to interact with industry and other agencies for contract projects. Income arising out of such initiatives will become additional resources for furthering their infrastructure and other R&D activities.... All measures will be taken to accelerate the process of transforming of a laboratory technology to an industrial operation through strengthening and involvement of design, consultancy, and project implementation groups.

The lack of strong linkages between universities and the industry has led to the present situation where:

- The faculty, in general, have no industrial experience or exposure.
- There is not much provision for continuing education in the universities and institutions for practising engineers to update their technological competence.
- State of art research in the industry prevents flow between organised research in the universities and institutions and evolution of industrial R&D.
- There is no suitable mechanisms available for collaboration in most of the departments of the universities and institutions.
- Some of the universities and institutions feel constrained to accept contracts with time bound results.
- There is chronic dependence of our industry on foreign collaboration.

The universities and professional institutions should come out of their ivory towers and interact with the outside world. Similarly, the industries should build confidence in the capabilities of the universities and the institutions and interact with them for mutual benefit. It should be recognised that the academic world, industries, and R&D organisations together hold the key to the technological development in many of the core sectors of our country. This requires insight into the problems of industry, and it provides a base for research and education. Survival of industry largely depends on improved, innovative, and new technologies and for this purpose it needs the support of the academic institutions. Unfortunately, in our country universities, including technological institutions, and the industry have been run on parallel lines without interaction.

The World Bank and Overseas Development Agencies of Britain have extended support to polytechnics and regional engineering colleges, respectively, for improving the collaboration between the two sectors.

The universities have, for the first time, been asked to generate, at least in part, their own resources, and find that they must assist business to ensure survival. It is evident that, in the coming years, industry, universities, and research institutions will, out of necessity, have to assist each other. In order to do so they will, however, have to first overcome attitudinal differences, and remove some obvious impediments. With the policy of liberalisation, globalisation, and privatisation, Indian industries have to face stiff competition with large multinational giants. To meet the challenges, the Indian higher technical education system needs revamping and restructuring. Not only has the science and technology base to be strong, but also our human resource has to rise to the occasion and meet the emerging challenges. This calls for major emphasis on close industry-institute partnership, resource generation, and faculty exposure by the technical education institutes.

## Benefits of Industry-Academia Interaction

It goes without saying that the training of technical manpower in the country must be consistent with the needs of the country, both in terms of numbers, and the nature of the training. Naturally, therefore, the curricula and course structures have to be designed keeping in mind the nature of work that the graduating students are expected to undertake. The vast majority of the graduates of engineering colleges and diploma polytechnics are employed by industry, both in the private sector and the public sector. Relatively smaller numbers go into entrepreneurship. Some find employment in government organisations. Only a few go in for higher education with the ultimate objective of taking up a career in the academic institutions. Thus, the needs of the industry, which is the major employer of our graduates, should constitute an important factor in the design of our curricula.

With an aim to strengthen the industry-academia linkage, the MHRD has taken steps for setting up of an "incubation fund". To have an industry incubation fund is worth considering, though the operational and logistics details need to be worked out. The All India Council for Technical Education (AICTE) also has initiated a scheme where one crore rupees will be provided for starting an incubation centre on the campus, if there are matching grants available from the industry. The institute will need to provide about 2500-3000 sq. ft. on the campus for this to happen. Cluster colleges can also participate in this.

MHRD is in the process of enabling institutions to have collaborations with other institutions globally, so as to help them evolve as 'centres of excellence'. The MHRD is also establishing 50 centres of excellence in frontier areas of science. There is a need for greater private sector involvement. The industry should engage itself more in terms of not only funding, but also skill development, innovation, and entrepreneurship. The target of enhancing access to higher education by creating ten million additional seats aligned to the skill needs of the economy, calls for more innovative and viable models of funding higher education. The National Vocational Qualification Framework (NVQF) offers students an alternate path that can offer employment and provides an opportunity to acquire a degree or diploma. Skill building can only be imparted by the industry or its associates. The same needs a greater involvement of the industry not only in providing skills, but also in promotion of innovation and encouragement of entrepreneurship among our youth.

The MHRD will also launch the National Employability Enhancement Mission (NEEM) through the AICTE. The objective of NEEM is to offer on-the-job practical training to enhance the employability of a person either pursuing his/her graduation/diploma in any technical or non-technical stream, or someone who has discontinued his/her degree or diploma course to increase employability. Any society/trust/company registered under Companies Act shall be eligible to apply for registration as a NEEM agent.

It is expected that the educational institutes and industry will work together for training, internships, and consequently better employability of students. The framework will provide a vehicle for companies and entrepreneurs to provide employability skills and internship as value added proposition to students of all fields.

The Ministry of Human Resources Development (MHRD) announced key initiatives to promote industries-academia collaborations in the country for greater national productivity including the setting up of an incubation fund for 100 institutions. MHRD will setup an Academia-Industry Interface Council with representatives of industry and academia. The Council will promote collaboration between the two and create a culture of innovation. The MHRD will identify ten institutes with the potential to have research parks at tier one, two, or three, depending on the optimum size of industry presence required and current level of academia-industry engagement in the institute. As in the case of IIT Madras Research Park, while the initial funding would come from the government, the research park would be expected to raise resources from the market and generate its own revenues later on.

The MHRD will explore the possibility of funding for research on competitive basis for national priorities where industries and academia collaborate. It has begun documenting case studies as an MHRD-CII collaboration initiative. The MHRD will recognise good works of collaboration between industry and academia through annual awards. In coordination with industry, the MHRD will put in place a mechanism to invite applications for best outcomes of industry-academia partnerships. The gap between industry and academia has to be bridged to enhance the employability of our people.

### Recent Initiatives of CII in Industry-Academia Linkages

Indian industry is keen to work with academia for its own benefit as the quality of manpower in industry cannot be improved without focusing on quality in academic institutions. The Confederation of Indian Industry (CII) has taken several steps in this direction, including increasing the number of PhD fellowships from one hundred to one thousand and funding of global innovation alliance. However, the scale of collaboration is low between these two sectors.

### Suggested Modes of Industry-Academia Linkages

There are various ways in which academia and industry can help each other. It is believed that the Swaminadhan Model for University, Industry, R&D Organisation symbiosis, if implemented, will result in pooling, sharing, and optimisation of the use of resources in terms of men, materials, and finance in these sectors and help towards national development through industrial growth. Teaching and research activities in universities get enriched. There would be better and relevant industrial R&D output and the industries will thus be well prepared to face the global competition.

Academia and industry are increasingly seeing greater value in collaboration. The academic world is eager to bring in cutting edge knowledge that practising industry professionals can provide to bring curricula abreast of contemporary developments and make it relevant. In turn industry is also realising the value of collaboration, especially by exposing the faculty and students to the latest industry and technology trends, and ways to improve employability of students.

India is steadily shifting to a fast track of economic and industrial development, which has led to mounting demands on education, and calls for a highly diversified human resource. Already India is witnessing several paradigms shift in the social, business, and industrial environment. The shift from low tech to high tech, national to global, production to service economy, state to private sector, and the changing occupational patterns create demand for a new workforce with a different skills profile than was demanded in the yester years. The onus of making available this resource lies on our system of higher education. This supply of competent human resource is vital for our economic restructuring and achieving global competitiveness.

# 19

# Commissions and Committees on Critical Issues

## Expansion and Research; Reform and Improvement in Higher Education

### *University Education Commission, 1949*

- To avoid overcrowding, limit enrolment to 3000 in teaching universities, and 1500 in affiliated colleges.
- Mass lecture is the most common form of instruction, and, therefore, should be supplemented by library work, tutorials, and written exercises, ensuring that tutorials do not become "coaching for exams".
- Standards of M.A. and M.Sc. degrees should be raised by regulating admissions as per facilities and faculty.
- Introduce at the earliest, reliable, objective examinations in universities.
- Given the critical role of teacher in transmission of knowledge, replace their differential scales of pay across different disciplines and institutions with uniform scales of pay comparable to provincial services to retain talent, extend PF benefits, retirement age should be 60, and extension till 64 years.

### *Education Commission, 1964-66*

- Plan HE expansion as per manpower needs of next 20 years and enrolment in UG level to double from 1.5 lakhs to 3.5 lakhs and at PG and research level, from 45,000 to 7.5 lakhs.
- Give up open-door policy and adopt selective approach in admissions in Arts and Science courses.
- Establish a second university in a state in case of university with unmanageable under-graduate population in affiliated colleges.
- Specialisation immediately after school at UG level is undesirable and should allow flexibility in choice of courses, like combining physics, chemistry with biology.
- Same should be the approach at PG level.
- Social sciences should be given a significant place in subjects of study in Indian universities, with adequate provision of scholarships, flexibility in choice of subjects, and higher allocation of funds.
- Develop and promote area studies of different regions like America, China, Asia-West, East, South, South-East, Latin America, etc.

- External examinations will continue for a long time. Introduce more frequent periodic assessment to reduce undue emphasis on external examinations.
- Each department should have a personal advisory committee to search outstanding young persons across India for teaching and research. Teachers must be provided with attractive salaries and research opportunities.
- UGC should sponsor fellowships at Lecturer, Reader, and Professor levels to attract outstanding persons to the teaching profession.

### *National Commission on Teachers in Higher Education, 1985*

- Rigorous merit-based selection crucial for teaching profession and education system should not be fragmented on basis of language, region, caste, and religion.
- Give teachers a place of honour, good salary, prospects of good career development, but also insist on work and accountability from teachers and HE managements.

### *National Policy on Education, 1986 and POA, 1992*

- HE expansion uneven, not conforming to UGC norms, with many universities and colleges without minimum infrastructure. Hence, only consolidation and improvement of facilities rather than quantitative expansion in the previous years.
- Reorganise UG programme on modular pattern with option to combine courses to meet growing demands of specialisation and facilitate mobility among courses.
- Reorganise boards of studies in universities to facilitate course redesign and promote inter-disciplinary programmes.
- Recast examination system with continuous comprehensive internal evaluation, introduce semester system, and use of grades in place of marks.
- Specially designed orientation programmes will be organised for professional and career development of teachers.

### *National Knowledge Commission, 2006 (NKC)*

- Open 1,500 universities to boost GER to 15 per cent by 2015.
- Reform universities through revision of curricula every three years, supplement annual examination with internal assessment, transit to a course credit system, attract talented faculty by improving working conditions and incentives.
- Through central legislation, form Independent Regulatory Authority for Higher Education (IRAHE) independent of all stakeholders, subsuming regulatory functions of UGC, AICTE, MCI, BCI, etc. such as entry, license, arbitration of disputes, etc. and avoid policy inconsistencies.

- UGC and other regulatory bodies would disburse grants and maintain public HEIs.
- Enhance quality of education by stringent information disclosure norms, evaluation of courses by teachers and students, retain talented facility by differential salary packages across universities, formulate policies for entry of foreign institutions in India, and promote Indian institutions abroad.
- Syllabi of courses in universities remains unchanged for decades. But they need to be upgraded constantly, and revised frequently, with more autonomy for teachers, through decentralisation to departments.
- Start internal assessment with at least 25 per cent weightage and raise it to 50 per cent over time.
- Conscious effort should be made to attract and retain talented students–the potential faculty–and provide them with office and research opportunities along with rewards for performance for individuals and institutions.

***Committee on Renovation and Rejuvenation of Higher Education (Yash Pal Committee), 2009***

- Form National Commission for Higher Education and Research (NCHER) to subsume academic functions of UGC, AICTE, MCI, BCI, etc. These bodies should conduct regular qualifying examinations.
- Establish a National Education Tribunal to adjudicate on disputes within and between institutions and reduce litigation in courts.
- NCHER's top priority should be curricular reform, with mobility within a full range of curricular areas.
- Bring vocational education within universities purview.
- NCHER to create National Research Foundation to promote research in universities.
- Pending NCHER's clear policy stand, stop recognising new deemed universities.
- NCHER to identify 1500 best colleges to upgrade as universities.
- Set up a National Testing Scheme, open to all aspirants of university education, to be held more than once a year.
- Enhance quantum of central financial support to state-funded universities.

***Committee on Corporate Participation in Higher Education***

(N.R. Narayana Murthy Committee) 2012

- India's GER in HE must increase 20 per cent by next decade and HE needs additional capacity of 26 million seats.
- For this, remove all barriers to corporate participation.

### *Governance and Reorganisation of Higher Education Commission (1964-66)*

- Teaching, research, and service to community, any university's core functions need autonomy from regimentation of ideas and freedom from pressure of party politics.
- Vice-Chancellor, necessarily a distinguished educationist or eminent scholar of any discipline or profession, should embody the spirit of academic freedom, and principles of good management in university.
- Higher appointments should be left to the university, with Chancellor appointing from a panel of three persons.
- Adequate powers should be vested with VC to ensure effective working of the university.
- Important authorities of university include the core policy-making body; the executive council–a small body of 10-15 members, and the academic council which is the sole authority to decide courses of study and standards.

### *Committee on Governance of Universities and Colleges, (also known as Gajendragadkar Committee), 1972*

- Universities and colleges should devise mechanism and machinery to redress grievances of its different constituents, adopt the principle of rotation rather than election to different management bodies.
- UGC as custodian of university autonomy should be consulted before the state enacts or amends any laws on universities.
- Respect autonomy and supremacy of Academic Councils and Boards of Studies in academic matters.

### NPE, 1986 and POA, 1992

*SCHE* a state level body for planning and coordination of HE to protect it from degradation (an euphemism for socio-political pressures and interferences).

### *Gnanam Committee, 1990*

- Central government legislated that UGC's regulations are binding on all universities.
- No new university can be established by a state without UGC's concurrence and without reference to special needs for new university,

### *CABE Committee on Autonomy, 2005*

- In academic matters the universities provide the broad framework, and leave freedom to individual HEIs to design courses, and teachers to try out paedagogical innovations.
- UGC and AICTE should guide curriculum revision ensuring inclusion of frontier areas in curriculum.

- All universities quickly shift towards adoption of choice-based credit courses and semester system.
- All universities establish linkages with open and distance learning universities to enhance enrolment.
- Disband teacher appointment on contract and allow institutions to fill up vacancies expeditiously.
- Allow universities to offer courses as per emerging realities of the region.
- In administrative matters, it called for a review of all university acts and statutes periodically for better management, and to grant autonomy to affiliated colleges.
- Let institutional heads decide number and rank of faculty positions.
- University and college authorities and bodies to have a mix of elected and nominated persons.
- VC's selection only by search-cum-selection process.
- Recognised the need for training and development of academic administrators of HEIs to improve quality of governance.
- In financial matters, it recommended that one third investment on education should be for HE.
- Bring all government universities and government-aided college sunder UGC funding pattern and increase allocations to UGC.
- Full public funding of HEIs no longer possible, and alternative fund generation needed to encourage and incentivise.
- Set a ceiling on fee levels and ensure HEIs do not indulge in malpractices in fees.
- Give HEIs autonomy to take up consultancy and sponsored research projects. Make UGC more effective for maintenance of standards. HEIs need to be given full autonomy for academic and research collaborations with their counterpart industry and professional organisations in India and abroad.
- Need to encourage private participation in HE with adequate social control.
- Need professional ethics and norms of accountability from teachers.

### Privatisation and Private Higher Education NPE, 1986 and POA, 1986

- State Council of Higher Education (SCHE) cannot legislate creation of colleges without UGC's consent and sanction.
- Statutory bodies like UGC would regulate admission as per physical facilities and faculty strength.
- SCHE would prepare coordinated plans of HE development in a state which would be endorsed by UGC.

#### *NPE, 1986 and Revised POA, 1992*

- Government of India should set up a High-Powered Committee for mobilisation of resources for higher education, and also a High-Powered Committee on Technical Education for the same purpose.

***Punnaya Committee 1992***

- Rather than penalise any university or college, the UGC should incentivise them with a matching grant. Universities and colleges need to generate own funds for development purposes.
- Cent per cent income tax exemptions to endowments and contributions to HEIs.
- Self-financing courses only for those who can afford to pay, and adequate subsidy loan provisions for economically weaker students unable to pay high fees.
- Funding for HE is essentially the state's responsibility.

***Swaminathan Committee on Technical Education, 1994***

- Public technical education institutions should raise internal and external resources from industry, alumni, consultancy, sponsored research/ projects, etc.
- Fix fees at a higher level, and revise them periodically.

***Ambani-Birla Group, 2000***

- Establish world-class HE facility at each district HQ.
- Foster a healthy mix of state and affordable private initiatives.
- Enforce strictly "user pays" principle in HEIs with state support for economically weaker sections.
- Complete freedom to private agency without reference to UGC, AICTE, etc. to establish HEIs.
- HEIs to be out of bounds for politics and political parties.

***NKC, 2009***

- Private investment in HE is welcome and should be encouraged by offering land grants and other facilities.

***Yash Pal Committee, 2009***

- To double the current capacity of HEIs all three approaches are necessary, viz., public, private, and PPP, but with consistent ground rules to do away with ills associated with private initiatives.
- Private initiatives should not be driven by profit motives and
- Confine attention to commercially viable sectors like professional courses but should also offer social and natural science courses.
- Given considerable misuse of provisions and pending decisions of Tandon Committee on Deemed Universities, UGC should suspend sanction or recognition of new deemed universities.

***Tandon Committee on Deemed Universities, 2009***

- Abolish 44 out of 126 deemed universities, which neither on past performance nor on future potential, hold hope and deserve their status, and a national committee needs to be set up to salvage future of affected students.

- VCs, as in traditional universities, should head governing bodies of deemed universities like Board of Management, Executive Council, and Governing Council, and its membership should include more than 50 per cent of academicians and with not more than one or two of Trust/President's representatives.
- Trust/President cannot nominate VC, PVC, etc.
- Centralised admission test to govern admissions.
- Fees should be reasonable to the cost of the course.
- Ensure that private participation does not slip into crass commercialisation.

### *Narayan Murthy Committee, 2012*

- Create enabling conditions to make HE system robust and useful to attract private investments. Improve quality of HE with corporate participation.
- Engage corporate sector to invest in existing institutions, set up new ones, and develop new knowledge clusters.

### *FICCI Education Summit, 2013*

- Create enabling environment with fewer barriers for private and foreign participation
- Change from government as a single provider of funds to a situation where students, researchers, and faculty can source funds from multiple sources to ensure autonomy and freedom from any control or accountability.

## Commission/Committee/Reports on Evaluation of Higher Education System

Commission/Committee/Reports on Evaluation of Higher Education System

| *Year* | *Commission/Committee/Reports* | *Salient Features/Brief Note* |
|---|---|---|
| 1823 | Mountstuart Elphinstone's Minutes of 1823 | It stressed on the need for establishing schools for teaching English and the European sciences |
| 1835 | Lord Macaulay's Minutes of 1835 | It advocated efforts to make natives of the country thoroughly good English scholars |
| 1854 | Wood's Dispatch 1854 | Sir Charles Wood's Dispatch of 1854, famously known as the Magna Carta of English Education in India, recommended creating a properly articulated scheme of education from the primary school to the university. It sought to encourage indigenous education and planned the formation of a coherent policy of education. |

| Year | Commission/Committee/Reports | Salient Features/Brief Note |
|---|---|---|
| 1857 | Establishment of First 3 Universities in India | The University of Calcutta, University of Bombay (now Mumbai) and University of Madras were established. |
| 1887 | Establishment of 4th University in India | University of Allahabad |
| 1925 | Establishment of Inter-University Board: which is presently known as the Association of Indian Universities [registered in 1973] | The Lord Reading, the then Viceroy of India, convened a conference of Vice-Chancellors of the Indian Universities in 1924 at Shimla. On the basis of the recommendation of the Sadler Commission in 1919, a resolution was adopted in this conference of the Vice-Chancellors and the Inter-University Board was established in 1925 to promote university activities, by sharing information and cooperation in the field of education, culture, sports and allied areas.<br>In 1973, the Inter-University Board had been registered under the Societies Registration Act of 1860 in 1967 and renamed as the Association of Indian Universities (AIU).<br>Prior to establishment of UGC this Inter-University Board was coordinating amongst all Indian Universities; and at present AIU is carrying out that responsibilities and maintaining the legacy. |
| 1944 | Sargeant Report, the Report of the Central Advisory Board of Education | Report of the Central Advisory Board of Education, known as Sargeant Report on Post War Educational Development in India was the first attempt for formulating a National System of Education in India. |
| 1945 | Establishment of University Grants Committee | The Central Advisory Board of Education had recommended the formation of a University Grants Committee; and it was formed in 1945 to oversee the work of the three central universities of Aligarh, Banaras, and Delhi. |

| *Year* | *Commission/Committee/Reports* | *Salient Features/Brief Note* |
|---|---|---|
| 1948 | Recommendation of University Education Commission (i.e., Radhakrishnan Commission) to establish UGC | Soon after Independence, the University Education Commission, under the Chairmanship of Dr. S Radhakrishnan was set up in 1948 – "to report on Indian university education and suggest improvements and extensions that might be desirable to suit the present and future needs and aspirations of the country".<br>It recommended that the University Grants Committee be reconstituted on the general model of the University Grants Commission of the United Kingdom with a full-time Chairman and other members to be appointed from amongst educationists of repute. |
| 1952 | Central Govt. entrusted UGC for distribution of Grants-in-Aids to HEIs. | In 1952, the Union Government decided that all cases pertaining to the allocation of grants-in-aid from public funds to the Central Universities and other Universities and Institutions of higher learning might be referred to the University Grants Commission. |
| 1953 | Inauguration of the UGC | The University Grants Commission (UGC) was formally inaugurated by Maulana Abul Kalam Azad, the then Minister of Education, Natural Resources and Scientific Research on 28 December 1953. |
| 1956 | UGC formally established through the "University Grants Commission Act, 1956" | The UGC, however, was formally established only in November 1956 as a statutory body of the Government of India through the "University Grants Commission Act, 1956" of Parliament for the coordination, determination and maintenance of standards of university education in India.<br>Now UGC has decentralised its operations by setting up six regional centres at Pune, Hyderabad, Kolkata, Bhopal, Guwahati and Bengaluru |
| 27th June 2018 | Draft HECI (Repeal of UGC Act) Act 2018 | Draft of the 'Higher Education Commission of India (Repeal of University Grants Commission Act) Act 2018' has been uploaded in the public domain seeking suggestions from all stakeholders. |

# References


Adams, J D and others (2002). Industry-University Cooperative Research Centers. *The Journal of Technology Transfer.* 36(1)

Aggarwal, J C (2012), *Development of Education System in India* (Revised edition), Delhi: Shipra Publications.

Agarwal, P (2013). *Indian Higher Education: Envisioning the Future.* New Delhi: Sage

Ahmed, F and Garg, S (2015). *Higher Education in Knowledge Eva: Innovation, Excellence and Values.* New Delhi: Viva

AIU (2001). *Round Table on Internationalisation of Indian Higher Education (The Mysore Statement).* New Delhi: AIU

Azad, Prof. Jagdish Lal (2021). *Indian Education Since Independence: A Critical Study.* Delhi: Shipra Publications.

Ali, Z and Jamal, R (2006). An Impact Study of UGC Academic Staff Colleges. *Journal of All India Association for Educational Research.* AMU

*Annual Status of Higher Education* (2014) New Delhi: AIU

Antony, S (2001). Impact and Assessment and Accreditation of Institutions of Higher Learning. *University News* 39(8)

Arya. S (1995). University-Industry Linkage. *University News.* 33(15)

Arya, A (2000). *Indian Woman Education and Empowerment.* Delhi: Gunjan Publishing House

Asha, K and Neela J (eds.) (1995). *Speaking for Ourselves: Women in Distance Education.* New Delhi: Manohar

Asha, K and Margaret, T (eds.). *Brave New Women of Asia: How Distance Education Changed Their Lives.* Vancouver, COL

Department of Higher Education, Govt of India (2015). *A Methodology of Universities and Colleges in India.* New Delhi: MHRD

Dongekery, SR (1997) *Universities in India.* Mumbai: Manaktala

Elton, L (1998). Dimensions of Excellence in University Teaching. *International Journal of Academic Development,* 3(1)

FICCI (2014). *Higher Education in India: Moving Towards Global Relevance and Competitiveness.* New Delhi: FICCI

Ghosh, SC (2000). *The History of Education in Modern India.* New Delhi: Orient Longman

Government of India (1971). *Report of the Committee on the Status of Women in India: Towards Equality.* New Delhi: Ministry of Education and Social Welfare

Government of India (1968). *National Policy on Education.* New Delhi: Govt. of India

Gore, MS (1995). *Indian Education Structure and Process.* Jaipur: Rawat

Government of India (1986). *National Policy on Education,* New Delhi: Govt of India

Janardhan Raddy, N (1992). *Report of the CABE Committee on Policy.* New Delhi: Govt of India

Kurup, MR (2015), Quest for Excellence and Efficiency in Higher Education. *University News,* 52(20) Kothari Commission

Kothari Commission (1964-66). *Education and National Development (Report of the Education Commission).* New Delhi: Govt. of India

Ministry of HRD (1992). *National Policy on Education 1986 with Modifications in 1992* New Delhi: Govt. of India

Ministry of HRD (2020). *New Education Policy 2020*. New Delhi: Govt of India

Mishra, Ravi (2020) NEP 2020 and inclusion: How to bridge the gender gap in education https://www.academics4nation.org/post/nep-2020-and-inclusion-how-to-bridge-the-gender-gap-in-education

Mohanty, SB (2009). Should the Nation have a New Policy on Education? *Journal of All India Association for Educational Research*, 21(2)

Mohanty, SB and Pani, A (2016). Role of Higher Education in Leveraging the Transformation. *University News,* 54(5)

Mohnaty, SB (2016). Formulating A New National Policy on Education. *Journal of All India Association for Educational Research* 28(1)

National Knowledge Commission (2007) *Report of the Nation – 2006*, New Delhi

Powar, KB (1998). *Accountability in Higher Education*, New Delhi: AIU

Satyanarayana, P (2017). *Higher Education in Contemporary India*. Delhi: Shipra Publications

Satyanarayana P, Lakshmi Mantha, Sesharatnam, C (2020). *ICT Use in Indian Education.* Delhi: Shipra Publications

Satyanarayana P, Lakshmi Mantha, Sesharatnam, C (2021). *Professional Education in India*. Delhi: Shipra Publications

Srivastav, M (2012). *Open Universities: India's Answer to Challenges in Higher Education.* New Delhi: Vikas

Sharma, S (2004). *History of Education.* New Delhi: Anmol Publications

Sujatha, K and Rani, P. Geetha (2011), *Development of Secondary Education in India.* Delhi: Shipra Publications.

Tilak, J B G (2014). Private Higher Education in India. *Economic and Political Weekly* 49(40)

Twelfth Five Year Plan (2012-17). New Delhi: Govt. of India

Yashpal Committee (2009). *Report of the Committee to Advise on Renovation and Rejuvenation of Higher Education.* New Delhi, Govt. of India